Milestone Visual Documents in American History

The Images, Cartoons, and Other Visual Sources That Shaped America

MILESTONE VISUAL DOCUMENTS IN AMERICAN HISTORY

THE IMAGES, CARTOONS, AND OTHER VISUAL SOURCES
THAT SHAPED AMERICA

VOLUME 1: 1540–1858

Craig Kaplowitz
Editor in Chief

Dallas, TX

MILESTONE VISUAL DOCUMENTS IN AMERICAN HISTORY:
THE IMAGES, CARTOONS, AND OTHER VISUAL SOURCES THAT SHAPED AMERICA

Copyright © 2023 by Schlager Group Inc.

All rights reserved. No part of this book may be reproduced or utilized in any form or by any means, electronic or mechanical, including photocopying, recording, or by any information storage or retrieval systems, without permission in writing from the publisher. For information, contact:

Schlager Group Inc.
10228 E. Northwest HWY, STE 1151
Dallas, TX 75238
USA
(888) 416-5727
info@schlagergroup.com

You can find Schlager Group online at https://www.schlagergroup.com

For Schlager Group:
Vice President, Editorial: Sarah Robertson
Vice President, Operations and Strategy: Benjamin Painter
Founder and President: Neil Schlager

Printed in the United States of America 10 9 8 7 6 5 4 3 2 1
Print ISBN: 9781935306726
eBook: 9781935306733

Library of Congress Control Number: 2022943991

Contents

Reader's Guide...viii
Contributors...ix
Acknowledgments..x
Introduction...xi

Volume 1
Smallpox Epidemic among the Aztec Illustration..2
John White: Village of Secotan Illustration..8
Nova totius Map of the World..14
Nova Britannia Recruiting to the Colonies Flyer...20
Brockett's Map of New Haven..26
The Castello Plan: New Amsterdam Map..30
John Foster's Gravestone...36
Cherokee Delegation to England Portrait..42
"A View of Savannah" Map..48
Robert Feke: Portrait of Isaac Royall and Family..54
Dockside at Virginia Tobacco Warehouse Illustration...60
Benjamin Franklin: "Join, or Die" Cartoon..66
Slaves for Sale Advertisement..72
William Bradford: "Expiring: In Hopes of a Resurrection to Life Again" Newspaper Protest.........78
Thomas Jefferson: Advertisement for a Runaway Slave...84
Paul Revere: *The Bloody Massacre* Flyer..90
Philip Dawe: "Tarring & Feathering" Satirical Print..96
Philip Dawe: *Edenton Tea Party* Satirical Print...102
The Old Plantation Painting..108
"The Times, a Political Portrait" Cartoon..114
Colonial Cloth Makers Illustration...120
Painting of a Newly Cleared Small Farm Site...126
Elkanah Tisdale: "The Gerry-mander" Cartoon...132
The Plantation Painting...138
Carl Rakeman: "The Iron Horse Wins—1830" Painting...142
"Camp-Meeting" Lithograph..148
"King Andrew the First" Cartoon...154
William Henry Bartlett: Erie Canal, Lockport Illustration...160
Robert Cruikshank: "President's Levee" Illustration...166
Lowell Offering Masthead..172
Nathaniel Currier: "The Drunkard's Progress" Cartoon...178
Richard Doyle: "The Land of Liberty" Cartoon...184
Nathaniel Currier "The Way They Go to California" Cartoon...190
Currier & Ives: "Congressional Scales" Cartoon..196
McCormick's Patent Virginia Reaper Flyer...202
"Emerson School for Girls" Photograph...208
John H. Goater: "Irish Whiskey and Lager Bier" Cartoon..214
George Caleb Bingham: *The County Election* Painting...220
John L. Magee: "Forcing Slavery Down the Throat of a Freesoiler" Cartoon.......................226
"Picking Cotton, Georgia, 1858" Illustration..232

Volume 2
Cartoon Mocking Women's Rights Conventions...238
Louis Maurer: "Progressive Democracy—Prospect of a Smash Up" Cartoon......................244
Photograph of Powder Monkey on USS *New Hampshire*...250

Andrew J. Russell: Ruins of Richmond Photograph...........256
Photograph of the 107th U.S. Colored Infantry...........262
James E. Taylor: "Selling a Freedman to Pay His Fine" Engraving...........268
Alfred Rudolph Waud: "The First Vote" Illustration...........274
"Reconstruction" Cartoon...........280
Thomas Nast: "This Is a White Man's Government" Cartoon...........286
Thomas Nast: "The American River Ganges: The Priests and the Children" Cartoon...........292
John Gast: *American Progress* Painting...........298
Photograph of Nicodemus, Kansas...........304
Joseph Keppler: "The Modern Colossus of (Rail) Roads" Cartoon...........310
Haymarket Mass Meeting Flyer...........316
Photograph of Carlisle Indian School Students...........322
Jacob Riis: "Bayard Street Tenement" Photograph...........328
Louis Dalrymple: "School Begins" Cartoon...........334
Photograph of Freed Slaves at a County Almshouse...........340
Buffalo Bill's Wild West Flyer...........346
William McKinley Campaign Poster...........352
"Dreamland at Night" Photograph of Coney Island...........358
Edgar Thomson Steel Works Photograph...........362
Louis Wickes Hines: Photograph of Boys Working in Arcade Bowling Alley...........368
Photograph of Congested Chicago Intersection...........374
Photograph of Garment Workers Strike...........380
"Indian Land for Sale" Poster...........386
Photograph of Health Inspection of New Immigrants, Ellis Island...........392
Woman's Party Campaign Billboard...........398
"Gee! I Wish I Were a Man": Navy Recruiting Poster...........404
Photograph of Harlem Hellfighters Regiment...........410
Photograph after Raid on IWW Headquarters...........416
"The Only Way to Handle It" Cartoon...........420
Assembly Line Photograph...........426
Judge Magazine Cover: The Roaring Twenties...........432
Edward Hopper: *Automat* Painting...........438
Fazil Movie Poster...........444
Photograph of Bread Line, New York City...........448
John T. McCutcheon: "A Wise Economist Asks a Question" Cartoon...........454
NAACP: "A Man Was Lynched Yesterday" Photograph...........460
Photograph of Cab Calloway and Dancing Couples...........466
Jacob Lawrence: *The Great Migration* Painting...........472

Volume 3
Civilian Conservation Corps Poster...........478
"We Can Do It!" Rosie the Riveter Poster...........484
Photograph of B-17 Formation over Schweinfurt, Germany...........490
Ansel Adams: "Manzanar Relocation Center" Photograph...........496
Photograph of Navajo Code Talkers...........502
"Kultur-terror" Pro-German, Anti-American Propaganda Poster...........508
Alfred T. Palmer: "Detroit Arsenal Tank Plant (Chrysler)" Photograph...........514
Rube Goldberg: "Peace Today" Cartoon...........520
Photograph of Joseph McCarthy...........526
Photograph of the 101st Airborne Division outside Little Rock Central High School...........532
Thomas J. O'Halloran: "Kitchen" Debate Photograph of Richard Nixon and Nikita Khrushchev...........538
Photograph of Levittown, Pennsylvania...........544
Photograph of Interstate 10 under Construction in California...........550
Fred Blackwell: Woolworths Lunch Counter Sit-In Photograph...........556

Hélène Roger-Viollet: Drive-in Restaurant Photograph..........562
Herbert Block: "I Got One of 'em" Cartoon about Selma, Alabama..........568
Photograph of Black Panther Party Demonstration..........574
American Indians Occupy Alcatraz Photograph..........580
United Farm Workers Strike Photograph..........586
Photograph of Vietnam War Destruction..........590
Herbert Block: "National Security Blanket" Cartoon..........596
"Remember Wounded Knee" Patch..........602
Marty Lederhandler: Photograph of Gasoline Rationing..........608
Photograph of Anti-Busing Rally in Boston..........614
Warren K. Leffler: Photograph of Phyllis Schlafly at White House Demonstration..........620
Herbert Block: "Strange How Some Choose to Live Like That" Cartoon..........626
Pat Oliphant: "There He Goes Again" Cartoon..........632
"Silence = Death" Flyer..........638
Photograph of Berlin Wall Teardown..........644
Tom Olin: "Wheels of Justice" March Photograph..........648
Greg Gibson: Photograph of Anita Hill Testifying before the Senate Judiciary Committee..........654
Steve Greenberg: "Bill Clinton's Foreign Policy Vehicle" Cartoon..........660
Steve Greenberg: "Contract with America" Cartoon..........666
Oklahoma City Bombing Photograph..........672
Bush v. Gore Election Photograph..........678
Photograph of World Trade Center Towers after 9/11 Terrorist Attack..........684
J. Scott Applewhite: "Mission Accomplished" Photograph..........690
"We the People Are Greater Than Fear" Flyer..........696
Mihoko Owada: Photograph of Rioters Breaching the U.S. Capitol..........702
Steve Helber: Photograph of Robert E. Lee Statue Removal..........708

List of Documents by Category..........713
Index..........717

Reader's Guide

Overview
Milestone Visual Documents in American History focuses on visual images as documents to be analyzed and understood in their own right, just as written documents are. Including primary sources from early America to the present day, this 3-volume set features iconic photographs, paintings, cartoons, maps, and more. The 121 images ranging from the 1500s to the present day are combined with associated commentary providing detailed information about the image, the artist, and the times in which it was produced.

Organization
The set is organized chronologically in three volumes:

- Volume 1: 1540–1858
- Volume 2: 1859–1940
- Volume 3: 1941–2021

Within each volume, entries likewise are arranged chronologically by year.

Entry Format
Each entry in *Milestone Visual Documents in American History* follows the same structure using the same standardized headings. The entries are divided into three main sections: Fact Box, Document Image, and Analysis. Following is the full list of entry headings:

- The **Fact Box** includes the basic facts of the visual source: Title, Author/Creator, Date, Image Type, and a brief statement outlining the document's Significance.
- **Document Image** includes the full image.
- **Overview** gives a brief summary of the visual document and its importance in history.
- **About the Artist** presents a brief biographical profile of the person or persons who created the visual document.
- **Context** places the document in its historical framework.
- **Explanation and Analysis of the Document** consists of a detailed examination of the visual document.
- **Questions for Further Study** proposes study questions for students.
- **Further Reading** lists articles, books, websites, and documentaries for further research.
- Each entry features the byline of the scholar who wrote the analysis.

Features
At the end of Volume 3, readers will find a List of Documents by Category and a cumulative Index.

Questions
We welcome questions and comments about the set. Readers may direct any such questions to the following address:

The Editor
Schlager Group Inc.
10228 E. Northwest HWY
Suite 1151
Dallas, TX 75238
info@schlagergroup.com

Contributors

Editor in Chief

Craig Kaplowitz
Auburn University

Contributors

David Adkins
Roane State Community College

Antoinette Bettasso
Kansas State University

Elizabeth Boyle
St. Maria Goretti Catholic High School

Michael Martin Carver
Bowling Green State University

Jon Chandler
University College London

Ryan Fontanella
St. Philip's College

Richard Filipink
Western Illinois University

Elizabeth George
Taylor University

Raymond Hylton
Virginia Union University

Matthew Jagel
St. Xavier University

Tom Lansford
University of Southern Mississippi

Bryant Macfarlane
Kansas State University

Robert Malick
Harrisburg Area Community College

Mike O'Neal
Independent Scholar

David Price
Santa Fe College

Jonathan Rees
Colorado State University–Pueblo

Kenneth Shepherd
Henry Ford College

David Simonelli
Youngstown State University

Mallory Szymanski
Alfred University

Michelle Valletta
Roger Williams University

Belinda Vavlas
Kent State University

Seth A. Weitz
Dalton State College

Acknowledgments

Jacob Riis: "Bayard Street Tenement" Photograph: Jacob A. (Jacob August) Riis (1849-1914). Museum of the City of New York. 90.13.4.158.

Herbert Block: "National Security Blanket" Cartoon: A Herblock Cartoon, copyright The Herb Block Foundation.

Herbert Block: "I got one of 'em just as she almost made it back to the church" Cartoon: A Herblock Cartoon, copyright The Herb Block Foundation.

Herbert Block: "Strange How Some Choose to Live Like That Instead of Choosing to Be Rich Like Us:" A Herblock Cartoon, copyright The Herb Block Foundation.

Photograph after Raid on IWW Headquarters: University of Michigan Library (Special Collections Research Center, Joseph A. Labadie Collection).

"Wheels of Justice" March Photograph: Used by permission. © Tom Olin Collection, MSS-294. Ward M. Canaday Center for Special Collections, The University of Toledo Libraries.

Steve Greenberg: "Betsy Ross Gingrich: Contract with America" Cartoon: Steve Greenberg, Seattle Post-Intelligencer, 1995.

Steve Greenberg: "Bill Clinton's Foreign Policy Vehicle" Cartoon: Steve Greenberg, Seattle Post-Intelligencer, 1994.

Fred Blackwell: Woolworth's Lunch Counter Sit-In Photograph: Photographed by Fred Blackwell.

McCormick's Patent Virginia Reaper Flyer: Wisconsin Historical Society.

Photograph of Congested Chicago Intersection: Chicago History Museum, ICHi-004192; Frank M. Hallenbeck, photographer.

Anti-Busing Rally in South Boston Photograph: Photographed by Spencer Grant.

"Kultur-terror" Pro-German, Anti-American Propaganda Poster: "Kultur-terror," Poster NE 224, Hoover Institution Library & Archives.

"Remember Wounded Knee" Patch: Minnesota Historical Society.

Cherokee Delegation to England Portrait: Collection of the Museum of Early Southern Decorative Arts, Old Salem Museums & Gardens.

INTRODUCTION

Visual images have been used to influence and interpret American history as long as there has been American history. From gravestones and woodcarvings to political cartoons and photojournalism, images have told the stories and pushed the arguments of history every bit as much as written sources. History as a discipline is devoted primarily to written texts (my first book contained no images at all). But over the course of twenty years in the history classroom, I have developed a deep appreciation for visual sources as an aid to student learning. People do not experience their lives primarily through the written word, and our understanding of those who lived in the past is enhanced greatly by the unique access into their lives that visual sources provide.

Looking at a visual document is not exactly like looking through a window into others' lives, however. These images have creators, just as textual documents do, and we must consider the creator's purpose and intended audience just as we do for authors of written sources. Images, again like textual documents, also often reveal more than the creator intended, including their preferences, assumptions, and blind-spots. These sources cannot be interpreted or analyzed well in isolation but require an understanding of the larger context. We intentionally titled this a collection of *visual documents* as an encouragement to approach these images as we would approach the speeches, letters, and other written documents that dominate most primary source collections—by subjecting them to good historical analysis in order to add the resulting insights to our historical understanding.

For this reason, each visual document is accompanied by in-depth commentary that analyzes the image as a primary source, examining who created it, its historical setting, and what it can tell us about its era. The commentary includes a high-level overview to situate the document, including key facts about the image, a biographical sketch of the creator(s), and an explanation of what was going on in the creator's life and in the country leading up to creation. This contextual information is followed by an explanation and analysis of the image—its meaning, intended purpose, and argument—along with questions for further study and suggestions for further reading. The commentary works on two levels—it provides the context necessary to help students interpret these specific sources, and it models how contextual information can be used to analyze visual sources, to help students learn the process of historical examination to be able to apply elsewhere.

I selected images with two primary criteria in mind: 1) each visual document should represent a significant development, theme, or event in American history; and 2) each should be effective for use in the classroom. I have used many of these images successfully in classes for years, and I hope they all will prompt curiosity, provoke a response, or raise questions. Of course, a collection of 121 sources cannot touch on every important event or topic in U.S. history, but I have tried to include images for key topics addressed in U.S. history courses at the high school and college level from a wide range of creators and perspectives. Some of these images are well known, and some are quite obscure. Some are of famous events and deal with famous people, while others document the lived experience of unknown individuals and families. All reveal something about the actions, decisions, and events that have shaped the American story.

As single works created by an individual or group, each of these images represents a particular view, argument, or claim about American history, and as such they offer us much to think about on their own. In some cases, it can be quite effective to examine the single representative image in this collection along with similar images available online (by using the image in this collection as the anchor term for an online search). A few examples where such an approach may be fruitful include: Reconstruction political cartoons reveal competing arguments about how to restore the nation—examine the cartoons of Thomas Nast in particular to see changing attitudes across time within the work of a single cartoonist; Spanish-American-Cuban-Filipino war cartoons offer countless examples of common turn-of-the-twentieth-century assumptions about race, gender, class, and culture (even among those who disagreed on policy), and how those assumptions could be used to make arguments about policy and culture; war recruiting posters reveal assumptions about American national identity, history, and gender roles that were relied upon to motivate Americans of all stripes to contribute to the war effort; and photographs from the civil rights movement of the 1950s and 1960s reveal both the brutality of the forces of segregation and also the fortitude of those seeking change, and gain power with each image added for consideration. Each of these topics is represented by a document in this collection, which can be used to begin an online search to create a small image essay for comparison and contrast, if desired.

Many thanks to Neil Schlager, Sarah Robertson, and all the folks at Schlager Group / Milestone Documents. I have been involved with Schlager Group for over a decade, both as an instructor using the resources and as an editor and author, and it has always been a pleasure. Thanks, too, to the many scholars who contributed the commentary to make this a truly educational resource, and to my students over the past twenty years who have helped me make historical sense of many of the documents in this collection, and helped me learn what does and does not work well in the history classroom. Finally, Alli, Merrill, and Seth have waited, mostly patiently, to be included in acknowledgements. For their constant reminder of what's most important, I am grateful.

—Craig Kaplowitz

Milestone Visual Documents in American History

The Images, Cartoons, and Other Visual Sources That Shaped America

Smallpox Epidemic Among the Aztec Illustration

Author/Creator
unknown Aztec artist/Bernardino de Sahagún

Date
c. 1540

Image Type
Illustrations

Significance
Illustration by an Aztec elder showing the smallpox epidemic, brought to New Spain (Mexico) by Hernán Cortés and his soldiers, that killed millions and weakened the Aztec Empire

Overview

This illustration was drawn by a Nahua Aztec elder to accompany the research compiled in Father Bernardino de Sahagún's sixteenth-century work *General History of the Things of New Spain*. It shows people suffering from smallpox, which devastated the Aztec Empire and allowed for Spain to conquer Aztec land and people. When European explorers first encountered Native populations in North America and South America, an exchange of goods and ideas began that became known as the Columbian Exchange. In addition to the exchange of food and crops, there was an exchange of disease. The introduction of European diseases proved fatal to communities in the Americas, where people had not developed immunity or resistance to them.

Variously called the Age of Exploration, Age of Discovery, and Age of Encounter, the fifteenth and sixteenth centuries are often characterized by the exploration of North America, South America, and the Caribbean by European explorers searching for everything from land to gold to mythic treasure. The first European to visit Mexican territory is believed to have been Francisco Hernández de Córdoba in 1517, who arrived in Yucatán. His reports upon his return to Cuba would encourage Diego Velásquez, the Spanish governor in Cuba, to send Hernán Cortés to further explore the area of modern-day Mexico.

This illustration shows the suffering that resulted when Hernán Cortés and his soldiers brought smallpox with them to Mexico. Since the Native Aztec population had not been exposed to smallpox previously, they had little immunity to the disease, which allowed the community to be ravaged by the disease. This image shows one Aztec Native that had fallen ill to the disease being treated by a local physician. Unfortunately, there was little the community could do either to relieve the suffering or to resist the invaders, given the population reduction from the disease.

About the Artist

While the illustrator of this image remains unknown, the illustration was first included in Father Bernardino de Sahagún's *Historia general de las cosas de Nueva España* which translates to *General History of the Things of New Spain* and served as an encyclopedia about the people and culture the Spaniards found in

Document Image

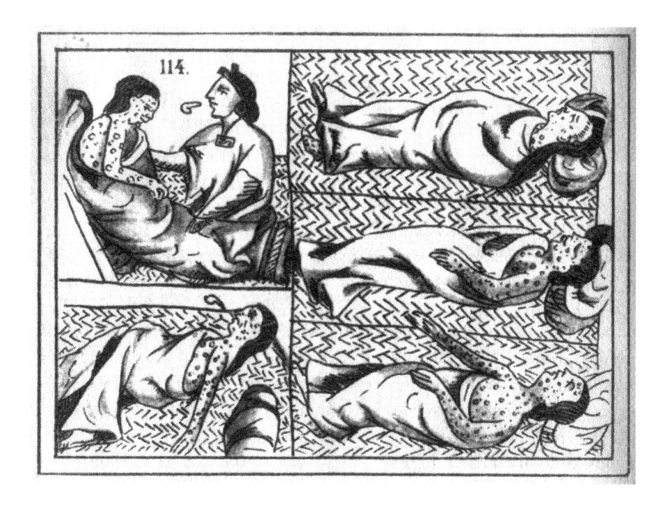

Illustration by an Aztec elder showing the smallpox epidemic
(Sarin Images / Granger)

Mexico. Bernardino de Sahagún (c. 1499–1590) was a Franciscan friar and missionary who hoped to explain Indigenous history, culture, and religious beliefs through his writings. Though the goal was for other Franciscan missionaries to use this information to evangelize the Aztec people as requested for the Spanish crown, an unintended consequence was that he preserved Aztec culture. Little is known about Bernardino de Sahagún's life in Spain except that he studied at the University of Salamanca and entered the Franciscan Order. The Franciscan Order is a Roman Catholic religious order, founded in 1209 by Saint Francis of Assisi, that emphasizes ideals of poverty and charity. The first group of Franciscan missionaries landed in Mexico around 1524, but Bernardino de Sahagún would not arrive in Mexico until 1529. This would be eight years after Hernán Cortés's conquest of Mexico, which ended in 1521. The timing allowed Bernardino de Sahagún to chronicle the effect of this conquest in addition to the culture that existed before the conquest. He would compile this writing and research into his encyclopedia of "New Spain" from 1545 to 1590.

Bernardino de Sahagún's compilation filled a total of twelve books devoted to various subjects related to the Aztecs. It is often referred to as the *Florentine Codex*. As a Franciscan missionary, much of Sahagún's initial research was focused on a religious objective, so he regarded the religion practiced by the Aztec people as rather barbarian. While his overall goal as a missionary was to convert the Native Aztec people to Christianity, his work allowed for a more thorough understanding of the people and culture. His research included interviewing elders of towns in Central Mexico who answered questions about their own history, culture, and religion through a pictorial form of writing. This specific illustration was included in his anthology's *Book XII: The Conquest of Mexico*, which was the final in his series focused on the history of "New Spain."

Context

European exploration of the Americas began when the sailors and warriors from Scandinavia, known as Vikings, reached Newfoundland around 932 CE, but they would stop their exploration around 1010 CE. What is considered the Age of Exploration began in the 1400s and continued through the 1600s. Though their goals varied as some sought gold and new land while others hoped to find a faster route to India and East Asia for trading purposes, the result was that European countries began to invest in exploration of the Western Hemisphere. European countries that focused on exploring the Americas included Portugal, Spain, France, England, and the Netherlands. Once explorers crossed the Atlantic in hopes of finding riches in what they called the New World, they also began interacting with the Indigenous peoples who had long inhabited that land. These interactions prompted an exchange of goods, plants, animals, germs, and people known as the Columbian Exchange. This exchange included explorers bringing various crops and goods from Europe to the Americas and trading with Indigenous groups for crops they had previously never seen. As these exchanges continued, a more globalized world was created as reliance developed for products originating an ocean away. This drastically affected the economy, and it also affected entire societies, sometimes devastatingly so. As a positive example, European explorers like Christopher Columbus and Hernán Cortés imported Iberian horses that helped Native Americans hunt more effectively. More negatively, this trade relationship was often founded on the idea that European culture was superior to that of the Native people, and European explorers immediately began to take without giving as they felt entitled to the land, goods, and even people they found in this "New World."

Many countries explored the Americas during this time, including Spain, which funded the voyages of Christopher Columbus, among others. Arguably one of the most famous explorers from this period, Columbus led four voyages beginning in 1492. However, there were many other prominent explorers funded by the Spanish crown, such as Amerigo Vespucci, Vasco Núñez de Balboa, Juan Ponce de León, Hernán Cortés, Francisco Pizarro, and Francisco Vásquez de Coronado. Exclusive to Spain, these explorers are often referred to as conquistadors, or conquerors. Their goal was usually to conquer the Native people of the land they explored and to acquire land and gold. Of the Spanish conquistadors, Cortés and Pizarro are remembered for their conquest of Indigenous populations. Cortés defeated the Aztec Empire in 1519, and Pizarro defeated the Incan Empire in 1533.

Explanation and Analysis of the Document

This illustration of smallpox was probably created by an elder from the Nahua Aztec community and was published in Father Bernardino de Sahagún's *General History of the Things of New Spain*. The five-panel pictorial drawing shows an individual who had fallen ill with smallpox. Smallpox is an infectious disease caused by the variola virus. Some of the early symptoms of the virus are fever, vomiting, and the development of mouth sores. As the disease progresses, those infected develop fluid-filled blisters, which then scab over. Complications can include scarring of the skin from the rashes and lesions that develop from the disease as well as malaise, headaches, and back pain. This illustration seems to show the progression of the smallpox as the individual falls ill and ultimately remains in bed. The elder drawing this would likely have seen many friends and family members fall ill to smallpox in the years after the arrival of the Spanish conquistador Hernán Cortés. The illustration also highlights another figure, the physician or medicine man, who is attempting to heal the infected patient. Though Aztec medicine was advanced, focused on herbal treatments, there was little that could be done once someone fell ill to smallpox. The first successful smallpox vaccine would not be developed until 1796, nearly two centuries after this epidemic.

Although Cortés is often credited with defeating the Aztec Empire, much of his success was due to the weakening of the Aztec population from the disease that infiltrated their community. Since the Native people had no immunity to the European diseases brought by the explorers, they were greatly affected by such diseases, and morbidity was high. Smallpox, influenza, and measles were some of the diseases that proved to be extremely deadly to Native American populations. While Europeans were accustomed to these diseases and therefore had a relatively low mortality rate, such diseases are believed to have killed up to 90 percent of the Indigenous American populations. The Aztec population therefore dwindled rapidly, which made them incapable of fighting back against repeated invasions.

Such devastation also affected the Spaniards' encomienda system, whereby the Spanish crown granted sections of land to Spanish colonists and permission to force Native inhabitants to work the land. This system of enslaving Native Americans to perform labor for the colonists was popular until 1542, when the encomienda system was abolished. In any case, as more and more Native people died from disease, the Spanish looked to other populations for labor. In particular, they began to import enslaved Africans to work their land. Many Africans had already been exposed to European diseases, meaning they had some immunity and were less likely to fall ill. In the shift from a reliance on the coerced labor of Native Americans to that of enslaved Africans, we see the destruction the Spanish wrought on one community and a precursor to the destruction that would be done to another. More than affecting the conquistadors' source of labor, however, the smallpox epidemic killed the workforce, defense, and morale of a previously strong and prosperous community. Though the Spanish conquistadors would talk of noble conquests, this illustration shows the truth: that a weakened nation had been ravaged more by disease than superior warfare.

The Aztec Empire not only had fallen to Spain but also had dwindled due to the death of most of its population. Even without such devastation, it is likely that Aztec culture would have been quickly assimilated into that of the Spanish over the next decade. This would have been done through a forced assimilation that accompanied Native enslavement through the encomienda system and evangelization by missionaries like Bernardino de Sahagún. However, the *General History of the Things of New Spain* allowed an opportunity for Aztec language, history, religion, and culture to be preserved before the community disappeared or assimilated to a Spanish way of life. Through this understanding of the preservation of culture, this image is equally as important to future generations as it was to the generation using this pictorial writing to tell its own history.

—Elizabeth Boyle

Questions for Further Study

1. This artistic representation of the smallpox epidemic in Mexico is divided into five panels. What story does this illustration show about this individual's experience with smallpox? What symptoms are depicted?

2. Why would Bernardino de Sahagún include this illustration in *General History of the Things of New Spain*? What does it show about how the Aztec Empire was affected by the arrival of the Spanish in Mexico?

3. These illustrations and writings were created for an audience in Spain. How do you think the *Historia general de las cosas de Nueva España* was received in Spain by its intended audience?

Further Reading

Books

Giblin, James C. *When Plague Strikes: The Black Death, Smallpox, AIDS*. Harper Collins, 1995.

Oldstone, Michael B. A. *Viruses, Plagues, and History*. Oxford University Press, 2009.

Sahagún, Bernardino De. *General History of the Things of New Spain by Fray Bernardino de Sahagún: The Florentine Codex. Introduction, Indices, and Book I: The Gods*. 1577. PDF reproduction, Library of Congress. https://www.loc.gov/item/2021667846/.

Documentaries

In Search of History: The Aztec Empire. Eduardo Matos Moctezuma, director. History Channel, 2020.

John White: Village Of Secotan Illustration

Author/Creator John White; Theodor de Bry	**Image Type** Maps; Illustrations
Date 1585	**Significance** A detailed illustration of a Native American settlement in the late sixteenth century that stimulated an interest in colonization across Europe

Overview

This drawing of the village of Secotan was created by John White, an artist and colonist, in 1585. White accompanied the first expedition to Roanoke Island as its official artist and cartographer. Over thirteen months, White produced over seventy watercolor drawings of the plants, animals, and people of the region. This illustration of the village of Secotan (spelled "Secoton" in the drawing) provides a unique insight into indigenous settlement patterns, subsistence practices, and ceremonial life in the sixteenth century. White's drawings are some of the earliest surviving images of Native Americans.

The village of Secotan was located close to Roanoke Island on the northern shore of the Pamlico River. The Secotans initially welcomed the settlers and provided them with food. White visited the village in 1585 and made this illustration. However, as winter approached, the Secotans began to grow frustrated at the colonists' incessant demands. In early 1786, the Secotans refused to provide any more food. The English responded with a surprise attack that was intended to secure a supply of maize but instead prompted the Secotans to flee. The starving colonists abandoned the colony later that year.

White's illustrations were later obtained by the engraver Theodor de Bry (1528–1598) and reproduced alongside Thomas Harriot's *A Briefe and True Report of the New Found Land of Virginia* in 1590, where they obtained a much wider audience. De Bry's engravings were less accurate and less stylistic than White's original drawing, but they nonetheless captured the imagination of Europe. The images, alongside Harriot's text, kindled an interest in colonization across Europe and influenced pictorial representations of Native peoples for centuries to come.

About the Artist

John White (c. 1540–1593) was an artist and colonist who is best known as the governor of the second expedition to establish an English colony at Roanoke Island in modern North Carolina. Little is known about his early life, but by the 1580s he had become closely involved with efforts to establish an English claim to North America. In 1585, he accompanied the unsuccessful first expedition to establish a colony at Roanoke that was promoted by Walter Raleigh. White served as the expedition's official artist and cartogra-

Document Image

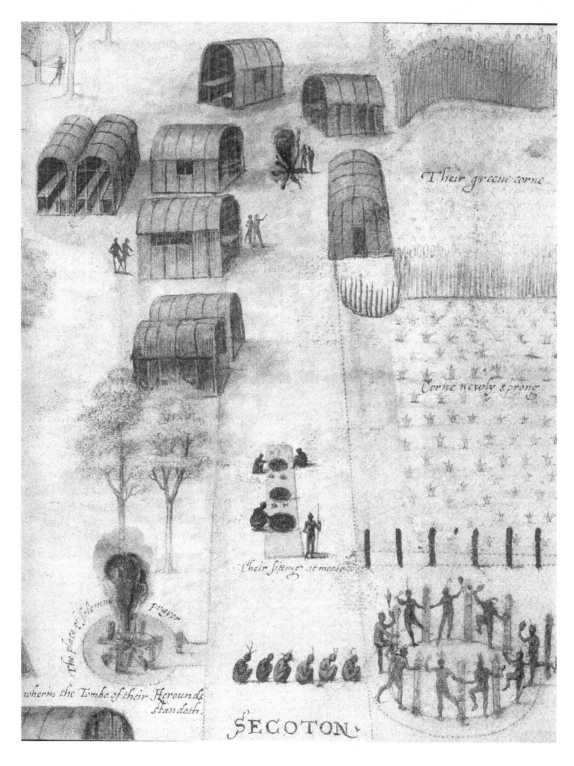

Illustration of the village of Secotan
(British Museum)

pher. He partnered with the scientist and philosopher Thomas Harriot (1560–1621) to acquire information about the people, plants, and animals of the region.

White returned to England following the failure of the expedition and was swiftly placed in charge of a new colonization venture. He was appointed governor of the new colony and instructed to raise money and recruit settlers. The prospective colonists departed from Portsmouth in April 1587 and arrived at Roanoke later that year. White's brief governorship was beset with difficulties, and with growing concerns over provisions, he decided to return to England to request aid. White departed for England in late August and arrived in November 1588. However, the threat of the Spanish Armada preoccupied English shipping, and it was not until 1590 that he could again raise ships and supplies. He arrived back at Roanoke later that year but found the colony abandoned. Among the missing colonists were his daughter, his son-in-law, and his granddaughter, Virginia Dare, who was the first child born to English parents in America. White returned to England and resettled in Ireland, but his later life is virtually unknown.

Context

In the early decades of the sixteenth century, mariners from France and Spain explored the long coastline between Florida and Nova Scotia but concluded that the region was of little value, while the English were preoccupied with the conquest and colonization of Ireland. Later in the century, after a successful campaign in Ireland, the English extended their colonial ambitions across the Atlantic. In 1784, Walter Raleigh, a wealthy landowner and a favorite courtier of Elizabeth I, sought permission from the queen to settle a colony in North America. A year later, after receiving the queen's approval, he dispatched about one hundred colonists, all of them male, to establish a colony on Roanoke, an island on the coast of modern North Carolina (then known to the English as part of "Virginia"). Raleigh's aim was to establish a base from which he could search for gold mines and launch raids against the Spanish treasure fleets. Roanoke was a perfect location, surrounded by dangerous shoals and long sandbanks that would protect it from Spanish attack. However, the shoals made it tricky for ships to land supplies, and the sandy soil was not suitable for growing crops.

The island's poor potential for agriculture did not worry the colonists at first who, commanded by the grizzled veteran Ralph Lane, expected to be fed by the local Algonquian peoples. Three major Algonquian-language peoples, the Chowanocs, the Weapemeocs, and the Secotans, inhabited the region in the late eighteenth century and numbered close to seven thousand. The Chowanocs were the most numerous and lived in towns dotted along the western shore of the Chowan River. The northern bank of the Albemarle Sound was settled by the Weapemeocs, and to the south, reaching as far as the Pamlico River, were the Secotans. Their capital of the same name was located on the northern bank of the Pamlico River and was the primary residence of their paramount chief, Wingina.

The Secotans who inhabited the region around Roanoke Island were hospitable at first, but they began to run out of patience as the English demanded ever more maize through the winter even as their own supplies ran low. Early in the spring of 1786, Wingina refused to provide any more food. Lane responded with a surprise attack during which Wingina and several others were killed. The attack was intended to secure a supply of maize, but instead it prompted the Secotans to flee, meaning that there was no new crop to feed the profligate colonists. The starving colonists deserted Roanoke later that spring when a flotilla of English ships passed by on the way home from raiding in the Caribbean.

In 1587, Raleigh dispatched a second group of colonists, this time including women and children, under the command of John White. Raleigh planned to locate the colony further north, in Chesapeake Bay, where the land was more fertile, but the impatient sailors dumped the colonists at Roanoke before hurrying on to pillage the Caribbean. White soon returned home in search of supplies and reinforcements, but the threat of the Spanish Armada resulted in the requisitioning of his ships, and he was prevented from returning to Roanoke for three years. Finally, in August 1590, he returned to Roanoke with a relief expedition to find the colony abandoned. The only clue was the name of a nearby island, "Croatoan," carved into a tree. The fearful mariners refused to venture to the island to investigate, and any surviving colonists were abandoned to their still unknown fate.

Explanation and Analysis of the Document

This image depicts the village of Secotan, which John White visited in 1585. A dozen houses are dotted between the trees and alongside the village's main street. The houses would have been made out of mats of reed or bark that could be lifted for ventilation. The various shapes of the buildings suggest that they had distinct functions. Closed structures may have been used for storage and ceremonial purposes, while open houses were likely to be summer residences. A central hearth would have been used to cook and smoke fish caught from the Pamlico River.

White was careful to illustrate the day-to-day activities of the village's inhabitants. At the top right is a house for guarding corn, which he indicates was sown in three stages (so that it would be ready to harvest throughout the summer). In the right foreground, wooden posts are shown in a circle around an area of beaten earth where people gathered to sing and dance. To the left is an open fire where people gathered to pray, and a tomb that housed the remains of the community's "kings and princes." These details provide us with a unique insight into the way of life of Algonquian Indians in the late sixteenth century.

White's illustration, however, is not entirely accurate. There would have been no need for a straight road through the community, and archeological evidence suggests that houses would not have been positioned in straight rows. Instead, houses would have been positioned around a central open space with no strict plan. Nor would there have been a series of neat open corn fields: rainfall in the area was not reliable enough to guarantee multiple harvests in one year (and White's visits to the town came during a period of drought). The Native peoples of eastern North America did not practice monoculture. Rather than growing in open fields, corn would have been grown in mounds surrounded by beans to introduce nitrogen, which was far more effective than the European method of ploughing and planting in rows that is depicted. They supplemented their diets through fishing, hunting, and gathering wild herbs and plants. They did not occupy their towns all year round, nor did they always return to the same site. Theodor de Bry added further details to his later copy, including a hunting scene, plots of tobacco and pumpkins, and neat pathways and gardens that gave the impression of an English country garden.

Europeans who viewed this image would have been left in little doubt that its subjects were savages who wore little clothing, worshipped idols, and possessed a primitive culture. But the image also hinted at signs that successful colonization would be possible. This illustration of Secotan reveals an orderly community whose inhabitants diligently cultivate crops and produce abundant yields. The broad street and sturdy houses are more impressive than those found in many contemporary villages in Europe. The sacred rites and ceremonies suggest a people who were deeply religious and receptive to conversion. The image, therefore, offers an idealized impression of the abundance of the region as well as the potential for its people to be civilized.

—Jon Chandler

Questions for Further Study

1. Carefully examine the drawing. Do you think this is a true illustration of the village of Secotan? Which aspects might be exaggerated or inaccurate?

2. John White was careful to depict the activities of the people who lived in Secotan. Which activities has he drawn attention to and why?

3. What do you think was the motivation behind White's depiction of the village?

Further Reading

Books

Fullam, Brandon. *The Lost Colony of Roanoke: New Perspectives.* Jefferson, NC: McFarland, 2017.

Kupperman, Karen Ordahl. *Roanoke: The Abandoned Colony.* Lanham, MD: Rowman & Littlefield, 2007.

Mancall, Peter C. *Hakluyt's Promise: An Elizabethan Obsession for an English America.* New Haven: Yale University Press, 2007.

Miller, Lee. *Roanoke: Solving the Mystery of England's Lost Colony.* London: Jonathan Cape, 2000.

Oberg, Michael Leroy. *The Head in Edward Nugent's Hand: Roanoke's Forgotten Indians.* Philadelphia: University of Pennsylvania Press, 2011.

Websites

The First Colony Foundation. https://www.firstcolonyfoundation.org.

NOVA TOTIUS MAP OF THE WORLD

AUTHOR/CREATOR Willem Janszoon Blaeu and Josua van den Ende	**IMAGE TYPE** MAPS
DATE 1606	**SIGNIFICANCE** Map of the world that includes North America at the time of Dutch exploration of the Hudson River

Overview

Nova totius terrarum orbis geographica ac hydrographica tabula—literally, "a new map of the world's land and seas"—is famous as one of the first maps to attempt to depict North America as one of the world's continents. Drawn up by the Dutch cartographer Willem Janszoon Blaeu, the map is a perfect depiction of everything that mattered about imperialism, colonialism, and the riches that came from them in the seventeenth century, especially in the United Provinces (today's Netherlands), then a major player in the European discovery and colonization of the world.

About the Artist

Willem Janszoon Blaeu headed a family firm of cartographers in Amsterdam in the seventeenth century, at the height of Dutch exploration of the world. Born Willem Janszoon, he added the "Blaeu" to his name to avoid being confused with another professional mapmaker, a sign of how widespread the importance and dissemination of geographical knowledge was considered at the time in the Netherlands. Janszoon Blaeu began his career as a student of the astronomer Tycho Brahe, discovering a star and learning the skills for making navigational instruments, maps, and globes during his studies. He eventually bought a publishing company and began producing maps and atlases, both for practical use by sailors and for simple decoration in homes. In fact, many of his maps are identifiable in portraits done by the Dutch Renaissance artist Johannes Vermeer.

Blaeu's ambition was as great as that of the Dutch government and Dutch overseas financiers and merchants: he wanted to be Europe's most prominent producer of maps. His firm hired the most talented engravers, scribes, and colorists in northwestern Europe, and his maps were produced on his own heavy paper. His maps became perceived as works of art, so much so that book publishers came to him to produce regular print books as well. In 1633 he was appointed the official mapmaker for the Dutch East India Company, the private company that had colonized what is today Indonesia. A year later, his publishing firm produced the *Theatrum Orbis Terrarum*, often called the *Atlas Novus* or New Atlas. Produced in larger and larger editions, it eventually covered twelve volumes, including 600 double-page maps and 3,000 pages of text, and was referred to as the *Atlas Major* or Big Atlas, the most expensive and most prestigious book in Europe. Blaeu died in Amsterdam in 1638, and his sons continued his

Document Image

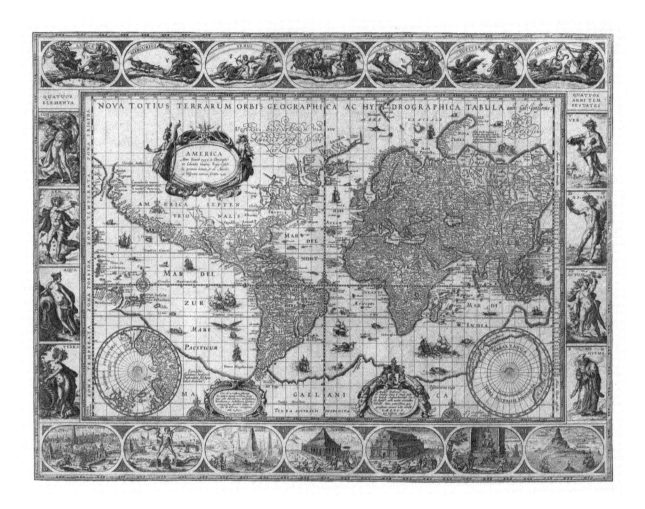

The Nova totius map of the world
(Library of Congress)

mapmaking firm until their offices were destroyed in the Great Fire of Amsterdam in 1672.

Context

Between 1400 and 1700, Europeans used the knowledge they had gained in shipping technology and weaponry developed during the Crusades and used it to travel the earth. This period is often referred to in Western histories as the Age of Exploration or the Age of Discovery, a time when Europeans began circumventing Asian land routes in favor of sea routes in search of spices, precious metals, foodstuffs, knowledge, and people to enslave. They accumulated commodities and ideas in droves. The Columbian Exchange—the triangular trade between Europe, Africa, and the Americas, where colonization of the Americas was the focus—saw new peoples, animals, plants, diseases, and ideas disseminated across the Atlantic. Native Americans were devastated in these encounters, often without ever seeing a European at all, while Africans offered up slaves for exploitation in Caribbean and American plantations. The result was the long-term division between a "first world" of industrial, financial, and service development and a "third world" of peoples lacking in that same development.

Europeans with means got rich, learned to navigate the world, and gained invaluable knowledge during the Age of Exploration, none more so than the Dutch, whose homeland was then referred to as the United Provinces. Having been a Spanish colony under the Hapsburg crown for a century, the "Low Countries," as they were referred to, were a hotbed of Protestantism and rebellion. The northern half of the territory broke free in 1581, declaring their independence as the United Provinces (U.P.), or Dutch Republic. Like the Spanish themselves, the Dutch were inspired by their religion and independence to expand their power around the world in the 1600s. The U.P. developed a powerful merchant and naval (and pirate) fleet operating out of Amsterdam, and the city became a financial power as well, funding expeditions to southeast Asia, southern Africa, and especially the Americas. Money flowing in and out of the United Provinces spawned a Dutch renaissance in which painters, scientists, and philosophers became prominent enough to build international and historical reputations.

The common method of Protestant colonization in the seventeenth century was to advertise for a group of investors to contribute money to a company of adventurers and settlers, who would buy a ship with the money and sail it to some section of the world and find a way to make a profit to repay those investors and make everyone involved in the company rich. These companies were referred to as joint stock companies, and no European joint stock company was richer than the Dutch East India Company, which established colonies in Indonesia and South Africa after its foundation in 1602. Looking to expand on its success, the VOC (as the company's initials were styled in Dutch) decided to send out an expedition to map and colonize in the Caribbean and North America. In 1609 the English sea captain Henry Hudson was hired by the VOC to establish a Dutch presence in North America. Hudson sailed up the river that today bears his name in New York State, and in 1614 a new joint stock company was formed, the New Netherland Company, to occupy the area and trade in furs with the Native Americans in the region. Later, the Dutch West India Company would be formed to exploit the West Africa slave trade and bring more colonists to the Caribbean and New Netherland to compete with French, Swedish, and English colonists in the same section of North America. At around this time, mapmakers and scientists in Europe and the United Provinces hurriedly published maps of the New World, as it was styled, especially in the context of the rest of the planet and the possessions of other European powers. Willem Blaeu's map of the world is a prime example of Dutch excitement over their new colonies, especially those in the Americas as depicted here.

Explanation and Analysis of the Document

This map is one of the most famous created in the era of Dutch exploration, produced just a few years before Henry Hudson's expedition to North America and the Hudson River. The map depicts the northeastern section of North America as broken up into a series of islands, a rather hopeful depiction of the navigability of northern North America. Hudson's expedition was meant to find a northern water passage through North America that would make the journey to East Asia and China quicker than having to sail south all the way around either the Americas or Africa and Asia. Europeans would continue looking for this fabled "northwest passage" for another 250 years to follow. No such river existed, but like all their European neighbors, the Dutch claimed all lands they found in North America on their way into the interior of the continent.

The map is an example of what became known as a Mercator projection, as designed by the Dutch cartographer Gerardus Mercator. Mercator was the first European to try to take all of the geographical knowledge gained by Europeans over the course of 150 years and put it on a flat piece of paper as a surface, making it useable by a ship's navigator as the ship sailed the world. More importantly for the purposes of Willem Blaeu and mapmakers like him, a Mercator projection was also a work of art, and many people bought them simply to decorate their homes and to display them as symbols of their excitement over the geographical discoveries of the age. Blaeu's "new map of the world," as it would be rendered in English, became the Dutch standard in world maps for most of the next sixty years. Issued as a standalone map on Blaeu's own paper and in expanding volumes of his family's published atlases, this map would have been one of the most famous maps in the Western world in its day.

The shape of the landmasses on Blaeu's map are, of course, wrong in their details if correct in their positions. North America is depicted as being massive in size, as big in width as Asia and Europe combined—surely a sign of what navigators considered the enormity of the project of making their way around the continent. Africa and South America, neither of them containing Dutch colonies at the time, are depicted as much smaller than they actually are, whereas Indonesia, the U.P.'s first and richest colony, is a gigantic collection of islands in the bottom right-hand corner of the map. As with all Mercator projections, the stretching out of the Arctic and Antarctic make them seem impossibly huge in size, and the continent of Australia does not exist because no European had discovered it yet.

Blaeu's map is equally famous for its elaborate ornamentation. It is littered with small ships, fanciful sea monsters, and decorative compasses. On the top and sides of the map are a series of border panels representing the knowledge that a trained astronomer and scientist like Blaeu would value in the early seventeenth century. Over the top of the map, gods are depicted as representations of the earth and the other known planets and satellites in the solar system—then only Mercury, Venus, Mars, Jupiter, and Saturn. The four seasons—spring, summer, autumn, and winter—are characters occupying the right border of the map. The bottom of the map depicts the seven wonders of the ancient world—the Hanging Gardens of Babylon, the Colossus of Rhodes, the Egyptian Pyramids, the Mausoleum at Halicarnassus, the Temple of Artemis (Diana) at Ephesus, the Statue of Zeus (Jupiter) at Olympia, and the Lighthouse (Pharos) at Alexandria. Aristotle's four basic elements of life—fire, air, water, and earth—are characters on the left border. Thus, the map was designed to be the centerpiece on the wall of a wealthy home, not just a tool of the navigator.

—David Simonelli

Questions for Further Study

1. Describe the continents as Blaeu depicted them on this map. What did Europeans know of the world, and what did they not know?

2. It is obvious that the map, with its little sea monsters and ships, was meant to be a work of art. How could it also have served as a navigational tool for a captain just setting out on a voyage to unknown lands? Why might it work better than, say, a more factually accurate globe?

3. Judging by the distortions on the map, what do you conclude the Dutch empire considered to be the most important sections of the world for them to conquer?

Further Reading

Books

Emmer, Pieter C., and Josef J. L. Gommans. *The Dutch Overseas Empire, 1600–1800*. New York: Cambridge University Press, 2021.

Kent, Alexander James, Soetkin Vervust, Imre Josef Demhardt, and Nick Millea, editors. *Mapping Empires: Colonial Cartographies of Land and Sea*. Springer Cham, 2020.

Websites

"Blaeu, Willem Janszoon (1571–October 18, 1638)." *Geographicus: Rare Antique Maps*. https://www.geographicus.com/P/ctgy&Category_Code=blaeuwillemjanszoon.

Luminet, Jean-Pierre. "Willem Janszoon Blaeu." https://arxiv.org/pdf/1503.08327.

Nova Britannia Recruiting To The Colonies Flyer

Author/Creator Robert Johnson	**Image Type** Flyers
Date 1609	**Significance** Example of seventeenth-century promotional pamphlet printed in the hope of enticing people to travel to the New World

Overview

Nova Britannia is an example of an English promotional pamphlet. During the seventeenth and eighteenth centuries, pamphlets were a common form of printed mass communication. Printed as small books, these tracts focused on topical subjects, such as religious, political, or promotional, to name a few. The first page of the tract often contained an image that was designed to attract the reader's attention, as is the case with *Nova Britannia*.

Often written in the vernacular of the day, pamphlets are important in the study of print media addressing a broad audience. It is important to note that print materials were expensive during this period. More often than not, these documents were written to be persuasive, informing audiences of a particular position. Along with broadsides, pamphlets served to inform the literate population of urban centers.

This particular pamphlet was used as a promotional tool to attract people to English colonies in North America after the founding of the English settlement at Jamestown in 1607. This piece was published to aid in the work of the Virginia Company of London. The early part of the seventeenth century saw a dramatic shift in European colonization efforts and trade in the Americas. Recruitment efforts became a vital part of the charter companies' work for the English to succeed in their new colony of Virginia. Unfortunately for those being recruited, these pamphlets often glossed over the difficult life of those living in the early English settlements. Many pamphlets were filled with untruths, including *Nova Britannia,* which promised great riches to those willing to make the expansive and challenging journey to the New World. Adventure and promises were vital to the success of promotional pamphlets. *Nova Britannia* and similar pamphlets, in showcasing the time's social, political, and cultural arguments, prove a significant literary source for period studies.

About the Creator

This document was created in support of the Virginia Company's efforts to populate the settlement at Jamestown. Authored by alderman Robert Johnson, a significant member of the Virginia Company of London, *Nova Britannia* was one of the first promotional pieces for the new colony. In the English context, an alderman was a member of the county or borough council, in this case, London. Johnson would have been powerful within his community, able to use his

Document Image

The Nova Britannia flyer
(Virginia Museum of History & Culture / Alamy)

status to author several tracts with the purpose of promoting English involvement in the colonization of the Americas. From what is known of him, Johnson held positions with the Virginia Company and the East India Company. Later on, Johnson would also become a stakeholder within the Virginia Company, which highlights the amount of wealth he would have had. Little is known about Johnson, but his tracts have become popular in the study of early English colonization. This pamphlet, taking the form of a letter or sermon, was addressed to "Sir Thomas Smith, of London." In his collective works, Captain John Smith briefly mentions Johnson's pamphlet *Nova Britannia* as being "entered for publication" on February 18, 1609. Later in his writing, he also notes other works written by Johnson.

The document's cover page shows that it was printed for Samuel Macham, who sold the pamphlets at "his Shop in Pauls Church-yard, at the Signe of the Bulhead." Macham was a seemingly popular London printer during the early 1600s and printed theological works. Records show that Macham was a printer and bookseller active between 1608 and 1615.

Context

In the fifteenth century, European exploration became a popular exploit. English exploration of the Americas began in the 1570s; however, it would not result in permanent settlement. During the early seventeenth century, England started a quest to expand its empire. The English hoped to find riches similar to those found by the Spanish. In 1606, a group of merchants came together to form the Virginia Company, which was chartered by King James I. A charter was a contract signed by the king that allowed for the establishment of a colony or corporation. In the English colonies, there were three types of charter: royal, proprietary, and joint-stock. Virginia was founded as a joint-stock charter with the explicit instructions to function as a religious mission bringing Christianity to the New World.

Many of the stockholders were more focused on profit than the religious aspect of the charter. Still, those men would not have foreseen the profits to be had from growing tobacco in the colony of Virginia. In May 1607, the colony was officially founded at Jamestown. Only thirty-eight of the original settlers survived, which meant that by 1609 the Virginia Company needed to supply more colonists. The company began to advertise to entice people to come, including several women. The winter of 1609–10 was disastrous and became known as the "starving time," as many people died of starvation and some even committed cannibalism. Due to its status as a joint-stock, the company was able to sell shares. The public's reaction to the enterprise was relatively positive until the death rate in the colonies became high, and the company began to lose favor.

Robert Johnson wrote and published *Nova Britannia* when the company desperately needed people to travel to Jamestown. As a stakeholder in the company, Johnson would have likely been aware of disasters plaguing the colony. His pamphlet was published before the "starving time," and it is plausible to wonder if anyone who read and was persuaded by his promises suffered during that period.

Following its disastrous start, Jamestown finally found a source of revenue in planting and harvesting tobacco. Tobacco already had a long history of being grown in the Caribbean, and it brought revenue to the monarchy once it was grown in Jamestown. Following this success, the Virginia Company changed its rules to allow laborers to purchase land in 1616. Nonetheless, Virginia would continue to be plagued by labor shortages.

Pamphlets such as *Nova Britannia* became vital to the success of the English colonies in the Americas. Promotional literature detailing the adventures of those living in the New World would become increasingly popular back in London, enticing still more people to migrate to the Anglo-American colonies.

Explanation and Analysis of the Document

Robert Johnson's *Nova Britannia* was tasked with the almost impossible mission of convincing English men and women to go to the colonies. By 1609, when he published his work, the colony at Jamestown had already suffered greatly. Recruitment relied heavily on ignoring the suffering and showcasing the New World as a place that brought prosperity to those who went. *Nova Britannia* focused on the religious aspects of the king's charter while also promoting the benefits to those who emigrated to the Virginia Company–owned colony. *Nova Britannia*'s main argument focused on the creation of a colony as a Christianizing mission that would lead to possible profits. Johnson outlined a simple task in the document: to colonize Virginia, spread the message of Christianity, and bring prosperity back to those in England. Johnson crafted his argument to resonate with readers, whether that be through talk of wealth, adventure, or the message of English Christianity to the New World.

Johnson used persuasion tactics to make the journey to Jamestown seem obtainable and profitable to men, boys, and even some women. *Nova Britannia* made the argument that it would be considered honorable to travel to the colonies and support the king in this new land. The settlement would bring resources to king and country.

On the document's title page, Johnson used the argument of planting prosperity in Virginia: "OFFERING MOST Excellent fruites by Planting in VIRGINIA. Exciting all such as be well affected to further the same." By joining the efforts of the Virginia Company, the colonists would be "planters" who would bring glory and honor to England while planting a seed of enlightenment in the New World. This rhetoric was used throughout the colonial period to convey spreading "Englishness," whether through religion or ideals, to the New World. In his pamphlet, Johnson took aim at the way the Spanish had so brutally colonized the Americas. By his emphasis on "planting," Johnson intended to convey that the English would be better suited to colonization efforts. *Nova Britannia* promised a land filled with opportunity and great fortune if the right "sort of" people sought passage. Johnson's piece attracted people who were literate and could afford the cost of going to the New World.

The image on the front of the *Nova Britannia* pamphlet showcased the "adventure" that would be given to those who made the journey to Jamestown. The ship's image on the cover would have conveyed excitement to those men who sought out the adventure that Virginia could bring. Many of the testimonies that were used to promote materials such as Johnson's focused on adventure and prosperity. The overall appearance and argument of the piece exemplify the promotional aspect of this type of literature.

When examining Johnson's *Nova Britannia* as a historical text, it cannot be overstated that this type of document is not a reliable source for understanding what life was like at Jamestown. The whole point was to bring new colonists into the colony after the failures in 1607 and 1608. That being said, promotional pamphlets such as *Nova Britannia* showcase the importance of studying this type of literature nonetheless because they reveal the time's social, political, religious, and cultural arguments. *Nova Britannia* demonstrates how enterprises promoted business in the seventeenth century. The idea of bringing the concept of "Englishness" into a colonizing effort would become a vital trope later in the colonial period. In *Nova Britannia*, Johnson begins to sow the seed of superiority as a cornerstone of the colonizing mission.

—Antoinette Bettasso

Questions for Further Study

1. This document states that "Nova Britannia"—New England—will offer the "MOST Excellent fruites by Planting in VIRGINIA." Briefly explain why promises such as these were essential to creating a promotional pamphlet.

2. Why was it important for the Virginia Company to invest in promotional materials? What did stakeholders such as Johnson hope to gain from people emigrating from England to Jamestown?

3. What does this document tell us about the importance of mass communication in the seventeenth century?

Further Reading

Books

Geiter, Mary K., and W. A. Speck. *Colonial America: From Jamestown to Yorktown*. Palgrave MacMillan. 2002.

Raymond, Joad. *Pamphlets and Pamphleteering in Early Modern Britain*. Cambridge University Press, 2003.

Taylor, Alan. *American Colonies: The Settling of North America*, Volume 1. Penguin Books. 2001.

Articles

Fitzmaurice, Andrew. "The Commercial Ideology of Colonization in Jacobean England: Robert Johnson, Giovanni Botero, and the Pursuit of Greatness." *The William and Mary Quarterly* 64, no. 4 (October 2007): 791–820. https://www.jstor.org/stable/25096750.

Websites

"The Virginia Company of London." Historic Jamestowne website. https://www.nps.gov/jame/learn/historyculture/the-virginia-company-of-london.htm.

Documentaries

The New World: Nightmare at Jamestown. National Geographic. 2006.

Brockett's Map Of New Haven

Author/Creator John R. Brockett; Frederick R. Honey	**Image Type** Maps
Date 1641	**Significance** Illustrates the innovative urban design of New Haven Colony based on nine large squares

Overview

This document is a copy of the earliest map of New Haven Colony and is usually credited to John Brockett, a surveyor and colonist, who was one of the first settlers of the colony. New Haven was founded by John Davenport, a leading clergyman, and Theophilus Eaton, a wealthy merchant, both of whom were from London. Their mission was to establish a colony that would become both a religious utopia and a center of commerce. The venture was supported by a number of wealthy and prominent individuals who established the colony in 1638. Brockett's map identifies the names and home lots of the first settlers. The names include a number of wealthy merchants as well as nine women.

The town is based around nine large squares. The middle square was designated as a public space, with the town meetinghouse at its center. The other eight squares were subdivided into housing lots, which were distributed to the first settlers relative to the amount they had invested into the venture. Those who were not investors were granted lots in two additional suburban sections southwest. The town was surrounded by agricultural land divided into "quarters." Farm plots were allocated to settlers who lived in adjacent squares to allow them quick and convenient access to their fields. New Haven was arguably the first planned town in North America, and its design would inspire later settlements.

About the Artist

John Brockett (c. 1610–1690) who was among the first settlers of New Haven Colony. Brockett was born in England, and little is known of his life until he migrated to America during the 1630s. In 1639 he was one of the signatories of the Fundamental Agreement of New Haven, which established the constitution of the new colony. Over the next few years the settlement grew around a grid of nine squares. Brockett is one of three men who may have been responsible for the design of the town. Brockett, a surveyor, certainly mapped out the town in 1638, but most experts believe that he was not the town's architect. In 1641, he produced a map of the colony listing the names and homes of the original settlers. Over the following decades Brockett became a prominent individual in the colony and held a number of public offices.

In 1880, this copy of the map was produced by Frederick R. Honey, an instructor in mechanical geometry at Yale University. It was possibly intended as a book illustration. Brockett's original map is now lost.

Document Image

Brockett's map of New Haven
(Yale University Art Gallery)

Context

On April 24, 1638, the clergyman John Davenport and his childhood friend Theophilus Eaton, a wealthy merchant, and some 500 colonists sailed into Long Island Sound. Davenport and Eaton were on a mission to establish a religious utopia as well as a mercantile empire. The colonists possessed no recognized charter or legal claim, so instead they purchased land from the local Quinnipiac people. By 1640, they had created a government, established a church, and named the colony New Haven. Eaton was the first governor of the colony and held the position until his death in 1658.

By 1641, New Haven had a population of around 800 people. The colony had expanded to include Stamford, Milford, and Guilford. Among the first settlers were a large number of rich merchants who had emigrated from the nonconformist and commercial center of London. Unlike the other settlements in New England, which were established primarily as sanctuaries from religious persecution, the founders of New Haven hoped to turn the colony into a commercial hub. In the seventeenth century, transportation by water was much faster and cheaper than transportation by land. New Haven, with its natural harbor and easy access to waterways, heralded a prosperous future. Its settlers hoped that the colony would dominate commerce around the Long Island Sound and even attempted to establish a trading post in Delaware Bay that was swiftly destroyed by the Dutch. The colony increasingly struggled to compete with merchants from Boston and New Amsterdam. In 1647, in an attempt to open a direct trade route, a ship filled with furs, grain, and lumber was dispatched for England. The ship was never seen again.

New Haven failed to become a commercial center and instead became a small agricultural settlement renowned for its religious zeal. Its churches closely regulated the lives of their members. The colony, declared its first constitution, would be "of such civil order as might be most pleasing unto GOD." As in Massachusetts, only members of the church were allowed to vote and hold office. In the 1640s and 1650s, no other colony would exceed New Haven in its zealous support of the English Puritan Revolution. Many settlers returned to England to fight alongside the parliamentarians against the king. Others supported the parliamentarian cause by writing pamphlets and holding public days of fast and prayer. In 1664, under political pressure from England and despite protests from conservatives like Davenport, the colony was absorbed into Connecticut.

Explanation and Analysis of the Document

This document is a copy of the earliest map of New Haven that was drawn by John Brockett in 1641. The town was divided into large nine squares measuring 825 square feet that were separated by two parallel streets running north to south and two parallel streets running east to west. The squares were bounded by four streets: today's George, State, York, and Grove Streets. The central square was designated a public space and was used as a marketplace, a cemetery, and a parade ground. At its center stood the town's meetinghouse. It also contained various public buildings, including a school, a prison, and three churches. The other eight squares were each subdivided into plots of land for housing lots. Two additional suburban sections extended to the waterfront.

The town was designed to function as part of an agrarian community. The central square provided common pasture and woodlands, while farm fields stretched beyond the boundary streets. The agricultural land was divided into "quarters," and farm plots were assigned to those living adjacent to the town square to ensure quick and easy access to the fields. The pattern of a square town surrounded by fields was later adopted elsewhere in North America, most notably in the design of Philadelphia.

Brockett's map tells us the names and home lots of the first settlers of New Haven who were allocated property relative to the amount of money they had invested into the enterprise. The settlers included a large number of wealthy merchants, such as Stephen Goodyear, William Hawkins, and Francis Brewster, who were each granted prominent plots adjacent to the central square. The largest plot belonged to Theophilus Eaton, the governor of the colony, in the bottom right square. His friend and cofounder of New Haven, John Davenport, has a sizeable plot in the square opposite. Those who had not been among the original investors (at least thirty-two families) were given lots in the suburbs outside the town. Nine of the residential plots are owned by women. Married women were not allowed to own property, but unmarried women could inherit from their fathers or brothers, and widows could inherit from their husbands. Unlike most of the men, the first names of the female property holders are not recorded, but several are identified as widows, such as the Widow Baldwin, whose husband died on ship while traveling to New Haven in 1638.

The town's detailed dimensions suggest it was designed well before the colonists arrived in New Haven, but it is not certain who or what inspired the plan. Some researchers have suggested that the colonists may have drawn inspiration from the Roman architect Vitruvius or from the description of New Jerusalem contained within the Bible. The most likely source, however, was the city of Londonderry in Northern Ireland. The city was designed in the early seventeenth century as a series of squares around a central diamond and, like New Haven, was pioneered by a group of London merchants. Nonetheless, with its large open square and its regular street system, the design of New Haven was still innovative. It was arguably the first planned town in North America.

The town did not retain its original form for long. The eight residential squares were later divided into four smaller blocks by the introduction of new streets. The middle square was itself split into two sections, with one part containing the public building and the churches while the other was left as an open park. Today, the center square is still visible as the town green, while the surrounding squares have been developed into the business district and Yale University.

—Jon Chandler

Questions for Further Study

1. Closely examine the map of New Haven. What, if anything, seems unusual or innovative about the design?

2. In the area shown in this map, nine out of 123 residential plots are owned by women. What does this tell us about the status of women in the colony?

3. New Haven was intended as a commercial center and a religious utopia. To what extent does the design of the town reflect either of these ambitions?

Further Reading

Books

Anderson, Virginia DeJohn. *New England's Generation: The Great Migration and the Formation of Society.* Cambridge: Cambridge University Press, 1991.

Bremer, Francis J. *The Puritan Experiment: New England Society from Bradford to Edwards.* Hanover: University Press of New England, 1995.

Daniels, Bruce C. *New England Nation: The Country the Puritans Built.* New York: Palgrave Macmillan, 2012.

Reps, John W. *The Making of Urban America: A History of City Planning in the United States.* Princeton: Princeton University Press, 1965.

Sletcher, Michael. *New Haven: From Puritanism to the Age of Terrorism.* Charleston, SC: Arcadia, 2004.

The Castello Plan: New Amsterdam Map

Author/Creator
Jacques Cortelyou, Johannes Vingboons

Date
1660

Image Type
Maps

Significance
A unique map of New Amsterdam—today's Lower Manhattan—that provides insight into the design and layout of the city just a few years before its conquest by the English

Overview

This document is a map of New Amsterdam that was created by Jacques Cortelyou, a French Huguenot surveyor. In 1660, Cortelyou was commissioned by the Dutch West India Company to make a detailed map of the city. The company was concerned that instead of building houses and contributing to the growth of the city, its inhabitants were engaging in land speculation by planting gardens and orchards and waiting for land values to increase. The map provides a rare view of the design of New Amsterdam, including buildings, streets, gardens, and the defensive wall that was constructed in 1653. The document is known as the Castello Plan, named after the Villa di Castello in Florence, where the map was rediscovered in 1900. The Castello Plan depicts New Amsterdam at the height of its prosperity when it was the administrative center of New Netherland and had a population of several thousand. Four years later, in 1664, the colony was conquered by the English in a surprise attack. New Netherland became New York, and New Amsterdam became New York City.

This document is the only surviving map of New Amsterdam from the seventeenth century. It therefore provides a unique insight into the design and layout of New Amsterdam. However, historians are uncertain of its accuracy. The original survey produced by Jacques Cortelyou no longer survives; this document is a later copy produced by the artist and cartographer Johannes Vingboons, who never set foot in America. It is possible that Vingboons embellished the drawing to create an idealized vision of the city that would appeal to a European market.

About the Artist

Jacques Cortelyou (1625–1693) was born in Utrecht, Holland, into a family of French Huguenots. Huguenots, or Protestants, were targets of violence and abuse in Catholic France. Many escaped to the Netherlands, as well as England, Switzerland, and Prussia. Cortelyou studied at Utrecht University and afterward became a tutor to the children of Cornelis van Werckhoven, an employee of the Dutch West India Company. He traveled with the family to New Amsterdam in 1652 after van Werckhoven was granted a large tract of land on western Long Island in what is now Brooklyn. Cortelyou was later appointed Surveyor

Document Image

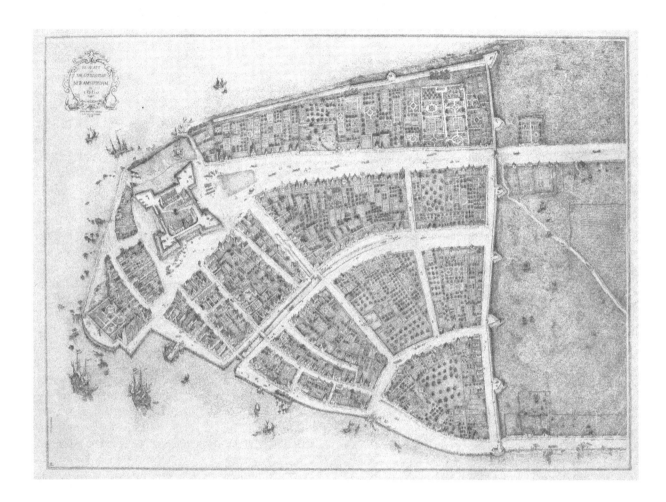

The 1660 map of New Amsterdam
(The New York Public Library Digital Collections)

General of New Netherland. In 1660, he was ordered by the Dutch West India Company to survey the city and its surrounding gardens. The company was concerned that too many of the city's inhabitants were involved in land speculation. Instead of building new houses, speculators planted gardens and orchards as they waited for land values to rise. Cortelyou had the skill and the knowledge to create an accurate picture of the city, which was passed on to the company.

Cartelyou's original survey has not survived. This document is a copy that was created by Johannes Vingboons (1616–1670), a Dutch cartographer and watercolorist. Vingboons never set foot in America, and there is some skepticism among historians about whether this is really an accurate depiction of New Amsterdam. Vingboons sold this copy to Cosimo de' Medici in 1667. Cosimo was an art collector who, on a trip to Amsterdam, purchased this map along with around sixty others. Cosimo, who would later become the Grand Duke of Tuscany, brought the map back to his home in Italy, the Villa di Castello, near Florence, where it lay forgotten until it was unearthed in 1900. The map is now commonly known as the Castello Plan after the villa in which it was discovered. It is the only surviving map made of New Amsterdam made during the period of Dutch rule.

Context

On September 3, 1609, Henry Hudson guided his ship into what would become known as New York Bay to establish a Dutch claim to the region. Hudson, an English mariner in the employ of the Dutch, had entered the area to find a northwest water passage to Asia. He navigated every estuary and bay along the coast, and after exploring the shoreline for a few days, he set out on large river that now carries his name. His ship could only ascend the river around 160 miles, as far as today's Albany, and he failed to discover a route to the Indies. He did, however, discover a region rich in furs and timber.

By 1614, Dutch merchants had established a permanent presence at Fort Nassau, near modern Albany, to trade for furs with Munsee, Lenape, and Mahican nations in a territory that was named New Netherland. The fort was later relocated and renamed Fort Orange, but it only ever contained a handful of Dutch soldiers and traders employed by the monopolistic Dutch West India Company. The company was a joint-stock enterprise financed by both private capital and government funds to attain a profit from the new colony.

The company soon realized that it would be necessary to establish a more populous settlement to guard the entrance to the Hudson River. In 1625, the company founded the fortified town of New Amsterdam on Manhattan Island. The provincial director, Peter Minuit, offered sixty guilders of trade goods to secure the settlement from the neighboring Lenape, who accepted the supplies as gifts to seal a defensive alliance and not, as was once assumed, as payment for the island of Manhattan. The company encouraged agricultural settlement to the east on Long Island, to the north besides the Hudson, and to the west in modern New Jersey.

The colony's expansion strained relations with the numerous Algonquian and Iroquoian residents of the region. In 1643, after the Algonquians had resisted the imposition of an annual tribute, the Dutch under the provincial director Willem Kieft surprised and slaughtered at least eighty Native Americans, including women and children. The massacre prompted a unified response from the Algonquians, who attacked the scattered settlements around New Amsterdam. Over the next two years, dozens of colonists and more than a thousand Native Americans lost their lives. Kieft's War devastated the Algonquians, but it almost destroyed New Netherland too.

In 1647, the company sent Peter Stuyvesant to restore order to the colony. Stuyvesant acquired a reputation as an autocratic administrator but under his watch New Amsterdam grew into a large and prosperous seaport. The colony's success, however, attracted attention from overseas. In 1660, the English Parliament passed legislation designed to restrict the Dutch from trading with its colonies in America. Four years later, the English decided to send an expedition to conquer New Netherland. Taken by surprise, the Dutch could not resist the three English warships that arrived carrying three hundred soldiers. Stuyvesant, enraged, surrendered without a fight. In 1667, the colony was formally handed over to the English. New Netherland became New York; New Amsterdam became New York City; and Fort Orange became Albany.

The Dutch, apart from a brief reconquest in 1673, were expelled from the continent and the English could consolidate their position in North America. However, Dutch New Yorkers resisted assimilation and preserved their identity, language, and culture well into the eighteenth century.

Explanation and Analysis of the Document

The Castello Plan provides a bird's-eye view of New Amsterdam in 1660. The map, oriented to the northwest, contains a detailed depiction of the buildings, streets, squares, and gardens of the fortified city. Although there are no physical remains of New Amsterdam, the town is preserved in the grid pattern of today's Lower Manhattan.

Fort Amsterdam, the large square structure on the left side of the map, dominates the city. The fort was the most important building in New Amsterdam. Constructed in 1625, its main purpose was military, but it also functioned as the center of trade and administration in the colony. Its location at the tip of Manhattan Island commanded access to the Hudson River. The fort was constructed in a standard seventeenth-century star design, with four bastions and several cannons. The walls were constructed from compacted earth or rubble to absorb cannon fire. Within the fort were a church, the governor's house, the barracks, a prison, and a store house. The soldiers of the Dutch West India Company were garrisoned within the fort along with the provincial director. In this image, the fort flies the flag of the Dutch West India Company, while the company's soldiers are depicted parading in regular formation outside the fort. The site of the fort is now occupied by the Smithsonian Institution's Museum of the American Indian. To the far left of the fort lies Peter Stuyvesant's house and garden. The provincial director's house was constructed from stone, and his garden was composed of four squares divided by a cruciform path. The size of his residence and its elaborate walled garden reflected his high status in the colony. The English renamed the building Whitehall, after the seat of government in London, and the name lives on as today's Whitehall Street.

The wide street that leads from Fort Amsterdam out of the city was called Heere Straat, or the Gentlemen's Street, and was later renamed Broadway by the English. The street followed a natural ridge that had long been used as a trail by the region's Native Americans. The Dutch simply widened the trail and built houses and farms alongside it. Heere Straat reaches a city wall that stretches across Manhattan Island: modern Wall Street. The wall, a wooden palisade, was constructed in 1653 to protect against the English. Below Heere Straat, bisecting the city, is a small inlet from the East River flanked by houses and paths. The inhabitants decided to turn the inlet into a canal known as the Heere Gracht, or the Gentlemen's Canal, that was later filled in and is now known as Broad Street. To the right of the canal, where it meets the east river, sits the Stadt Huys, a tavern that was built by the Dutch West India Company and was later converted into New Amsterdam's city hall. The waters surrounding Manhattan are surrounded by ships and boats along with several beached vessels. The busy port is symbolic of wealth and prosperity.

We do not know if the Castello Plan is an accurate depiction of New Amsterdam or an idealized representation. Jacques Cartelyou's original map is lost, and it is impossible to know for sure if this is a true copy. Johannes Vingboons, who produced this copy, never set foot in New Amsterdam, and some historians have argued that this image is too neat, with pretty canals, tidy gardens, and impressive fortifications. A more realistic depiction of New Amsterdam in 1660 might depict muddy roads, a crumbling fort, and rotting city walls. Vingboons's watercolor was perhaps inspired more by the old Amsterdam than the new and so offered an imaginary vision of the successful colonization of the New World. His patron, Cosimo de' Medici, would certainly have been more interested in the fantasy than the reality.

—Jon Chandler

Questions for Further Study

1. Jacques Cortelyou was commissioned to produce the original map of New Amsterdam by the Dutch West India Company, whose members were concerned that instead of building houses, the city's inhabitants were planting gardens and orchards instead. Why was this a concern? Do you think this map would have reassured them?

2. Fort Amsterdam, on the left, dominates the city. Why was this fort such an important building in seventeenth-century New Amsterdam?

3. Do you think the Castello Plan is an accurate depiction of New Amsterdam or just a fantasy? Why do you think so?

Further Reading

Books

Goodfriend, Joyce D., ed. *Revisiting New Netherland: Perspectives on Early Dutch America*. Leiden: Brill, 2005.

Jacobs, Jaap. *The Colony of New Netherland: A Dutch Settlement in Seventeenth-Century America*. Ithaca: Cornell University Press, 2009.

Shorto, Russell. *The Island at the Center of the World: The Epic Story of Dutch Manhattan and the Forgotten Colony That Shaped America*. New York: Doubleday, 2004.

Articles

Jacobs, Jaap. "'The Great North River of New Netherland': The Hudson River and Dutch Colonization." *The Hudson River Valley Review* 30, no. 2 (2014): 2–15.

van den Hurk, Jeroen. "Plan Versus Execution: The 'Ideal City,' of New Amsterdam. Seventeenth Century Town Planning in North America." *New York History* 96, no. 3–4 (2015): 265–83.

Websites

"A Tour of New Netherland: A Lost World." New Netherland Institute website. https://www.newnetherlandinstitute.org/history-and-heritage/digital-exhibitions/a-tour-of-new-netherland.

John Foster's Gravestone

Author/Creator
"The Stonecutter of Boston"

Date
1681

Image Type
Sculptures

Significance
An ornate gravestone that, through its epitaph, iconography, and inscription, reflects typical attitudes toward life and death among seventeenth-century Puritans

Overview

This gravestone was commissioned for John Foster of Boston, Massachusetts, in 1681. Its design is characteristic of the period. The decorative carving on early gravestones reflected philosophical attitudes toward life and death in seventeenth-century New England. The imagery on the markers derived from the stern religious beliefs of the Puritans. The Puritans discouraged most artistic endeavors as frivolous indulgences that distracted from spiritual pursuits. However, they tolerated gravestone carving because it promoted their beliefs. Gravestones were intended to remind observers of their own mortality and encourage them to reflect on their own spiritual preparedness for death. Bones, coffins, hourglasses, scythes, skeletons, and skulls were common symbols. Elaborate carvings, such as this gravestone, are considered to be the earliest sculptures produced in colonial America.

Foster was a printer, mathematician, and astronomer when he died of tuberculous at a young age. His brothers commissioned this gravestone from a local carver known today only as "the Stonecutter of Boston." It is not known who produced the exact design, although the imagery was copied from a well-known book of symbols. Foster's ornate gravestone reflects his status as a successful businessman and prominent citizen. The headstone employs typical imagery to symbolize the passage of time and the inevitability of death, while an inscription alludes to Foster's religious dedication. The footstone, however, offers a simple dedication to Foster's material prosperity. These sentiments were not a contradiction. For the Puritans, both the spiritual and the material aspects of his life were considered worthy of commemoration, with his affluence interpreted as a reward for his religious devotion. The gravestone, then, offered a reminder to any observer of the importance of living a life in preparation for death.

About the Artist

John Foster (1648–1681) was born in Dorchester, a suburb of Boston, Massachusetts. His father was the town brewer and a captain in the militia. Foster attended Harvard and, after graduation, became a schoolteacher for several years. In 1675, he opened the first successful printing press in Boston. He is best known for a wood block print of Richard Mather, produced in 1670. Foster later published books,

Document Image

John Foster's gravestone
(Graphic Arts Collection, Princeton University)

pamphlets, broadsides, almanacs, and other materials, including a large decorative map of New England. He was also involved in the study of astronomy, music, medicine, and mathematics. He died, aged thirty-three, in 1681 after suffering for seven months from tuberculosis (then known as consumption). In his will, he wrote, with "my body languishing but my understanding not distempered or impaired," he left twenty to thirty shillings "to pay for a pair of handsome Gravestones." His brothers then commissioned the best gravestone carver in the area, who is known today only as "the Stonecutter of Boston," to create an appropriate memorial.

"The Stonecutter of Boston" is known for the numerous gravestones, produced between 1653 and 1695, that can be found in the burying grounds around Boston. Most of his work was simple, with little ornamentation, but sometimes he attempted more ambitious pieces. John Foster's gravestone is considered his masterpiece. The imagery was not original: it was copied directly from Francis Quarles's *Hieroglyphiques of the Life of Man*, which was published in London in 1637. Such plagiarism was not uncommon; most images on colonial gravestones can be traced back to broadsides, engravings, or book illustrations. "The Stonecutter" first used the design on the gravestone of Joseph Tapping, which can be found in Boston's King's Chapel, in 1678. Foster's brothers were likely familiar with the gravestone and may have requested a similar design. Foster, too, may have had a say in the design of his own gravestone before he passed away.

Context

John Foster's life and death was shaped by the ideals and values of Puritanism. Puritans wished to purify what they considered an increasingly ritualized and hierarchical Anglican Church. They advocated for an elimination of ecclesiastical hierarchy and religious sacraments not rooted in the Bible. They believed in cultivating industry, self-discipline, and frugality. They were also notorious iconoclasts who were known for the destruction of religious imagery. The Puritans believed that the worship of an image distracted from the veneration of the religious figure that was depicted. They tolerated secular images, such as portraits, so long as the image was a realistic depiction of something that existed in the visible world. However, it was unacceptable for an artist to idealize or change a form because it implied that they could improve upon God's creation.

By the early seventeenth century, the Puritans were experiencing increasing persecution in England and began to seek refuge in North America. In 1620 a small group of Puritan Separatists, later known as the Pilgrims, established a town called Plymouth on the south coast of Massachusetts Bay. The settlers suffered through a hard winter, but thereafter more immigrants strengthened the colony. Ten years later, about 1,500 colonists lived in Plymouth Colony.

A much larger emigration of Puritans from England known as the "Great Migration" began in 1630. A syndicate of wealthy Puritans formed the Massachusetts Bay Company and obtained a royal charter to establish a colony north of Plymouth. The first families of colonists arrived in Massachusetts Bay in 1630. They were led by John Winthrop, a wealthy landowner, and founded the town of Boston. Over the next decade, around 14,000 English Puritans migrated to Massachusetts. They were attracted by the prospect of religious freedom and economic opportunities. Winthrop wrote of the new settlement as a "City upon a Hill" that would become a beacon for all believers. Puritans despaired at the poverty, corruption, and immorality of Old England, which they believed would soon suffer from divine punishment. Winthrop concluded that New England had been ordained by God as "a refuge for the manye, whom he meant to save out of the general destruction."

Puritanism emphasized the values of frugality, industry, and restraint that helped its adherents to prosper in the New World. Puritans suggested that diligence would be rewarded with material prosperity, but they also warned that wealth must not distract from the ultimate purpose of human existence: preparation for salvation in the next world. Puritans denounced excessive consumption, but they could never escape temptation since their values helped them to become successful entrepreneurs. Boston became a thriving seaport that prospered on the export of fish and lumber. Wine, sugar, and tobacco were imported alongside books, newspapers, and printing presses. John Foster was to become a prominent figure in this emerging urban culture.

Explanation and Analysis of the Document

Gravestones provide a glimpse into the religious, intellectual, and social life of seventeenth-century New England. The oldest stones are scattered throughout the region's early settlements adjacent to a church or meetinghouse or on the town common. The gravestones were carved by local tradesmen who used a hammer and chisel to sculpt often ingenious artistic designs. Early gravestones were produced with a headstone and a footstone that were placed at the head and the foot of the grave to resemble the headboard and footboard of a bed. The stones were organized in random family groupings: it is only in modern times that the stones have been rearranged into rows to facilitate mowing. The stones were usually made from easily available slate, sandstone, or schist. Gravestones for prominent citizens and clergymen were often larger in size and with a more elaborate design that those made for less-important individuals or children.

John Foster's ornate slate gravestone indicates his prominent status in Boston and reflects the stern religious beliefs of the Puritans. Death, the Puritans believed, was to be welcomed as the gateway from the mortal world of sin to the glory of the afterlife, but because salvation was never certain, death was also an occasion of great anxiety. In this way, Puritan culture was riven by a significant inner tension: death was to both dreaded and embraced. Gravestones, then, became a constant reminder of the precariousness of life and the uncertainty of salvation. Members of the congregation would pass the gravestones every day, and the inscriptions, epitaphs, and imagery were intended to remind them to prepare for their own impending death. Even the shape of the gravestones was intentional, meant to symbolize an arch or a doorway through which the deceased could travel from one life to the next.

On this gravestone the imagery within the central arch represents the passage of time and the inevitability of death. Time, depicted as an old man with a scythe and hourglass, attempts to hold back Death, depicted as a skeleton, who reaches across to snuff out a candle, representing life, that burns above a globe. The handles on the globe resemble a snake with the head of a bird and the tail of a fish: symbols of regeneration. The sun, shining brightly at the top of the scene, promises eternal life in heaven. This iconography was typical of contemporary gravestones and would have been familiar to ordinary people in Puritan New England. Below the illustration reads an epitaph that emphasizes the brilliance of the deceased: "The *INGENIOUS* / Mathematician & printer / Mr John Foster / AGED 33 YEARS DYED SEPTR 9th / 1681."

Beneath this inscription, a verse in Latin next to the letters "IM" reads: "Living thou studiest the stars; dying mayst though, Foster / I pray, mount above the skies, and learn to measure the highest heaven." This verse was written by the clergyman Increase Mather after learning that his friend did not have long to live and alludes to Foster's work as an astronomer. Below, next to the letters "JF," is Foster's reply: "I measure it, and it is mine; the Lord Jesus has bought it for me / Nor am I held to pay aught for it but thanks." In contrast to the decorative headstone, the accompanying footstone is much plainer. Foster's name appears at the top, and below is a short phrase from Ovid's *Metamorphoses* that alludes to his commercial success as a printer: "SKILL WAS HIS CASH."

The two gravestones symbolize the significance of both the material and the spiritual worlds in Puritan New England. The headstone and its imagery provide a familiar scene of the ultimate triumph of death. It was intended to remind the observer of their own mortality and to inspire a moment of personal reflection. The footstone, meanwhile, commemorates Foster's own ability and prosperity. Both the universalist and the individualist aspects of his life are worthy of commemoration: Foster's material success was interpreted as a reward for his religious dedication.

—Jon Chandler

Questions for Further Study

1. Examine the imagery at the top of John Foster's headstone. What do the symbols represent? What message or messages were they intended to convey?

2. The inscription on the headstone praises the deceased as an "ingenious mathematician and printer," and the footstone simply pronounces that "skill was his cash." Do these images contradict or complement the imagery?

3. What does this gravestone reveal about the philosophical attitudes toward life and death of the Puritans in seventeenth-century New England?

Further Reading

Books

Bremer, Francis J. *The Puritan Experiment: New England Society from Bradford to Edwards*. Hanover: University Press of New England, 1995.

Ludwig, Allan I. *Graven Images: New England Stonecarving and Its Symbols, 1650–1815*. Hanover, NH: University Press of New England, 1999.

Roark, Elisabeth Louise. *Artists of Colonial America*. Westport: Greenwood Press, 2003.

Stannard, David E. *The Puritan Way of Death: A Study of Religion, Culture, and Social Change*. New York: Oxford University Press, 1977.

Websites

"Farber Gravestone Collection." American Antiquarian Society. https://www.americanantiquarian.org/farber-gravestone-collection.

Cherokee Delegation To England Portrait

Author/Creator "Markham"; Isaac Basire	**Image Type** Paintings, Flyers
Date 1730	**Significance** A portrait of the seven delegates from the Cherokee who visited London in 1730 to conclude a controversial treaty of alliance with Britain

Overview

This printed engraving is the only surviving depiction of the seven Cherokee delegates who visited London in 1730. The delegates were accompanied by Sir Alexander Cuming, an eccentric Scottish aristocrat who had traveled to South Carolina the previous year (without any government credentials) with a scheme to secure the allegiance of the Cherokees to Great Britain. The Cherokees were increasingly recognized in Britain as a powerful player in the region. Cuming believed that he could establish an alliance between Britain and the Cherokees that would erode French influence in the region and in turn make him rich and famous.

Cuming's success probably came through freakish luck rather than any actual understanding of Cherokee politics. In town after town, Cuming gained a positive reception for his promises of a new and stronger relationship with Britain and protection from the French. His plans probably coincided with the personal ambitions of an Overhill Cherokee chief called Moytoy who saw an opportunity to enhance his own political power. Cuming convened a meeting at the town of Nequassee in which he demanded a single point of contact, and the Cherokee found themselves electing Moytoy as "emperor" of the Cherokee nation. In return, Moytoy was only too happy to acknowledge King George II as the nation's sovereign, a term that meant little to the Cherokees.

Cuming immediately assembled a delegation of Cherokees to accompany him to England to conclude a formal treaty. Moytoy declined the invitation but appears to have given his blessing to the seven men who did decide to embark on the journey. The delegates arrived in England in June 1730. They remained there for three and a half months, during which time they met the king four times and visited a number of popular attractions such as the Tower of London and the Houses of Parliament. Everywhere they went, they were greeted by crowds of spectators who were fascinated by the visitors. This print was probably produced to sell to spectators who wanted a souvenir. The lengthy caption provides a detailed description of their visit. The document depicts the Cherokees as both savage outsiders and powerful allies.

About the Artist

The original painting was by an artist known only as "Markham" and is now lost. The surviving image is

Document Image

Portrait of the Cherokee delegation in 1730
(Collection of the Museum of Early Southern Decorative Arts, Old Salem Museums & Gardens)

CHEROKEE DELEGATION TO ENGLAND PORTRAIT 43

from an engraving made by Isaac Basire who specialized in cartographic prints and, like many other printmakers at the time, regularly plagiarized and undersold his competitors. It is likely, then, that this was not an authorized copy of the original painting. Images of Indigenous peoples had become increasingly popular in eighteenth-century Europe. In the eighteenth century, portraits, paintings, and prints of Indigenous visitors proliferated, particularly in Britain. These images were produced not just by obscure artists such as the mysterious Markham but also by artistic luminaries like George Romney and Sir Joshua Reynolds.

It is likely that Basire's work circulated at several different levels: first as an expensive painting for the wealthy, then as a cheaper mezzotint for the middling sort, then as an illicit copy produced by other artists to undercut the original versions. The cheap reproductions would have been sold to the general public as a souvenir. Large crowds gathered everywhere the Cherokee went around the city of London and created a market for people who wanted to purchase a memento of their visit. Basire doubtless created this plagiarized piece to profit from the popular fascination with the Cherokee delegates.

Context

In 1729, an eccentric Scottish aristocrat called Sir Alexander Cuming sailed to Charles Town (later named Charleston), the capital of the colony of South Carolina. Cuming, who had a history of speculation and recklessness, was supposedly inspired by his wife, who had dreamt that he would find great wealth in America. Cuming, with no credentials from the government, had decided that he would persuade the Cherokee to acknowledge their allegiance to the king and establish a lasting economic and military alliance between Britain and the Cherokee. He would then escort a delegation of Cherokees to England to formally seal the alliance. The British Crown, he hoped, would reward him handsomely, and he would become rich and famous.

Cuming spent several months in Charles Town, where most of the residents shunned him as a lunatic, before finally securing a guide who was willing to take him into Cherokee country.

He ventured northwest out of Charles Town and journeyed 300 miles into what is today Georgia and North Carolina, passing through various constellations of linguistically, culturally, and historically connected villages. The Cherokees had traded enslaved people and deerskins with Charles Town for at least a generation. Although depopulated by war, disease, and slave raids, they still numbered around fifteen thousand people who were dispersed in some fifty settlements, each housing around fifty inhabitants. However, most people continued to identify strongly with their matrilineal clans: there was no such thing as a Cherokee nation-state. In the late 1720s, the Cherokees were increasingly caught between the imperial rivalry of Britain and France. The Cherokees had allied with the British during the Yamasee War of 1715, but they were now increasingly divided between those who supported a continued relationship with Britain and those who wished to seek a new partnership with the French.

Cuming traveled through the Cherokee towns, oblivious to the political tensions he encountered, meeting dignitaries and shaking hands. In town after town, Cuming gained a positive reception for his promises of a new and stronger relationship with Britain and protection from the French. His plans coincided with the personal ambitions of an Overhill Cherokee chief called Moytoy who saw an opportunity to enhance his political power. Cuming convened a meeting at the town of Nequassee in which he demanded that the Cherokee nominate a single leader would carry out his plans. Moytoy likely stacked the meeting in advance to ensure that the assembly would elect him as "emperor" of all the Cherokee. In return, Moytoy was only too happy to acknowledge Cuming as the nation's "lawgiver" and King George II as its "sovereign," neither of which meant much to the Cherokees. The Cherokees interpreted the events as a sign of friendship, not allegiance; no one except Cuming believed that they had participated in a ceremony of subjection.

Cuming, desperate to publicize his apparent success, immediately assembled a delegation of Cherokees to accompany him to England to conclude a formal treaty. Moytoy himself declined the invitation but appears to have given his blessing to the seven men who did decide to embark on the journey. The motivations of these men are not clear, except perhaps personal ambitions that matched Moytoy's own. Cuming and the seven Cherokee traveled to Charles Town, from where they set sail on May 4, 1730, and arrived in England a month later.

Explanation and Analysis of the Document

This document depicts the seven delegates from the Cherokee, Ouka Ulah, Kettagustah, Tethtowie, Clogoittah, Collonnah, Onaconoa, and Oukanaekah, who visited England in 1730. For three and a half months, the Cherokees toured Britain. First they traveled to Windsor Castle, where they attended an installation ceremony for the Order of the Garter and met King George II and his sons. Four days later, accompanied by Cuming, they met the king again. They spotted their faces and shoulders with red, blue, and green paint, carried bows, and wore feathers on their heads. Cuming laid the Crown of Tanasi—a certain symbolic headdress Moytoy had obtained for Cuming, which to the Cherokees was little more than a token gift—at the feet of the king. The Cherokees then presented eagles' tails and four enemy scalps before posing for a group portrait that survives today in the form of this print.

Like all portraits, this one was carefully staged by both artist and subjects, and it is impossible to know for sure who was responsible for its specific features or exactly what messages were intended. The subjects' savagery is illustrated through their facial tattoos, their distinctive hairstyles (including the feathered plume worn by Ouka Ulah in the center), and their moccasins. Each delegate also carries a weapon—swords, a club, a rifle, a bow and arrow, a tomahawk, and a dagger—while on the far right Oukanaekah holds aloft a heart-shaped gourd rattle. For good measure, the subjects are situated within a fanciful forest that emphasizes their belonging to foreign and presumably primitive climes. However, the Cherokees do not appear to be particularly alarming or threatening. Instead, they adopt relaxed poses that resemble a "conversation piece," a popular genre of portraiture in the mid-eighteenth century that depicted its subjects in informal dialogue. Two of the men are identified, in language that would have been familiar to every reader but not to the Cherokees themselves, as a "King" and a "Prince." The delegates are each clothed from "the Royal Wardrobe" with fashionable breeches, fitted jackets, and shirts, which distinguished them as men of wealth and status in eighteenth-century Britain.

The image assumes, then, that the visitors are representatives of a type of savagery that is also seen as a promise of strength: however fierce the delegates may appear, they have now become friends and allies of Britain. The accompanying caption informs the reader of the "infinite Surpize and Wonder" expressed by the Cherokees during their tour during which they visited popular attractions such as the Tower of London, Parliament, Greenwich, and many theaters, spas, and fairs. The delegates, we are informed, have concluded a treaty of commerce and friendship and have offered their gratitude to the king. The lengthy caption concludes with a note informing the reader that Britain has won a valuable ally, since "the marks on their faces & bodys are tokens of Victory."

Britain had secured an agreement that obliged the Cherokees to assist the British in war, to trade only with the British, to live under British law, and to exclude the settlement of non-Britons in their land. However, none of the delegates had received the authority to sign on behalf of the nonexistent "Cherokee Nation." They believed they were participating in a ceremony of friendship rather than a binding treaty. When they finally received a full translation of the treaty, the delegates were furious. For twenty-two days they deliberated, but since they were stuck in England, they decided that they had no choice but to sign the agreement. They concluded that the language was purely figurative and that they had no authority to make such an agreement anyway. On October 7, laden with gifts of guns, kettles, clothing, and wampum, the delegates sailed for home.

The British had hoped to formalize an exclusive alliance and trade agreement, but the treaty did not reflect the wishes of the majority of the Cherokees, and the influence of the French remained strong. In 1734, a council held at Great Tellico disavowed the agreement, and the delegates renounced the treaty they had signed. Nonetheless, the visit left a lasting impression on the young man on the far right, Oukanaehah, who later came to be known as Attakullakulla, or Little Carpenter. He became one of the most eminent leaders and diplomatic negotiators of the Cherokee. A shrewd politician, he consistently opposed war with the British and sought peace and prosperity for his people.

—Jon Chandler

Questions for Further Study

1. Carefully examine the image. What messages do you think the artist is trying to convey?

2. Now examine the caption. Do you think this is an accurate description of the Cherokees' visit to England?

3. The man on the far right, Oukanaehah, later came to be known as Attakullakulla, or Little Carpenter, and was a staunch ally of the British. How do you think he was influenced by his visit to England?

Further Reading

Books

Fullagar, Kate. *The Savage Visit: New World People and Popular Imperial Culture in Britain, 1710–1795*. Berkeley: University of California Press, 2012.

Thrush, Coll. *Indigenous London: Native Travelers at the Heart of Empire*. New Haven: Yale University Press, 2016.

Tortora, Daniel J. *Carolina in Crisis: Cherokees, Colonists, and Slaves in the American Southeast, 1756–1763*. Chapel Hill: University of North Carolina Press, 2015.

Vaughn, Alden T. *Transatlantic Encounters: American Indians in Britain, 1500–1776*. Cambridge: Cambridge University Press, 2006.

Weaver, Jace. *The Red Atlantic: American Indigenes and the Making of the Modern World, 1000–1927*. Chapel Hill: University of North Carolina Press, 2014.

Websites

Fear-Segal, Jacqueline. "The Long and Enduring Relationship between the Cherokee and British People." *Beyond the Spectacle: Native North American Presence in Britain*, University of Kent. https://blogs.kent.ac.uk/bts/2019/02/12/the-long-and-enduring-relationship-between-the-cherokee-and-british-people/.

"A View Of Savannah" Map

Author/Creator
Paul Fourdrinier, Peter Gordon, George Jones, Noble Jones, James Oglethorpe

Date
1734

Image Type
Maps

Significance
A perspective view of Savannah, Georgia, that illustrates the utopian intentions of the colony's founders and has had an important influence on urban planning in America

Overview

This print offers an oblique perspective view of the streets, squares, and buildings of Savannah, the first settlement in Georgia. It was commissioned by the Georgia Trustees, a group of merchants, politicians, and clergy who were instrumental in the establishment of a new colony in America. The colony was conceived by James Edward Oglethorpe, a member of Parliament and a former army officer who had taken a keen interest in social and moral concerns. Oglethorpe and the trustees hoped to alleviate urban poverty in England by shipping the unemployed and the unemployable to America. In the new colony they would be granted their own farms, and though agricultural labor they would become productive subjects. These settlers would become the citizen-soldiers who would defend the flourishing colony of South Carolina from the hostile Spanish in Florida.

In 1732 the trustees were awarded a royal charter to establish a new colony that would be named Georgia after King George II. In 1733 Oglethorpe accompanied the first colonists to America, and over the next decade he played a critical and often controversial part in almost every aspect of life in the colony. His influence remains visible today in his design for the town of Savannah. Oglethorpe planned the city around a series of streets and open squares laid out in a grid pattern. Oglethorpe was a utopian, and he expressed his ideals in the design, layout, and operation of Savannah and the surrounding region. He was certain that the organization of the built environment would ensure the growth of an egalitarian, industrious, and loyal citizenry. His plan, captured in this image, has become an icon of urban planning in the New World.

The Georgia Trustees were eager to advertise their new settlement and raise money through charitable subscriptions and donations. The trustees embarked on an ambitious campaign to promote the colony, producing promotional literature and prints like this one, which were circulated widely to raise publicity about the venture. The trustees never raised enough funds from donations, however, and the colony relied on financial assistance from Parliament. In 1752, the trustees surrendered their charter to the colony, and Georgia came under the direct rule of the government in London.

Document Image

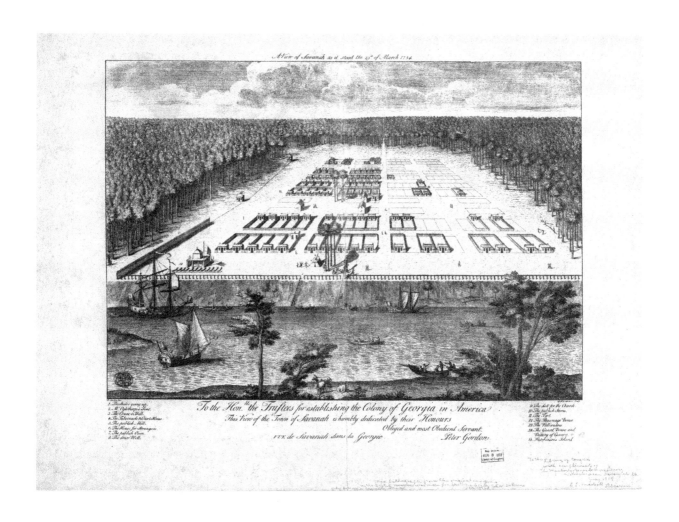

The 1734 map of Savannah, Georgia
(Library of Congress)

"A View of Savannah" Map

About the Artist

This print is often credited to Peter Gordon, who is named in the elaborate dedication found at the bottom of the scene. Recent research, however, has established that this is incorrect. Gordon was an unemployed upholster and one of the original settlers who sailed to Georgia with Oglethorpe in 1733. Later that year, he was given permission to return to England and carried with him a copy of the town plan. The original plan was probably drawn up by Noble Jones, the first surveyor of Georgia. Gordon was entrusted with carrying it to George Jones, a London draughtsman, who converted it into a perspective view of the town. Gordon presented this to the Georgia Trustees, who directed him to have it engraved. Engraving was a popular method of reproducing images in the eighteenth century by incising a design onto a metal plate, which was then covered in ink before a piece of paper was laid over the surface to create a printed impression. The engraving ensured that the plan would be accessible to a larger number of people, and the trustees ordered that all proceeds be donated to the poor. Gordon, following instructions, took the image to Paul Fourdrinier, a noted engraver, who created the print with its dedication. Gordon was simply the messenger, but it appears likely that he claimed credit for the image to try to profit from its sale.

However, the most influential individual involved in the creation of this image was James Edward Oglethorpe (1696–1785). It was Oglethorpe who oversaw all the propaganda for the colony, who must have had the idea to produce the print, who must have instructed the surveyor to create the initial plan, and who then deputized Gordon to carry it to the draughtsman and thence to the trustees and the engraver. Oglethorpe was a landed gentleman who, after a military career, entered politics. In 1729, after the death of a friend who had been imprisoned for debt, he was appointed to head a committee to investigate conditions in English prisons. He was horrified by what he found and became an advocate for prison reform. By 1730 he had formulated a far more ambitious plan to establish a new colony in America that would provide opportunities for the poor. He partnered with like-minded individuals to form the Georgia Trustees, who successfully petitioned for a royal charter for the new colony. In 1733 he accompanied the first settlers across the Atlantic to Georgia and for the next decade was the most important figure in the colony, acting as de facto governor and leading military campaigns against the Spanish. In 1743 he departed Georgia for the last time and returned to England. He continued to serve in Parliament until 1754 and then resumed his military career before his retirement.

Context

Oglethorpe believed that the establishment of a new colony would provide social and moral redemption for poor Englishmen to improve themselves and defend the frontier of the empire. Georgia, unlike the existing colonies, was to be a charitable venture administered by twenty-one philanthropists and social reformers known as the Georgia Trustees. According to Oglethorpe, Georgia was a bountiful haven containing "fertile Lands sufficient to subsist all the useless Poor in England, and distressed Protestants in Europe." He argued that agrarian labor would transform the poor into useful subjects who would defend the imperial frontier. In 1733 Oglethorpe arrived with the first settlers to establish the town of Savannah. His paternalistic, almost authoritarian, attitude produced mixed results. His conviction was critical in securing the colony's survival during the first years of settlement, but his inappropriate choice of officials, and his unflinching loyalty to them, created considerable resentment.

By the mid-1730s, Oglethorpe and the trustees were battling protests that they were stunting the economic development of the colony due to the prohibition of Black slavery. Early on, Oglethorpe had decided that slavery was not compatible with his utopian intentions. His opposition to slavery was pragmatic rather than ideological. South Carolina, with is large plantations and Black majority, had a dispersed free white population and was vulnerable to uprisings of the enslaved. Oglethorpe believed that slavery would jeopardize the creation of a militia that was necessary to defend the frontier. Moreover, he was convinced that slavery was degrading to free men, who would aspire to own slaves themselves instead of dedicating themselves to hard work. Instead, Oglethorpe and the trustees wanted to increase the number of whites willing to bear arms by establishing numerous small farms worked by free families instead of a smaller number of large plantations dependent on enslaved laborers. To promote their vision, the trustees restricted new settlers to just fifty acres (significantly smaller than plantations in South Carolina) and prohibited the importation or possession of enslaved workers. Rather than replicating South Carolina's rice economy, the trustees promoted the production of silk and wine, which were not seen as requiring slave labor. Georgia's free and industrious settlers would create a formidable barrier against the Spanish in Florida.

The trustees were obsessed with creating a society that was free of social and moral corruption. However, except Oglethorpe, none of the trustees ever visited Georgia, and they had no comprehension of the new world in which they were concerned. The trustees did not trust their subjects to improve themselves without strict guidelines, so in addition to prohibiting slavery and limiting landholdings, they banned alcohol as deterrent to hard work, prevented lawyers from practicing in the new colony to discourage agitation, and governed the colony through a court of four officials rather than an elected assembly. These restrictions provoked deep discontent among the colonists, who contrasted their hardships against the relative prosperity of South Carolina's plantation owners. Pro-slavery Georgians began to pressure Parliament to lift the probation, and when Oglethorpe returned to England, the trustees finally conceded defeat. The ban on slavery was lifted in 1751, and the following year the colony was handed over to the crown. Georgia received the common colonial political structure of an elected assembly, an appointed council, and a royal governor.

Georgia quickly diverged from the reformist vision of its founders and established a plantation society with a strict slave code that virtually replicated South Carolina. The new administration stimulated an economic and demographic explosion, with most of the new growth dependent on emigrants from South Carolina establishing rice and indigo plantations. The experiments in wine and silk collapsed, and, as the trustees had feared, the introduction of Black slavery concentrated wealth and power into a small number of large plantations.

Explanation and Analysis of the Document

This widely reproduced print depicts a dramatic perspective view of Savannah a year after its founding. The image, looking south from the Savannah River, depicts a grid of streets and squares that had been designed and surveyed by James Edward Oglethorpe. The central street running from the river through the town into the forest is Whitaker Street, which is still a main throughfare in Savannah's historic district. The other two streets on either side are Bull Street on the left (east) and Barnard Street on the right (west). The image presents an orderly and symmetrical plan of the city that was organized into rectangular wards centered on open areas called squares. Only four squares are depicted, but it is certain that Oglethorpe surveyed six. Each square was organized into a ward containing residential housing as well as space for civic buildings. The housing was organized into tythings on the north and south sides of the square; each tything consisted of ten houses. The east and west sides of the square was reserved for public buildings such as courthouses or churches.

Every freeman who came to the settle in the new colony was awarded fifty acres of land. This included their house within Savannah, a five-acre garden outside the city, and a forty-five-acre farm beyond the gardens. The settlers generally lived in the city and worked on their garden and farm for food. The wards were designed to correlate with the exterior garden and farm lots so that communities stayed together both inside and outside of the city. Oglethorpe's plan reflects his utopian intentions for the city. The design is repetitive and egalitarian, with every house, garden, and farm of an equal size.

In the foreground, the Savannah River is bustling with traffic, as large ships and small boats visit the port and goods are hauled up a steep embankment. The print's metropolitan audience would no doubt be impressed by the scale of economic activity. The engraving identifies several important locations in the new city. A staircase from the river to the city is adjacent to Oglethorpe's tent, which served as the first public building in the settlement. Oglethorpe's original intention was to return swiftly to London, and he probably had no plan to construct a permanent home. He also no doubt realized the important of setting an example of self-sacrifice. Four figures are gathered around the tent, perhaps including Oglethorpe himself. Adjacent to the tent is a crane that was built a week after the colonists arrived at the site to hoist barrels and boxes from the river. Slightly behind the tent is the tabernacle and courthouse where church services were held, while the location of the town mill, public oven, and communal well in the center of the city is a reminder of the colony's utopian mission. Nearby, "The House for Strangers" was designed for a formal meeting between Oglethorpe and Tomochichi, the chief of the Yamacraw, who lived in coastal Georgia when the settlers arrived. Tomochichi welcomed the colonists because it was an opportunity to establish trade and diplomatic relations with the English. Oglethorpe and Tomochici spoke through interpreters and established a friendly relationship. In 1734 Tomochici, his wife, their adopted son, and six tribesmen accompanied Oglethorpe on a trip to England. "The House for Strangers" was later occupied by a group of German Protestants known as Salzburgers. The engraving also identified the future location of the church as well as a fort and guardhouse. In the bottom left, next to the guardhouse, are the town stocks. Punishments were harsh for those who did not abide by the code of conduct insisted upon the trustees.

Oglethorpe only laid out the first six squares, but his design was followed for decades after he returned to England. The city grew to include twenty-four squares, and twenty-two of these remain today. The towns of Ebenezer and New Inverness, later known as Darien, were also laid out with squares and wards, and Oglethorpe's influence on urban planning continues to the present day.

—Jon Chandler

Questions for Further Study

1. Examine the engraving of Savannah. How has the city been designed? How does its design contribute to its utopian mission?

2. James Oglethorpe and the Georgia Trustees decided to produce this print in London, where it circulated widely. Why do you think they chose to produce this image in particular? What did they want their audience to take away from it?

3. If you examine the engraving carefully, you'll see that important locations throughout the city are identified by numbers that match captions at the bottom. But the town stocks, which are toward the bottom left of the image, are not captioned. Why not?

Further Reading

Books

Wilson, Thomas D. *The Oglethorpe Plan: Enlightenment Design in Savannah and Beyond.* Charlottesville: University of Virginia Press, 2012.

Wood, Betty. *Slavery in Colonial Georgia, 1730–1775.* Athens: University of Georgia Press, 1984.

Articles

Baine, Rodney M., and Louis de Vorsey. "The Provenance and Historical Accuracy of 'A View of Savannah as It Stood the 29th of March 1734.'" *Georgia Historical Quarterly* 73, no. 4 (1989): 784–813.

de Vorsey, Louis. "The Origin and Appreciation of Savannah, Georgia's Historic City Squares." *Southeastern Geographer* 52, no. 1 (2012): 90–99.

Websites

"James Edward Oglethorpe." Georgia Historical Society website. https://georgiahistory.com/education-outreach/online-exhibits/featured-historical-figures/james-edward-oglethorpe/.

Robert Feke: Portrait Of Isaac Royall And Family

Author/Creator Robert Feke	**Image Type** Painting
Date 1741	**Significance** A family portrait reflecting the growing prosperity and status of some North American families before the American Revolution

Overview

This 1741 group portrait by Robert Feke of Isaac Royall Jr., one of the wealthiest men in colonial New England, and his wife, daughter, sister, and sister-in-law is an example of the fledgling school of American artists who drew upon established artistic practices that first developed in Europe while cultivating their own unique style. Given the high prices portrait painters commanded for their commissions, such works tended to be limited to households in the upper echelons and, when displayed in a home's entryway or parlor, reflected the wealth and prestige of its occupants. Colonial elites obviously sought to emulate their British counterparts by sitting for portrait artists, which indicated both the close connections between Great Britain and its North American colonies and the emergence of powerful colonial leaders, some of whom wished to remain loyal to the British government and others who came to challenge British rule in the 1760s and 1770s.

Royall's father, Squire Isaac Royall Sr., rose from comparatively humble beginnings to acquire a substantial fortune as a seller of rum, sugar, and enslaved people. In 1700 Royall Sr. relocated from Dorchester, Massachusetts, to the Caribbean Island of Antigua, where his son was born in 1719. In the face of mounting challenges, Royall Sr. acquired a large parcel of Massachusetts and returned to New England with his family and several enslaved people in 1737. The estate passed to the younger Royall two years later following his father's death, whereupon he began to greatly increase the family's already considerable assets. The younger Royall held numerous posts in local and colonial government, including a tenure as the representative of Medford, the location of the family estate, in the colonial assembly.

Feke's painting of the Royall family reveals their obvious wealth but also something of colonial gender dynamics, with the male head of the household standing to the right of the four seated female relatives under his care. The work offers insight into how colonial elites such as Royall viewed themselves as members of colonial society and invites consideration of how their growing economic and political influence might have either encouraged a sense of American autonomy that influenced the development of an independence movement or strengthened their ties to Great Britain.

Document Image

The Royall family portrait from 1741
(HOLLIS Images, Harvard Library)

ROBERT FEKE: PORTRAIT OF ISAAC ROYALL AND FAMILY 55

About the Artist

While a great many of Robert Feke's paintings survived to the present day, comparatively little is known about the artist who produced them, one of the first notable colonial artists. His great-grandfather left Norfolk, England, for Watertown, Massachusetts, in 1631. The Fekes later relocated to Oyster Bay, Long Island, where Feke's father worked as a blacksmith and Baptist minister. Feke was born between 1705 and 1710 and spent several years as a sailor, which allowed his to voyage to England and Europe. According to some accounts, Feke developed his painting technique without any formal training while imprisoned in Spain. He first gained notoriety as a portrait painter in New York City; his earliest known painting, that of a young boy, was dated to sometime in the 1730s. Feke relocated to Boston in the early 1740s and gained notoriety for painting portraits of New England elites. Feke's group portrait of Harvard Law School cofounder Isaac Royall and his family from 1741 is perhaps his best-known work.

In 1742 Feke married Eleanor Cozzens, the daughter of a prosperous tailor in Newport, Rhode Island, and resided in his wife's hometown for the next several years. The couple raised three sons and two daughters. Feke continued to paint wealthy personages, primarily merchants from Boston and Philadelphia, until poor health supposedly compelled him to travel to either Bermuda or Barbados in search of a more favorable climate. There is no official record of his death, but some evidence suggests it occurred in 1752.

The nearly sixty paintings either signed by Feke or believed to be by him convey a style that emphasizes a sense of realism and sophistication that matches the work produced by European artists of the era. His portraits of such colonial luminaries as Benjamin Franklin, whom Feke painted in the late 1740s, are invaluable in presenting images of those from the highest ranks of colonial society before the American Revolution.

Context

By the mid-eighteenth century, Britain's North American colonies were considerably more populous and prosperous than the modest enclaves established by the ambitious opportunists and religious dissidents who first inhabited Jamestown and Plymouth a century before. The rapid growth of shipbuilding and fishing in New England and tobacco and cotton production in the South increased the colonies' financial importance to the British government, particularly as the English colonies, despite their small size, came to be significant participants in the expanding Atlantic economy. Colonial merchants traded domestically with the indigenous and French-Canadian inhabitants of North America and exported an increasingly large amount of goods to Europe. Subsistence farmers, who made up most of the colonial population, grasped the potential profits that might be gained by producing a surplus of crops to be sold for both intercolonial and export markets.

Against this backdrop of a growing capitalist awakening, some enterprising, driven individuals sought enormous growth, taking advantage of the rising demand in Europe for such products as tobacco and rum. The economies of the southern colonies came to depend on the large-scale production of specific cash crops, such as rice, indigo, and cotton, that offered considerable financial gain if harvests were bountiful and the prospect of ruin if the crops failed. Southern entrepreneurs showed little interest in investing in manufacturing in their region, which resulted in the development of few large cities and the general absence of local merchant communities. Instead, investments went into the acquisition of more land and more enslaved people to perform backbreaking labor in all conditions to enrich their owners.

Colder temperatures and less-fertile soil in many locations discouraged northerners from undertaking the sort of extensive commercial agriculture that came to define the South's economy. Northern farmers tended to grow staple crops, such as wheat, for the purposes of feeding their families and selling or bartering the surplus on a local or possibly regional market. Such subsistence farming encouraged northerners to engage in small-scale manufacturing to supplement their incomes and discouraged the widespread use of enslaved labor. But none of the northern colonies abolished slavery before the American Revolution, and some northern colonists, such as Isaac Royall, participated in the slave trade and acquired large profits by negotiating the sale of human cargoes to plantations located in the southern colonies and in the Caribbean. Such transactions were part of the increasingly complicated trade network that linked together the economies of Europe, Africa, and the Americas. Entrepreneurs like Royall grew in number and influence in northern coastal cities such as Boston, New York, and Philadelphia, becoming members of a vibrant merchant class that took full advantage of British protectionism when it benefitted them and seeking ways of avoiding it when the lure of higher profits from deals with the French, Dutch, or Spanish were possible.

Explanation and Analysis of the Document

In 1741 when the members of the Royall family posed for this portrait, Isaac Royall Jr., while just in his early twenties, was already overseeing a large and rapidly growing estate bequeathed to him by his recently departed father. Isaac Royall Sr. had purchased the 500 acres located in Medford, Massachusetts, for the family estate in 1732 while still overseeing his sugar cane plantation on the island of Antigua in the West Indies, which he established in the early 1690s. His success as a merchant trading sugar, rum, and, especially, enslaved people between the Caribbean and Boston resulted in his acquisition of considerable wealth. At the time of the Royalls' relocation to Massachusetts, father and son co-owned more than sixty enslaved people, more than any other family in the colony at that time.

In 1737, at the age of nineteen, Royall Jr. married fifteen-year-old Elizabeth McIntosh. The young bride also came from a privileged background, having inherited the estates of both her parents and most of the holdings of her grandfather, Colonel Henry McIntosh, who had left his granddaughter a considerable amount of land in Suriname, a Dutch colony located on the coast of South America. The union both increased Royall Jr.'s assets and served to consolidate his position as a member of the Massachusetts elect. The Royalls brought twenty-seven enslaved people to live and work on the estate.

Following the death of Isaac Sr. in 1739, his young son assumed control over his father's many properties, which he augmented with several real estate acquisitions while also holding such important public offices as justice of the peace and Medford's representative to the colonial legislature. Royall also added to his wealth as one of New England's most successful slave traders. He and his wife hosted a number of social gatherings at their estate that allowed them to showcase their fine home and its furnishings, including the family portrait painted in 1741.

Feke's painting of the Royalls draws upon some of the elements of the Grand Manner or Great Style aesthetic popular with British and American artists in the eighteenth century. The Grand Manner movement emphasized the use of large-scale and visual metaphors to communicate the high rank and noble traits of those appearing on canvas. The large, paned glass windows revealing mature trees and soaring clouds are meant to invoke a sense of the virtuous natural world, an homage to works by artists of the Renaissance often found in Grand Manner portraits. With its large dimensions of 56 3/16 inches by 77 3/4 inches, the group portrait's figures are close to life size. This is consistent with works painted in the Grand Manner, which attempt to instill a sense of awe in the viewer.

The subjects' elegant and obviously expensive clothing and graceful poses leave little ambiguity as to their high social standing. Dressed in a waistcoat and jacket made from rich velvet, Royall Jr. appears relaxed while still projecting an air of patriarchal authority emphasized by being the only standing figure. Seated to the immediate left of Royall Jr. is his wife and their infant daughter, both named Elizabeth, then his sister-in-law Mary McIntosh Palmer and his sister Penelope Royall Vassall, the wife of an owner of a planation in Jamaica. All the females in the portrait, including the eight-month-old Elizabeth, appear to be wearing satin dresses. The table they are seated at displays a carpet done in the "turkey-work" style that was popular among the well-to-do in England and America during the 1700s. The infant Elizabeth clutches a teether made from coral set in a handle of gold and ivory as a final symbol of the Royalls' elevated status.

As was the case with many wealthy colonists, Royall found his loyalties divided during the American Revolution. While he expressed sympathies for those advocating for the colonies' independence, his wealth was too dependent upon his connections to Loyalist families and the British government to break ranks and become a Patriot. Royall hurriedly departed Medford for Nova Scotia, Canada, just as hostilities commenced between British troops and colonial militiamen in Massachusetts in April 1775, leaving instructions that his enslaved people be given their freedom. Despite his sympathy for the cause of America independence, Royall's name appeared in the

Massachusetts Banishment Act of 1778, and he ultimately went into exile in England with his daughters. He died of smallpox in 1781, unable to return to Massachusetts. His influence continued after his death with the bequeathment of a sum of money to Harvard College, for the purpose of establishing either a medical or law school, the latter being selected.

—Michael Carver

Questions for Further Study

1. How would you describe the five figures' facial expressions? Are there detectable differences between the only male figure and the three adult women?

2. Why might the small girl located at the center of the painting be represented almost as an adult?

3. What does the positioning of the three women in the picture reveal about the status of women in Colonial America?

Further Reading

Books

Craven, Wayne. *Colonial American Portraiture*. New York: Cambridge University Press, 1986.

Procter, Alice. *The Whole Picture: The Colonial Story of the Art in Our Museums and Why We Need to Talk about It*. London: Cassell, 2021.

Saunders, Richard H. *American Faces: A Cultural History of Portraiture and Identity*. Hanover: University Press of New England, 2016.

Websites

"Examining Colonial Portraits with Boldt and Ackermann." *Decorative Arts Trust Bulletin*, October 28, 2020. https://decorativeartstrust.org/colonial-portraits-boldt-ackermann-post/.

"Faces of America: Portraits." *Uncovering America*, National Gallery of Art. https://www.nga.gov/learn/teachers/lessons-activities/uncovering-america/faces-portraits.html.

Royall House and Slave Quarters. https://royallhouse.org.

Dockside At Virginia Tobacco Warehouse Illustration

Author/Creator
Joshua Fry, Peter Jefferson, Francis Hayman, Charles Grignion, Thomas Jefferys

Date
1753

Image Type
Maps; Flyers; Illustrations

Significance
An illustration of a wharf in mid-eighteenth-century Virginia that emphasizes the importance of tobacco cultivation and the corresponding growth of slavery in the colony

Overview

This document is an example of a cartouche, a decorative emblem that was often included in published maps until the nineteenth century. A cartouche usually contained the map's title, its date and place of publication, the names of the mapmakers, and a dedication. This extravagant cartouche provides an imagined interpretation of what a mid-eighteenth-century tobacco wharf in Virginia may have looked like.

This particular cartouche was attached to Joshua Fry and Peter Jefferson's *A Map of the Most Inhabited Part of Virginia*, which was first published in 1753. That map was the first to accurately represent the interior regions of Virginia beyond the coastal plain known as the tidewater. Its preparation and publication were prompted by the struggle between Great Britain and France for control over North America. By the late 1740s, the British had become increasingly concerned about French activities in the Ohio Valley and the potential exposure of western Pennsylvania and Virginia. In 1750, the Board of Trade in London commissioned several new and more detailed maps to provide more precise information about the region. To this end, the governor of Virginia employed two surveyors, Fry and Jefferson, to develop a new map of the colony. The surveyors sent their original draft to London in 1751, and it was published in 1753. The following year, tensions between Britain and France in the Ohio Valley erupted into war.

The map may have been intended initially for use by a small number of officials rather than for wider publication. However, by 1753, escalating tensions with France had increased the popular demand for maps of the colonies. The publisher, Thomas Jeffreys, commissioned this lavish cartouche to increase its appeal with the popular market. Its artistic design emphasizes the importance of tobacco in mid-eighteenth-century Virginia. It focuses on the commercial exchange of tobacco with planters in the foreground while four enslaved Black men, minimally dressed, labor around them. The map, complete with this cartouche, was reprinted eight times and remained the most authoritative map of Virginia and the surrounding regions for over forty years.

Document Image

Virginia wharf illustration from 1753
(Library of Virginia)

About the Artist

The two mapmakers, Joshua Fry and Peter Jefferson, were the most experienced surveyors and cartographers in Virginia at the time. Fry was born in England, studied at Oxford, and migrated to Virginia around 1720. He taught mathematics at the College of William and Mary and married a wealthy young widow. He immediately resigned his position and took over the management of his wife's plantation and its enslaved laborers. He later moved his family further west and established a plantation in Albemarle County. He became the county's judge as well as its official surveyor. In 1749 he partnered with Peter Jefferson (a major landowner in the county and the father of Thomas Jefferson) to survey the boundary between North Carolina and Virginia. That same year, the two men along with several others established the Loyal Company of Virginia, a land speculation company that had obtained 800,000 acres south of the Ohio River. Their involvement with several surveying projects for the colony ensured that when the Board of Trade commissioned a new map of Virginia, Fry and Jefferson were the obvious choice.

Fry and Jefferson's draft map was completed in 1751 and published two years later by Thomas Jefferys. Jefferys had begun his career as an engraver and established himself as one of the most prominent cartographic publishers in London. His appointment as Geographer to the Prince of Wales meant that he was effectively the government's official geographer. This gave him access to official manuscripts as well as government commissions. We do not know for certain how Jefferys acquired the map. We do know that before its publication he decided to embellish the map with an elaborate cartouche. He commissioned two famous artists, Francis Hayman and Charles Grignion, to design and engrave the cartouche. Hayman was known for history paintings, theatrical scenes, and portraits, while Grignion was a historical engraver and book illustrator. Neither of these men had ever visited America. The cartouche was intended to be eye-catching rather than accurate to make the map more appealing to a general market.

Context

This document was produced in the mid-eighteenth century when Virginia was at the peak of its success in the tobacco trade. Tobacco was introduced to the colony in 1612, where it was grown in the first settlements around Jamestown. From there, the crop expanded north until it dominated the Chesapeake Bay area. Tobacco became the foundation of the colony's economy: it could be used to remit taxes, purchase goods, and even pay salaries. Promissory notes payable in tobacco circulated as readily as currency. Virginia was home to the most extensive and navigable river system on the seaboard. These rivers brought ships into the heart of the colony and connected many tobacco planters directly to markets in Europe. Large planters usually shipped their tobacco straight to England or Scotland, where an agent would, for a fee, store the tobacco, pay all customs duties, sell it, and use the profits as directed by his client. British merchants also sent agents, known as factors, to Virginia to liaise with the planters from whom they purchased tobacco. Smaller planters sold tobacco directly to these factors, who operated in exchange for manufactured goods.

By 1750, tobacco had become the continent's most valuable export. Virginia had been enriched by the tobacco trade and had experienced a corresponding boom in population. In the mid-eighteenth century, the colony's population of around 260,00 was the largest in British North America. Fully one-quarter of these people were enslaved. Tobacco was a notoriously labor-intensive crop, and as cultivation increased, so did the demand for workers. This labor demand was initially fulfilled by indentured servants from Britain, who worked for a predetermined number of years to pay back the cost of their passage before they became free. There was an ample supply of indentured servants during the middle decades of the seventeenth century, but as pay and conditions improved in Britain, this source of labor began to dry up and was replaced by slaves. By the turn of the eighteenth century, white indentured servants were outnumbered by enslaved Blacks. Between 1698 and 1774, as many as 100,000 enslaved captives had been transported to Virginia, with the largest numbers arriving in the 1730s and 1740s. The profits from slavery and tobacco allowed Virginia to replicate the English model of a landed gentry, which imposed a political, social, and economic hierarchy on the colony.

Virginia was by now tightly integrated into the global economy, and changes in tobacco prices could have significant ramifications. Prices had remained stable in the 1740s and 1750s, but fluctuations in the 1760s began to put planters in financial trouble. Most planters traded on credit, which meant that they were perpetually in debt to British merchants. After a major banking crisis in 1772, those merchants called in their debts, creating significant discontent among planters and traders. When war broke out between Britain and its colonies in 1775, tobacco exports stopped almost completely. Tobacco production fell from 55 million to 14.5 million pounds in the first year of war alone. Virginian planters were forced to diversify into foodstuffs and other products. Virginia's gentry remained preeminent, however, and many became leaders during the revolutionary and early national periods.

Explanation and Analysis of the Document

This cartouche illustrates the importance of tobacco cultivation in mid-eighteenth-century Virginia. It is concentrated on a detailed engraving of a dockside wharf. It depicts eight men on a dock where barrels of tobacco are being loaded on board an English ship. Amid the barrels are an assortment of characters. In the foreground, a ship's captain negotiates with two planters. The planters are finely dressed in the style of English gentlemen, and one of them symbolically smokes a pipe of tobacco. To the right, an inspector with his back turned carefully checks the cargo. Four Black men, who are clearly enslaved, are dressed only in loincloths. Three are preparing the tobacco for shipment, rolling the huge barrels to the dock to be weighed and then rowing them to the waiting ship. A fourth serves wine and pineapple, symbols of hospitality in colonial Virginia, to the white men. Their labor is essential to the entire enterprise, but they are infantilized through their near-nakedness and their diminutive stature. In contrast, the white men look and behave like proper Englishmen. The cartouche emphasizes the colony's prosperity as well as its continued cultural connections to Britain.

In the background looms a large warehouse where tobacco intended for export and imported manufactured goods were stored. Warehouses were built in ports and on major rivers throughout Virginia. Legislation passed by the colonial assembly required that all tobacco be stored in dockside warehouses such as these so that it could be easily inspected to ensure its quality. Two inspectors were employed at every warehouse to ensure that only tobacco of the best quality was exported. The tobacco was packed into barrels known as hogsheads that were of a regulated size. Inspectors, like the man in this image, looked through the barrels and checked at least two samples for substandard tobacco. Inspectors who allowed a shipment of inferior tobacco or who accepted bribes would face a heavy penalty. If a planter or merchant refused to release his tobacco for inspection, the entire shipment would be destroyed. The law was extremely unpopular, particularly with small planters, who had to pay to store their tobacco in dockside warehouses such as the one in this image. Regardless, because of the tobacco trade and the warehouse system, major towns emerged around major ports in the eighteenth century.

At the bottom of the cartouche is a dedication to the Earl of Halifax. Halifax was the president of the Board of Trade, an organization that had been established in the seventeenth century to promote colonial trade, but it had largely stagnated over the subsequent decades. Halifax, appointed in 1748, was determined to revive the organization and reclaim some its powers from colonial governments. One of his initiatives was to acquire better knowledge of the empire by commissioning new maps of each colony, including the map of Virginia to which this cartouche was attached. In 1751, the surveyors Joshua Fry and Peter Jefferson sent their map of Virginia to London, where it would have been received by the Board of Trade. Two years later, the map was published by Thomas Jefferys with the addition of this cartouche. It is not known how Jeffreys acquired the map, but the dedication implies that he obtained it directly from Halifax.

The artistic cartouche was designed to make the map more marketable to a general audience. It was produced by two artists who had never been to America, but who used their imagination and probably discussions with traders and travelers to create this scene of commercial exchange on a Virginia wharf. Published in London and intended for domestic as well as colonial markets, the cartouche was intended to remind viewers of the colony's prosperity and refinement. It presented the colony as a prime location for investment at a time when the tobacco trade was booming amid looming tensions with France.

—Jon Chandler

Questions for Further Study

1. This image, or cartouche, was attached to a map of colonial Virginia that was published in London. Why do you think the publisher decided to include this image?

2. Compare and contrast the depiction of the four white men with the four Black men. What message are the artists trying to convey?

3. What, if anything, does this cartouche tell us about the tobacco trade in colonial Virginia?

Further Reading

Books

Breen, T. H. *Tobacco Culture: The Mentality of the Great Tidewater Planters on the Eve of Revolution*. Princeton: Princeton University Press, 2009.

Kulikoff, Allan. *Tobacco and Slaves: The Development of Southern Cultures in the Chesapeake, 1680–1800*. Chapel Hill: University of North Carolina Press, 2012.

Articles

Taliaferro, Henry. "Fry and Jefferson Revisited." *Journal of Southern Decorative Arts* 34 (2013).

Verner, Coolie. "The Fry and Jefferson Map." *Imago Mundi* 21 (1967): 70–94.

Websites

"From Williamsburg to Wills's Creek: The Fry-Jefferson Map of Virginia." Library of Virginia website. https://www.lva.virginia.gov/exhibits/fry-jefferson/.

Sellers, John R. "Mapping the American Revolution and Its Era," Library of Congress website. https://www.loc.gov/collections/american-revolutionary-war-maps/articles-and-essays/mapping-the-american-revolution-and-its-era/.

Benjamin Franklin: "Join, or Die" Cartoon

Author/Creator
Benjamin Franklin

Date
1754

Image Type
Cartoons

Significance
One of the first political cartoons to call for unity among the American colonies, used initially during the French and Indian War and again during the American Revolution

Overview

The "Join, or Die" illustration was one of the first images used to promote unity among the thirteen colonies that would become the United States. The cartoon accompanied a May 1754 essay by Benjamin Franklin in the *Pennsylvania Gazette*, Franklin's newspaper. At the time, fighting had broken out between the British and French colonists in North America in what would become the French and Indian War (1754–63). This was one theater in a global war, the Seven Years' War (1756–63), between Britain and its allies and a French-led coalition. The image depicts a snake that has been cut into pieces, presumably by the French and their allies, and each segment of the serpent is labeled as a different colony. At the time, snakes were often viewed favorably as a symbol of renewal and transformation because of their ability to shed their skins. Hence, the snake could be viewed as a symbol of the colonies as they evolved from separate entities into a single, more potent creature.

In his essay, Franklin warned that if the British colonies did not cooperate and coordinate their efforts, the French and their Native American allies would be able to conquer them one by one. At the time, the author and some others, meeting in Albany, New York, were seeking to create a single colonial government. The ambitious goal was finalized on July 10, 1754, and would be dubbed the Albany Plan of Union. That effort failed, but the Albany Congress marked the first time representatives from all of the colonies gathered to discuss and debate their future. The Albany Congress served as a model for later efforts by the colonists to unite on the eve of the American Revolution (1775–83). The "Join, or Die" illustration would be reused during the Revolution to call for unity against the British. It would be replicated on flyers and even on flags during the fight for independence from Great Britain.

About the Artist

The artist who created the cartoon is unknown, but American publisher, writer, inventor, diplomat, and political leader Benjamin Franklin realized the potential power of the image and adroitly used it to illustrate the dangers of division against the French. Franklin is therefore usually credited as the creator of the image. Franklin was one of the most remarkable figures

Document Image

The "Join, or Die" cartoon
(Library of Congress)

in early U.S. history. A man of many talents and interests, he was born on January 17, 1706, in Boston, Massachusetts, but lived most of his life in Philadelphia, Pennsylvania. Franklin founded the *Pennsylvania Gazette* newspaper in 1729 and became well known as an author. Franklin would also serve as a colonial postmaster and achieve considerable fame as an amateur scientist for his contributions to fields such as oceanography and the study of electricity. Franklin was the founder and first president of the University of Pennsylvania. He would become noted as an abolitionist in his later years, and in 1774 he helped establish the Pennsylvania Society for Promoting the Abolition of Slavery.

Franklin was a supporter of democracy among the American colonies. In response to increasingly strict British rule in the colonies, he came to favor independence from Great Britain. In 1775, the newspaperman was elected as a representative from Pennsylvania to the Second Continental Congress, where he helped draft the Declaration of Independence, and he became the first postmaster of the new country. The Pennsylvanian was appointed ambassador to France by the Congress. While in Paris, he negotiated a treaty that secured French military assistance in 1778. Franklin also served as ambassador to Sweden. When he returned to the United States in 1785, he was elected president (governor) of Pennsylvania, a post he held until 1788. Franklin died on April 17, 1790.

Context

Through the first half of the 1700s, there were growing clashes between the British and French colonists in North America and the Native tribes who were allied to both empires. The British North American colonists sought to expand westward to accommodate a growing number of settlers. That brought them into conflict with the French and Native Americans in the West, and in 1754 militia groups on both sides engaged in a series of battles at the start of what would become known as the French and Indian War (1754–63). The British North American colonies at the time had significant differences in religion, economy, and social structure. The colonies tended to perceive themselves as separate, individual enclaves and often had rivalries with each other.

Colonial leaders such as Franklin sought to create a unified government to coordinate military strategy and resources against common enemies. The "Join, or Die" illustration was part of a campaign to garner support for the endeavor. In the first meeting of its kind, representatives from the colonies met at the Albany Congress from June to July 1754. The delegates at the congress endorsed the Albany Plan for a single colonial government that could collect taxes and raise a unified militia.

However, the various colonial legislatures did not approve the initiative because of fears over the loss of control to a central authority. The colonies supported less ambitious goals and instead simply wanted to cooperate on military steps and secure support from pro-British Native tribes such as the Iroquois Confederacy. The British Parliament also rejected the Albany Plan over concerns that it gave the central colonial government too much power. The colonial militias did cooperate, but the British military served as the main body to coordinate their campaigns.

The British won the war and were even able to conquer the French colonies in Canada. After the conflict was over in 1763, the government in London instituted a variety of measures in an effort to have Britain's American colonies pay for some of the costs of the war, which had almost doubled the crown's debt. For instance, in 1764, Parliament enacted a new tax on legal papers and other documents, the Stamp Act. In addition, the British government imposed limitations on new settlements in the West in an effort to prevent future conflicts with Native Americans through the Proclamation of 1763. There were also new rules on the importation and exportation of goods to the colonies as Britain sought to ensure that the colonies would only trade with British merchants. These restrictions and the various new taxes undermined the relationship between the colonies and Britain. In addition, many American colonists were angry that they were not represented in the British Parliament, as all of the members of Parliament were elected from districts in Britain.

In response to the British efforts to assert more control over the colonies, Franklin and other American colonial leaders called for collective action. For example, representatives from nine of the colonies met in Philadelphia in October 1765 in what became known as the Stamp Act Congress to craft a formal protest of the tax (the Stamp Act would be repealed in March 1766). Relations between Britain and the colonies continued to deteriorate, however, as Parliament enacted new restrictions. The "Join, or Die" illustration (sometimes rendered as "Unite, or Die!") again became popular as pro-independence Americans predicted dire consequences if the colonies did not stand together when confronting the British. A series of punitive laws, which came to be known as the 1774 Intolerable Acts, targeted Massachusetts in response to anti-British protests such as the December 1773 Boston Tea Party. Leaders in Massachusetts warned that the British would repress other colonies if the Americans did not join together. The "Join, or Die" slogan and cartoon would remain popular throughout the Revolutionary War.

Explanation and Analysis of the Document

"Join, or Die" was such an effective image because it was easily understood, even without Franklin's accompanying essay and arguments. The cartoon's snake presented a stark warning of what would happen if the colonies did not unite against their common foe (initially the French, and later the British). Each segment of the snake was identified as a different colony through the use of initials. South Carolina was the tail, followed, in order, by North Carolina, Virginia, Maryland, Pennsylvania, New Jersey, New York, and New England (the New England colonies, Connecticut, Massachusetts, New Hampshire, and Rhode Island, were simply grouped together as "N.E."). There were two colonies not listed. Delaware was omitted since it was generally viewed as part of Pennsylvania (and the governor of Pennsylvania was granted authority over Delaware). Finally, the status and future of Georgia was unclear. It had only been established in 1732, and it was the youngest of the colonies. Georgia's colonial charter had been rescinded in 1752 when the British monarchy took control of the territory away from the trustees who had founded the colony. Franklin likely did not think Georgia would be allowed to participate in the Albany Plan.

Snakes have generally had a negative connotation going back to the biblical story of the devil appearing as a serpent in the Garden of Eden. Snakes were also feared since some species were venomous. Nonetheless, in the 1700s many people in North America viewed snakes positively. Because they shed their skin, snakes were seen as a symbol of transformation. Hence, they could signify the transition of the colonies from individual territories into a single entity. In addition, snakes generally avoided contact with humans and only struck when forced to defend themselves. This paralleled a theme that Franklin discussed in his essay in the *Philadelphia Gazette*—that the British colonies did not seek war with the French or their allies, but they would fight if forced to. Snakes were also much more common in North America than in Europe. For instance, there were only three native species of snakes in Great Britain. When the cartoon was repurposed during the Revolution, it fit in with other representations that used the snake to symbolize the Americans. This included the Gadsden Flag, designed by Christopher Gadsden, which featured a rattlesnake with the motto "Don't Tread on Me."

The snake in "Join, or Die" symbolizes the colonies in another way. Its shape represents the coast of North America from South Carolina through the New England colonies. This provides a good visualization of what would happen if the French (and later the British) were to capture one or more of the colonies: it would divide the others and leave them isolated and potentially surrounded by enemy territory.

"Join, or Die" was in many ways a simple image, but it conveyed a powerful message about the importance of unity in the face of external threats. This message resonated with colonists, some of whom were not literate and others who did not have a good mastery of the English language. After its publication, the cartoon was reprinted by other colonial newspapers and journals as a testament to its popularity. On the eve of the American Revolution, it was again widely reprinted and made into banners and flags. "Join, or Die" would emerge as one of the most famous images of the American Revolution and one of the most successful political cartoons in U.S. history.

—Tom Lansford

Questions for Further Study

1. What was happening in the British North American colonies at the time the image was published? What issues caused these events?

2. What was Benjamin Franklin trying to accomplish with the cartoon? Was the image an effective way to convey his message?

3. How did the meaning of the cartoon change from the French and Indian War to the American Revolution? Was the image as powerful or important in the later conflict?

Further Reading

Books

Anderson, Fred. *The War That Made America: A Short History of the French and Indian War*. New York: Penguin Books, 2006.

Brands, H. W. *Our First Civil War: Patriots and Loyalists in the American Revolution*. New York: Doubleday, 2021.

Isaacson, Walter. *Benjamin Franklin: An American Life*. New York: Simon & Schuster, 2003.

Websites

Kiger, Patrick J. "How Ben Franklin's Viral Cartoon United the 13 Colonies." *History Stories*. History.com, October 23, 2018; updated September 28, 2021. https://www.history.com/news/ben-franklin-join-or-die-cartoon-french-indian-war.

Documentaries

Benjamin Franklin, episodes 1 and 2. Ken Burns, director. PBS, 2022.

Slaves For Sale Advertisement

Author/Creator
George Austin, Henry Laurens, and George Appleby

Date
1760

Image Type
Flyers

Significance
In one brief advertisement, illustrates the commercial and dehumanizing nature of the trade in enslaved people, a local concern over smallpox, and slave owners' fears of rebellion

Overview

This advertisement was first included in a newspaper local to Ashley Ferry, South Carolina, on April 26, 1760. It announced that 250 enslaved Africans would arrive through the port near Charleston on the following Tuesday, May 6, 1760. There is notably no price discussed as enslaved Africans were often sold at auctions to the highest bidder. By advertising a week in advance, the firm could hope to draw more people to attend the auction and drive the price of each enslaved person higher due to demand. While the advertisement is brief, it emphasizes the care that was taken with the people being sold. It also specifically mentions that no one on the boat contracted smallpox, which allows the writer to share explicitly that all individuals are healthy. This is important to include as many enslaved Africans would become ill or die on the journey to North America due to the inhumane conditions on the ships. This advertisement continues with its discussion on smallpox by stating that half of the individuals on the ship had previously had smallpox, a fact that would increase the market value of each person. Through this notation on the general medical history of the group, the firm attempts to make these enslaved Africans highly desirable to plantation owners, who may worry about their workers falling ill or dying shortly after their arrival.

The advertisement was submitted by Austin, Laurens, & Appleby, a prominent firm in the area, known for the importation of enslaved people and other goods. Originally a partnership between George Austin and Henry Laurens, it expanded to include George Appleby in 1759 after the immense success of the company. During the period of November of 1759 to November 1760, the firm imported 1,000 out of the 3,750 total slaves that were brought to South Carolina. They were the largest and wealthiest firm in the area. This advertisement shows one of the five cargoes that were imported during the year of 1759 to 1760.

About the Artist

The Austin, Laurens, & Appleby firm was founded by two South Carolinian merchants, George Austin and Henry Laurens, in 1747. However, Austin & Laurens would then become Austin, Laurens, & Appleby when the partnership expanded to include Austin's nephew George Appleby in 1759. This partnership would con-

Document Image

> TO BE SOLD, on board the Ship *Bance-Island*, on tuesday the 6th of *May* next, at *Ashley-Ferry*; a choice cargo of about 250 fine healthy
>
> # NEGROES,
>
> just arrived from the Windward & Rice Coast. —The utmost care has already been taken, and shall be continued, to keep them free from the least danger of being infected with the SMALL-POX, no boat having been on board, and all other communication with people from *Charles-Town* prevented.
>
> *Austin, Laurens, & Appleby.*
>
> N. B. Full one Half of the above Negroes have had the SMALL-POX in their own Country.

Slaves for sale advertisement from 1760
(Library of Congress)

tinue until 1762, when it dissolved through a mutual agreement.

While there is little recorded about George Austin and George Appleby outside of their business endeavors, Henry Laurens (1724–1792) has an interesting legacy as he was not only a merchant but also a politician, and one of the richest men in America. He was able to turn a large profit as a merchant. Laurens would export products like deerskin, rice, and indigo to Europe and the West Indies while importing products like wine, rum, sugar, and enslaved Africans to South Carolina. By 1750 the firm was one of the largest companies engaged in the slave trade. Around 1760, he expanded his enterprise to include rice and indigo planting to help bolster his profits. He owned six plantations: four in South Carolina and two in Georgia.

Despite owning several plantations and participating directly in the slave trade, he was one of the first in South Carolina to oppose slavery in America—as early as the 1770s. However, he continued to enslave people until his death and owned nearly 300 slaves in 1790. There is little to show that he applied his opposition to slavery to his own plantations by offering freedom to his slaves, but it seems that morally he saw the faults in institutional slavery. Having been involved in local politics in South Carolina, he would also become an active member of the Continental Congress, in which he served as the president of the organization from 1777 to 1778. He would also represent South Carolina for a year following his term before stepping back from political life.

Context

In 1739, the Stono Rebellion, one of the largest rebellions of enslaved people in the history of the United States, occurred in South Carolina only twenty miles from Charleston. This rebellion increased the worries felt by many plantation owners that the majority enslaved population was a constant threat to the colony's well-being. These fears were only exacerbated by the fact that in many areas in South Carolina, the enslaved outnumbered the free by three to one. In some low country areas, that number would be as high as seven or eight to one. This disparity showed that slave rebellions were a constant threat to those who regularly profited off of the institution of slavery through plantation labor. The sheer number of the enslaved population was concerning to those who found themselves as the minority. By 1740, there were explicit laws put in place in South Carolina to put to death to anyone who was involved or attempted to become involved in a slave rebellion. By 1741, corrective legislation was passed in South Carolina to impose a duty on new slaves in an effort to limit the growing Black majority found in the colony. However, despite any limitations, the economy of South Carolina was still heavily reliant on the labor of the enslaved. This made the institution of slavery necessary for economic prosperity despite the inherent social concerns.

The Stono Rebellion had occurred in 1739, but it was not the last; a number of other uprisings occurred subsequently in the area, including the New York Conspiracy of 1741 and Tacky's War in 1760 in Jamaica. Due to the uprisings occurring in the Caribbean, many plantation owners were skeptical about the origin of the enslaved people they sought to purchase for their labor. Many regarded enslaved people as less alien and less threatening if they had been born in the country where they worked. The believed that enslaved people who had been born locally not only would become compliant but also would have more to lose in rebelling. Foreign-born slaves, they surmised, had already lost all personal and cultural ties, so they had less to lose in rising up against their enslavement. In the South Carolina low country, more than half of the enslaved population was less than ten years removed from Africa, which increased the likelihood of uprising. These growing fears led to a proposal to ban the importation of slaves in 1760. While South Carolina passed this law as a security measure based on the fear of the growing number of African-born slaves, it was ultimately prevented by British authorities due to the economic impact it would have on the crown.

Since the concern of rebellions was high, those seeking to purchase enslaved labor would need to be convinced that the investment was worth it, which is why we see advertisements highlighting the health, productivity, and compliance of enslaved Africans. This firm would need to convince buyers to invest in purchasing enslaved Africans as there was a general distrust and skepticism that accompanied their arrival, highlighted by the recent proposal to ban the Atlantic slave trade outright. It is notable that there was no support for banning the domestic slave trade in the colony, as the fear was focused predominantly on enslaved Africans.

Explanation and Analysis of the Document

This advertisement, submitted by Austin, Laurens, & Appleby, focuses on the arrival of 250 Africans from the coast of Sierra Leone to South Carolina on Tuesday, May 6, 1760. The advertisement emphasizes the health of all onboard the ship and includes a specific reference that no communication with people from Charleston has been made. Given the concerns of the purchasing of foreign-born people, the emphasis on their health would have helped combat worries of potential buyers. Historically, Austin, Laurens, & Appleby represented about a quarter of all imports of enslaved people to South Carolina during this specific year. Since colonists had been close to banning the importation of slaves to South Carolina, it is evident that the fears surrounding increasing uprisings were present throughout the colony. With the Stono Rebellion in South Carolina having occurred only twenty years earlier, the presence of rebellion remained with the people.

Though these fears may have made it more difficult for firms to sell enslaved Africans for labor in the area, they were soon balanced by the smallpox epidemic of 1760. This epidemic infected over half of Charleston's population at about 2,000 people. Of these 2,000 people, around 900 ultimately lost their lives because of the infection. Mortality was particularly high among Africans, which would have severely impacted the labor available to sustain the Southern economy, founded as it was on the labor of the enslaved population. Because healthy laborers were needed, this advertisement would have likely been a relief to many plantation owners who had lost a portion of their workforce. Since Charleston was the center of this epidemic as the largest city in the area, the advertisement notes that there has been no contact made with the city. The last piece of reassurance at the end of the advertisement states that one-half of the Africans on the ship had been infected with smallpox prior to their journey. This was meant to reassure potential investors that these enslaved Africans would not easily fall ill to the virus despite its constant presence in the area. In Asia and Africa, there had also been a practice of inoculation that involved taking pus from one of the smallpox pustules and pricking a healthy person with it. Though risky, this helped a person develop immunity to the virus if successful. This process helped Africans, and later European colonists, develop immunity to smallpox without having suffered directly from the virus.

Ultimately, this advertisement shows a vignette from 1760 in which fears of African-born slaves competed with fears about a workforce dwindling because of the smallpox epidemic. In addition to the cultural commentary present in this advertisement, there is also the underlying evidence of the inhumanity inherent in slavery. Human beings were being brought by ships to an area struggling with an epidemic to help support the capitalist ventures of the elite. Their very lives were at risk, but the focus was on how they could best serve plantations given their possible immunity to a deadly virus. Austin, Laurens, & Appleby were able to secure some of the largest profits during this time by being complicit in the exploitation of human beings from across the globe. The ability to sell people into a labor system that indefinitely tied them to an exploitative market and inhumane working conditions ensured that individuals, like Henry Laurens and his colleagues, could become some of the richest men in America. Though Laurens would later separate himself from explicitly dealing with the slave trade and claim that slavery was immoral, he nonetheless secured his fortune selling the lives and futures of many to help farmers produce indigo and rice. This advertisement, in the context of its time, helps illustrate the hypocrisy that often accompanied any moral and economic arguments made surrounding the treatment of enslaved Africans.

—Elizabeth Boyle

Questions for Further Study

1. Why would an advertisement like this be included in the local newspaper? What does it show about the economy? What does it show about society at the time and how they viewed enslaved people?

2. This advertisement focused on the selling of enslaved people to work on plantations in South Carolina. After reading through the text of this advertisement, what qualities did you feel were emphasized? Why do you believe these qualities were chosen?

3. This advertisement specifies: "all other communication with people from Charles-Town prevented." Why do you think it would be important to emphasize the limited communication of these enslaved people with those who live in Charleston, South Carolina?

Further Reading

Books

Bailey, Anne C. *The Weeping Time: Memory and the Largest Slave Auction in American History.* New York: Cambridge University Press, 2017.

McInnis, Maurie D. *Slaves Waiting for Sale: Abolitionist Art and the American Slave Trade.* Chicago: University of Chicago Press, 2011.

Olwell, Robert. *Masters, Slaves, and Subjects: The Culture of Power in the South Carolina Low Country, 1740–1790.* Ithaca: Cornell University Press, 1998.

Wood, Peter. *Black Majority: Negroes in Colonial South Carolina from 1670 through the Stono Rebellion.* New York: Norton Library, 1975.

Websites

Costa, Tom. "The Geography of Slavery in Virginia." University of Virginia website, http://www2.vcdh.virginia.edu/gos/.

"Freedom on the Move: Rediscovering the Stories of Self-Liberating People: A Database of Fugitives from American Slavery." Freedom on the Move website. https://freedomonthemove.org/.

"Run Away from the Subscriber: Runaway Slave Advertisements 1745–1775: A Selection." National Humanities Center website. 2007.

William Bradford: "Expiring: In Hopes Of A Resurrection To Life Again" Newspaper Protest

Author/Creator William Bradford	**Image Type** Newspapers
Date 1765	**Significance** Newspaper masthead protesting the consequences that would affect American colonists if the Stamp Act were enacted

Overview

This image from October 31, 1765 shows the masthead of a popular American newspaper, *The Pennsylvania Journal and Weekly Advertiser*, warning that it may be forced out of business by the Stamp Act. Newspapers were an essential facet of print culture in colonial America, with the first successful newspaper being founded in the early 1700s. By the time of the Revolution, there were over thirty newspapers in the Anglo-American colonies. The typical American newspaper consisted of two pages and followed the style of London papers. These newspapers often featured news from Great Britain and the American colonies, local news, and advertisements. However, newspapers were not the only form of print media in the American colonies. The literate population was also informed through broadsides, proclamations, and almanacs.

This particular issue was a response to the looming fears surrounding the implementation of the Stamp Act of 1765, a tax on printed materials in the British colonies. Following the Seven Years' War (also known in America as the French and Indian War), tensions between the British colonies and the metropole (Britain) began to escalate. These early tensions concerned the new territories and unpopular taxes levied against the colonies. Accounts and positions concerning the tensions were published in newspapers, pamphlets, and broadsides as a way to inform readers how changes would soon affect them. In 1764, the British Parliament passed several other acts, including the Sugar and Currency Acts, that would prime the colonists for the tensions over the Stamp Act. Newspapers throughout Anglo-America began to protest these acts of Parliament that had an effect on the people of the colonies. This document allows the reader to understand the author's fears surrounding the implementation of the Stamp Act. *The Pennsylvania Journal and Weekly Advertiser*'s issue of October 31, 1765, would become synonymous with visual protests against the Stamp Act and the colonists' perception of threats levied against them by British leaders in London.

About the Artist

This document was written and printed by William Bradford, who published *The Pennsylvania Journal and Weekly Advertiser*. Bradford was born in New York City in the early 1700s. He was notably the grandson of William Bradford, with whom he shared a name, an

Document Image

William Bradford's newspaper masthead from 1765
(Library of Congress)

early printer and publisher who was credited with establishing the first printing press in the middle colonies. During Bradford's early life, he learned the art of printing from his grandfather and uncle, with whom he served an apprenticeship. Bradford announced in July 1742 that he would publish a weekly paper to convey the news in the colonies and abroad, as well as letters written by gentlemen. This was an acknowledgment of the vast networks of letters that shaped political discourse during the colonial period.

Early in his printing career, before the founding of *The Pennsylvania Journal and Weekly Advertiser*, Bradford focused on the publishing of religious texts. However, by December 1742 he had begun to print his newspaper, which would become very popular. During this period, Bradford was in competition with Benjamin Franklin's paper, the *Pennsylvania Gazette*, but he continued to gain popularity among readers. In addition, Bradford became a soldier in defense of the colonies during the Seven Years' War and would fight alongside the patriots during the American Revolution.

During the aftermath of the Seven Years' War, Bradford became a fierce opponent of the Stamp Act. He wrote up to its implementation about his open disagreement with Parliament's decision to enact the act. Bradford became a staunch supporter of the revolutionary zeal and was a member of the Sons of Liberty. The Sons of Liberty was an organization formed to oppose the Stamp Act and fought to advance the rights of colonists in the Americas. William Bradford's open opposition to the Stamp Act through his newspaper's commentary was influential throughout the colonies. Bradford's position was important when he became more entrenched in politics as the official printer of the First Continental Congress. Bradford's paper continued after his death in 1791, under the leadership of his son Thomas.

Context

Following the victory of Great Britain in the Seven Years' War (1756–63), British leaders found that they had to pay for the debt accrued during the conflict. The Seven Years' War was fought by the British and their Indigenous allies against the French and their allies, making this war a global conflict by European standards. The war was extremely costly for the British, and Parliament sought ways to replenish their finances. Much of the debt the British accrued came from the large numbers of troops stationed in the colonies during the war.

During the period directly following the Seven Years' War, tensions were heightened by a series of legislative decisions that affected the American colonists. In 1764, Parliament renewed the Sugar and Molasses Act, which was used to raise money to, in theory, protect the colonies as well as limit the smuggling of these items. The Currency Act was also extended, which regulated the use and creation of paper money. These acts of Parliament were met with anger and protests, including petitions from the colonists arguing against these acts. By March 1765, Parliament passed the Stamp Act, which went into effect in November. The Stamp Act was a direct tax on the colonists that consisted of taxes collected on all legal documents and printed materials, including playing cards, wills, contracts, newspapers, deeds, and pamphlets. Many colonists became angered that Parliament could pass these pieces of legislation without consulting them. The Stamp Act affected nearly everyone in the colonies, which led to these hostilities. Patrick Henry famously wrote the argument against "taxation without representation," which echoed the sentiments of many colonists. The Stamp Act also set forth that these taxes had to be paid in British sterling rather than the currency of the colonies. Furthermore, those who violated the act could be prosecuted without a jury of their peers.

With this backdrop, William Bradford published his now-famous newspaper masthead in opposition to the implementation of the Stamp Act. Many colonists were frustrated that they were not equally represented in Parliament when it came to legislation such as these acts. Some colonists feared that the Stamp Act could be used to strip them of the freedoms they were used to. Even though the colonists protested against this act, Parliament promoted it, which led to more debate and resistance. A group from nine colonies met in the Stamp Act Congress to discuss and draft petitions to the king and Parliament. It was from these protests that the Sons of Liberty were born. Angry mobs attacked those working as stamp distributors, and by 1766, many had resigned from their positions due to threats of violence. In 1766, Parliament repealed the Stamp Act, but colonists remained angry. At this moment, colonists considered that they had the power to unite against a "tyrannical" government. The camaraderie of those against the Stamp Act would light a fervor within colonists to protest other injustices, leading the road to the eventual revolution.

Explanation and Analysis of the Document

This issue of *The Pennsylvania Journal and Weekly Advertiser* has become one of the most easily recognizable newspapers of the eighteenth century because of its expression of opposition to the Stamp Act. Printed for October 31, the day before the Act was set to be enforced, Bradford's masthead would become known as the "tombstone edition." A masthead in this context refers to the title or heading of a newspaper. This edition of *The Pennsylvania Journal and Weekly Advertiser* was fashioned to resemble a tombstone, symbolizing the death of the newspaper upon the implementation of taxes on printed documents. The choice made by Bradford was to illustrate the seriousness of the Stamp Act and the cause for the newspaper's "expiring." Several features stand out about the document and highlight its unique argument.

The first thing that stands out is the design of the newspaper. Bradford conveyed his message concerning the Stamp Act by using the popular tombstone iconography of colonial America. A "mourning border" frames the newspaper's entirety; this was a black border found on paper to signify periods of mourning, such as death notifications and funerals. This "mourning border" is eye-catching and draws the gaze to the iconography found in the document. Bradford used the recognizable skull and crossbones motif in several places on the masthead. The skull and crossbones had long been established as a symbol of death. Headstones during the colonial period were highly stylized and a unique form of art that Bradford took into consideration when designing his piece. An aspect that stands out is the "stamp" created for this edition. Again using the skull and crossbones with the caption "An Emblem of the Effects of the STAMP. O! the fatal STAMP," Bradford makes his position very clear. The *Pennsylvania Journal* coopted the image of the royal stamp to resonate the anger of his readers.

Apart from the appearance of the paper, several critical lines that were written by Bradford stand out. He begins by informing the reader that "The Stamp Act, is fear'd to be obligatory upon us after the First of November ensuing, (the fatal Tomorrow)." Even in his rhetoric, Bradford uses the hyperbole of death to describe the tax. Bradford makes the claim that due to the Stamp Act, he would be "unable to bear the Birthen," or cost of publishing, and "has thought it expedient to stop awhile." William Bradford then uses the argument of enslavement by the British to further his claims of brutality caused by the Stamp Act, "whether any Methods can be found to elude the Chains forged on us" by this "insupportable Slavery." The invocation of slavery became an increasingly popular position in the lead-up to the Revolution, and this newspaper is an early example of that. This argument relied on the idea that the British had enslaved their American colonists by treating them unjustly. This position called for critiques of hypocrisy because of the American colony's involvement in the actual slave trade.

Poignantly, on the last page (page 4) of this issue, under the image of a colonial coffin, is an epitaph written for the paper: "The last Remains of The PENNSYLVANIA JOURNAL, which departed this Life, the 31st of October, 1765. Of a STAMP in her Vitals, Aged 23 Years." Even though he threatened the end of the newspaper, Bradford continued to publish following the implementation of the Act. In Philadelphia, the stamp distributor did not execute the Stamp Act out of fear of violence. That being said, Bradford's newspaper is still an important part of the rhetoric surrounding the tensions of 1765. This edition of *The Pennsylvania Journal and Weekly Advertiser* will remain important in the study of colonial protests against the Stamp Act. William Bradford's creativity inspired many during this crisis.

—Antoinette Bettasso

Questions for Further Study

1. Briefly summarize how this newspaper's appearance symbolized the Stamp Act as destroying American rights.

2. Why do you think Bradford wrote "The TIMES are Dreadful, Dismal, Doleful, Dolorous, and Dollar-less" in the top left-hand corner of the masthead of the newspaper? Do you believe this was an effective argument concerning the Stamp Act for the reader?

3. What does this newspaper tell the audience about forms of protest during the American colonial period?

Further Reading

Books

Bailyn, Bernard. *The Ideological Origins of the American Revolution: Fiftieth Anniversary Edition*. Harvard University Press, 2017.

Burgan, Michael. *The Stamp Act of 1765*. Compass Point Books. 2005.

Hutchins, Zachary McLeod, ed. *Community without Consent: New Perspectives on the Stamp Act*. Dartmouth College Press, 2016.

Morgan, Edmund S., and Helen M. Morgan. *The Stamp Act Crisis: Prologue to Revolution*. University of North Carolina Press, 1995.

Websites

"Documents from the Continental Congress and the Constitutional Convention, 1774 to 1789." Library of Congress, https://www.loc.gov/collections/continental-congress-and-constitutional-convention-from-1774-to-1789/articles-and-essays/timeline/1764-to-1765/.

"The Stamp Act." Colonial Williamsburg website, https://www.colonialwilliamsburg.org/learn/deep-dives/stamp-act/.

"The Stamp Act, 1765: A Spotlight on a Primary Source by George III." The Gilder Lehrman Institute of American History website, https://www.gilderlehrman.org/history-resources/spotlight-primary-source/stamp-act-1765.

Documentaries

The Stamp Act, excerpted from *Benjamin Franklin: A Film by Ken Burns*. Ken Burns, director. PBS, 2022. https://www.youtube.com/watch?v=hFVAvYw8-4w.

THOMAS JEFFERSON: ADVERTISEMENT FOR A RUNAWAY SLAVE

AUTHOR/CREATOR Thomas Jefferson	IMAGE TYPE NEWSPAPERS
DATE 1769	SIGNIFICANCE Shows the lengths to which slaveholders—even ones who held high ideals about the equality of all mankind—would go to recover fugitive slaves

Overview

The advertisement reproduced here was published in the *Virginia Gazette*, the first newspaper in Virginia, founded in 1736 in Williamsburg. The *Gazette* was the official newspaper of the colony of Virginia, in which official records and other government information appeared. It was published in the colonial capital of Williamsburg from its founding until 1780, when the capital shifted to Richmond. At that point, the *Gazette* itself moved to Richmond, and it continued to be published until the following year.

The ad for the escaped enslaved man named Sandy appeared at least twice, on September 7, 1769, and again on September 14. The September 7 edition of the newspaper has not survived, so the advertisement is reproduced from the September 14 edition.

The advertisement is typical of announcements about so-called runaway slaves. It gives the fugitive's name (Sandy), his approximate age, and a physical description. It also includes other information that might help identify him, such as his usual demeanor and the fact that he was a trained shoemaker. It suggests that he might be trying to leave Virginia and that he took property with him—including a horse and the tools of his trade. The ad also offers a reward for Sandy's return, and the amount of the reward varies depending on how far Sandy has gotten from Virginia.

Advertisements for fleeing captives were not uncommon in the *Virginia Gazette*, sometimes occupying one whole column of print in a three-column page. What makes Sandy's story significant, of course, is the name of the man claiming him: Thomas Jefferson, one of the largest landowners in Albemarle County. In 1769, Jefferson—already a lawyer and a member of the Virginia House of Burgesses—was about to become one of the key figures in American politics.

About the Artist

Thomas Jefferson (1743–1826) is one of the most famous, and one of the most contentious, figures in American history. He is best remembered as the author of the Declaration of Independence and as the third president of the United States. In more recent years, he has attracted notoriety because of his ownership of enslaved people. His father, Peter Jefferson, who died in 1757, left his son thirty enslaved people in his will. In the course of his lifetime, Thomas Jefferson

Document Image

> RUN away from the subscriber in *Albemarle*, a Mulatto slave called *Sandy*, about 35 years of age, his stature is rather low, inclining to corpulence, and his complexion light; he is a shoemaker by trade, in which he uses his left hand principally, can do coarse carpenters work, and is something of a horse jockey; he is greatly addicted to drink, and when drunk is insolent and disorderly, in his conversation he swears much, and in his behaviour is artful and knavish. He took with him a white horse, much scarred with traces, of which it is expected he will endeavour to dispose; he also carried his shoemakers tools, and will probably endeavour to get employment that way. Whoever conveys the said slave to me, in *Albemarle*, shall have 40 s. reward, if taken up within the county, 4 l. if elsewhere within the colony, and 10 l. if in any other colony, from
> THOMAS JEFFERSON.

Thomas Jefferson's 1769 advertisement for a runaway slave
(GRANGER)

would own around 600 enslaved people. By the time he died, he had set only seven of them free.

Historians agree that Jefferson's attitude toward slavery was ambiguous on many different levels. He was raised with slaves, and he staffed his house at Monticello with hundreds of enslaved laborers, both domestic and agricultural. In 1769, he was responsible for stopping a law that would have made it easier for slave owners to set their enslaved workers free. In addition, Jefferson had children with one of his slaves, Sally Hemings, who was also his late wife's half-sister, starting when Hemings was a teenager and Jefferson was in his forties. At the same time, he openly embraced and avowed ideals that slavery was immoral. His first draft of the Declaration of Independence contains a passage (later removed) condemning King George III for the African slave trade. In 1784, he was responsible for introducing legislation that would have prohibited the expansion of slavery into all American territory and into new states made up from that territory. It would have effectively stopped the expansion of the institution.

Sandy, the person who is the focus of the advertisement, appears in Jefferson's accounts in two places. Sandy apparently was one of the enslaved people Thomas Jefferson inherited from his father. An entry in Jefferson's accounts records hiring Sandy's labor out for a period of five and a half years, from Peter Jefferson's death to the end of December 1762. In 1773, four years after the date of the advertisement in the *Virginia Gazette*, Sandy was sold to Colonel Charles Lewis for £100. After that, he disappears from the historical record.

Context

Slavery is one of the most contentious subjects in American history. Enslaved Africans played crucial roles in establishing the economy and trade of the British colonies and the American states. And slavery was ubiquitous—all colonies permitted slavery before the war of American independence, and only some colonies ended the institution before the end of that war in 1783. In New York and New Jersey, slavery as an institution continued into the 1830s. In the region south of Pennsylvania, slavery continued until 1865.

The central irony of American history is the idea that a country founded on the concept that all were created equal held millions of people of African ancestry in slavery. The big question for slaves and slaveowners was this: *How do we justify a claim for freedom for a society that is about 20 percent enslaved, and that has no intention of giving up its slaves at any time in the foreseeable future?* In the mid-eighteenth century, many educated people, including slaveholders, recognized the dichotomy between calling for personal liberty while denying it to the enslaved. Major biographers of Thomas Jefferson suggest that he regarded slavery as a moral crime in his younger days but also felt unable to challenge the institution in his native Virginia. Over time, the community of wealthy, slave-owning white men came to believe that slavery was a necessary evil and that white supremacy was the only way they could protect their own interests.

The key to understanding the condemnation of slavery by some and the embracing of it by others during the War for American Independence is related to the spread of evangelical Christianity, which emerged in the Great Awakening of the mid-eighteenth century. The Great Awakening also launched an abolitionist movement present not only in the colonies but also in Great Britain. In 1772 a lawyer named Granville Sharp brought a case before the King's Bench. He pled for the freedom of an enslaved man named James Somerset on the grounds that slavery was illegal in England. Later that year, Lord Mansfield handed down the Somerset Decision, in which he essentially confirmed Sharp's point: for Somerset, at least, slavery ended when he reached England.

Mansfield carefully worded the Somerset Decision so that it applied only to James Somerset himself, but that did not stop many people from believing that slavery was extinct in England. The question was, did that mean that slavery was dead in the colonies as well? Many of the enslaved thought so.

Early in 1775 the royal governor of Virginia, Lord Dunmore, issued the Dunmore Proclamation, a call for a slave rebellion to end the American War for Independence. Dunmore said that indentured and enslaved servants who left their employers or owners and came into the British lines would be free forever. Within a couple of months, the number of enslaved workers who had fled their owners had exceeded 1,000. The irony of the situation was that enslaved and free colonists wanted the same things—freedom and liberty—but they had to fight each other to get them. Also ironic was the fact that Dunmore may have inadvertently caused the deaths of many self-emancipating slaves, because gathering them together in such numbers exposed them to disease—especially smallpox. Poor sanitation and poor food killed many of the freedom seekers, who found the freedom they sought only in death.

Explanation and Analysis of the Document

One of the few ways that we can envision the lives of enslaved Americans in the early years of the nation is through advertisements for runaway slaves. Sandy, Thomas Jefferson's escaped slave, is given a physical description in the historical record that most enslaved people at the time did not receive. Jefferson's ad tells us that Sandy was of mixed African and white ancestry, was heavyset, was prone to drinking, and was given to swearing when drunk.

We also know certain other things about him. He was left-handed. He had been trained as a shoemaker, and he had taken his tools with him when he left. In addition, Sandy was a skilled jockey, and when he fled he had taken with him a white horse, possibly one that Sandy himself had raced. Jefferson thought highly of Sandy's talents, offering a significant reward of 40 shillings (the equivalent of about $350 today), and scaling the reward up to £10 (about $1,750 today) if Sandy was captured after leaving Virginia altogether. Other records in Jefferson's archive show that Sandy was in fact recaptured, only to be sold to another Virginian slaveowner a few years later for a substantial sum.

Although we know that Sandy was in fact retaken, we know nothing of what happened to him after he was sold to Colonel Charles Lewis. We do know that the colonel only owned Sandy for a couple of years. In 1774 Lewis was killed in a war against Native Americans launched by the same Lord Dunmore who would later call for a massive slave rebellion during the American Revolution.

Two years after Lewis's death, the colonists declared independence, but they did not deal with the issue of slavery directly. Thomas Jefferson had avoided discussing slavery directly in the Declaration of Independence, referring only to "persons held to service." Within a few years, some leaders of the Revolution—including some who were major slaveowners—were beginning to talk about the possibility of arming enslaved people and awarding them their freedom for their support in the war. George Washington, for instance, talked about freeing and arming the enslaved to fight against the British in the South in the early 1780s, but he was quickly opposed by other slaveowners.

When the British finally surrendered at Yorktown in 1781, there were still hundreds of slaves within their camp. They made a half-hearted attempt to save as many as possible from recapture by Washington's army, but Loyalist slaveowners who supported the British were allowed to take their slaves with them into exile. Slaves who had escaped from Patriot owners were supposed to be returned to slavery, but many were allowed to escape on purpose or were taken away to Canada when the British evacuated the United States. Slaves who were sick or helpless were driven out or abandoned to die. Sandy might have been among them.

It is also possible that Sandy sought to support the Revolution in his own way. Black Americans (sometimes ex-slaves, but also freeborn) played a major role in the American Revolution through service in the Continental Army. Roughly 15 percent of the army was Black, in part because of the way the army's recruitment policy operated. Many Black Americans received their freedom or other awards commensurate with their service after the war—if they could collect it.

This meant that Sandy—if he was still alive and living in the United States a decade after he last appears in the historical record—might have been on the road to citizenship in the country that had once made him a slave. Service in the Continental Army spread the idea of African Americans as equal citizens throughout the country and helped establish a tradition of African American citizenship, especially in the North.

—Kenneth R. Shepherd

Questions for Further Study

1. How does Jefferson's ad describe Sandy? What are his outstanding characteristics?

2. Why do you think Jefferson feels it is necessary to describe Sandy's training and his accomplishments?

3. Based on what you see in the ad, do you believe that Jefferson values Sandy for his skills, or does he see him simply in terms of the money he is worth?

Further Reading

Books

Boles. John B. *Jefferson: Architect of American Liberty*. New York: Basic Books, 2017.

Gordon-Reed, Annette. *Thomas Jefferson and Sally Hemings: An American Controversy*.

Charlottesville: University of Virginia Press, 1998.

Jefferson, Thomas. *Notes on the State of Virginia: An Annotated Edition*, edited by Robert Pierce Forbes. New Haven: Yale University Press, 2022.

Riley, Padraig. *Slavery and the Democratic Conscience: Political Life in Jeffersonian America*. Philadelphia: University of Pennsylvania Press, 2016.

Websites

"Jefferson Papers." Founders Online, National Archives. https://founders.archives.gov/.

Documentaries

Thomas Jefferson. Ken Burns, director. Renaissance Films, 1997.

Paul Revere: *The Bloody Massacre* Flyer

Author/Creator
Paul Revere

Date
1770

Image Type
Flyers

Significance
A lurid depiction of the infamous altercation between a group of British troops stationed in Boston and large number of angry residents of the city that culminated the soldiers opening fire, killing five of the protestors

Overview

This engraving by noted Patriot Paul Revere is one of the most well-known images produced in the colonies before the American Revolution. Such engravings were widely popular in both Great Britain and its American colonies during the late eighteenth and early nineteenth centuries, serving as a way of spreading news and political commentary about current events. The popularity of engravings increased in the colonies in the aftermath of the French and Indian War (1754–63), when they became an effective means of expressing dissent to British policies intended to extract funds from the colonists to pay off the heavy debts caused by the conflict and pay for the British troops stationed in the colonies for their defense. These engravings, while comparatively unrefined, proved vitally important in calling attention to the increasingly domineering rule of the British government and fostering a sense of cohesion among the colonists. Powerful imagery was particularly important in more remote areas of the colonies, where literacy rates were often close to 50 percent.

As a lifelong resident of Boston and an active participant in the city's resistance movement after 1765, Revere was well positioned to experience events in the city during the tumultuous days before the Revolution, which he later reproduced as engravings. His hometown saw numerous altercations in the 1760s and 1770s, making it a place of particular concern for the British, which sought to suppress the growing discord by sending thousands of troops to keep the peace. The growing military presence only served to increase feelings of resentment and hostility, which led to a growing number of confrontations and brawls between British troops and Bostonians. The most infamous of these clashes occurred in early March of 1770 when an exchange of insults between a young colonist and a British sentry named Hugh White in front of the city's Custom House escalated to an all-out riot. Coming less than two weeks after a mob's attack against a store owned by a known Loyalist resulted in the shooting death of an eleven-year-old boy, both sides were on edge when scuffling gave way to gunfire that claimed the lives of five colonists and injured six more. While responsibility for the violence arguably lay more with the mob than the soldiers, news of the "Boston Massacre" spread quickly, helped greatly by the raw, visceral, and simplistic engraving by Revere. It

Document Image

Paul Revere's 1770 flyer
(Library of Congress)

became another entry in the growing catalog of British injustices.

About the Artist

This engraving was produced by Paul Revere, who is primarily remembered as the most famous of the riders who spread the word of the British troops advancing on Concord, Massachusetts, in April 1775, resulting in the first battles of the American Revolution. For his ride (and for the poem Henry Wadsworth Longfellow wrote about it much later), Revere has loomed large in the popular memory of the United States.

Revere was born in the Boston neighborhood of North End in late December 1734 to Apollos Rivoire, a silversmith who had immigrated from France due to religious persecution, and his wife, Deborah. The second of twelve children and the oldest surviving son, young Revere received a formal education at the North Writing School, from which he graduated at age thirteen and then began his apprenticeship to his father, learning the silversmith trade. Mastering the craft with impressive speed, nineteen-year-old Revere was well prepared to assume control of his father's business following his death in 1754.

While Revere came to be best known for the silverware and tea sets bought and prized by Boston's wealthiest residents, the demands of supporting such a large family necessitated his making a wide range of products and learning several other skills to make money, including engraving and dentistry. He served in the colonial artillery during the French and Indian War, rising to the rank of second lieutenant, and married Sarah Orne in August 1757 when his military service concluded. The couple ultimately had eight children together.

Still overseeing his silversmithing business and various side ventures, Revere came to be increasingly involved in Boston politics as a member of groups increasingly challenging British rule, most notably the Sons of Liberty. The imposition of the Stamp Act in 1765 sparked widespread anger across Massachusetts; the notion of an internal direct tax being collected from the colonists without their representation in Parliament led colonists to assault tax collectors and engage in increasingly violent riots. Revere volunteered to deliver messages on horseback on behalf of Boston's Committee of Safety in 1770, the same year the Boston Massacre took place. He participated in the Boston Tea Party three years later and founded an intelligence network dubbed the "mechanics" to collect information regarding the movement of British forces. An observed advance by British troops on Concord on April 18, 1775, resulted in Revere undertaking his famous race on horseback across the Massachusetts countryside to warn rebel leaders Samuel Adams and John Hancock of their possible capture.

Context

The fraying of ties between the American colonies and the British government occurred with a speed that surprised most on both sides of the Atlantic. From the standpoint of the Americans entering the 1760s, there seemed little incentive for breaking loose from the British Empire, which provided them with access to an ever-expanding global market and protection by one of the world's most formidable militaries. While the colonies lacked representation in Parliament and had to accept some regulation on their exports, such trade-offs seemed comparatively insubstantial considering the many benefits afforded by belonging to the empire.

But a cascading series of events during the 1760s and 1770s disillusioned a growing number of colonists, to the point where they insisted that a permanent separation from Great Britain was necessary, even if such a severing required armed conflict. Having long enjoyed relative autonomy, thanks to the establishment of colonial legislative bodies that controlled colonial budgets, the colonists bristled at new policies implemented by the British in the aftermath of the French and Indian War in 1763. These were intended to impose more control over colonial trade, extract funds from the colonies to cover their defense, and prevent the violation of Native American land rights by colonists seeking to expand westward.

A series of new policies from London further stoked the flames of anger: the Sugar Act of 1764 raised the duty on sugar and created new vice-admiralty courts in the colonies to try suspected smugglers; the Currency Act of 1764 called for colonial assemblies to cease the practice of issuing and circulating their own paper money; and the Stamp Act of 1765 obligated the purchasing of stamps for a wide range of legal documents and newspapers. Much of the colonists' fury over the acts, particularly the Stamp Act, hinged on their resentment over lacking direct representation in the British Parliament; they regarded the taxes levied on them without their official permission examples of increasingly oppressive rule by the imperial government. A growing number of British soldiers permanently stationed in the colonies to keep order on the western frontier deepened suspicion across the colonies.

Boston became in many respects the city most in the throes of a revolutionary fervor. As a key port city, Boston felt many of the new laws more acutely than most areas in the colonies. Major rioting began in the city during the summer of 1765, resulting in the assaults of stamp agents and even Massachusetts' lieutenant governor, Thomas Hutchinson, whose house protestors set on fire. Following the forced removal of British customs officials from the city in June 1768, London responded by dispatching additional British troops to Boston. The reinforcements' march through the city and setting up camp on the Boston commons further antagonized the city's inhabitants and set the stage for even more violent altercations.

A bitter fight between the employees of a ship-rigging factory and underpaid British soldiers looking for part-time jobs inflamed tension in the city, which boiled over on the night of March 5 in front of Boston's Custom House, located on King Street. On that night, a group of eight British soldiers and their captain, Thomas Preston, were protecting the building from an unruly group of 60 to 200 angry protestors, many young dockworkers, who began pelting the troops with snowballs, chunks of ice, and oyster shells. At some point during the confusion, the troops opened fire without Captain Preston giving the order, killing three members of the mob on the spot and wounding two others who succumbed to their wounds later. Six others also received wounds but survived.

Explanation and Analysis of the Document

Given the confused lead-up to the shootings and the ensuing panic, resistance leaders in Boston had little difficulty presenting the clash between the soldiers and the assembled laborers as the "Boston Massacre"—the latest and most vile example of British ruthlessness. One of the most indelible images produced in the colonies during the pre-revolutionary era, Paul Revere's engraving of the Boston Massacre, which he based with relatively few changes on a design by artist Henry Pelham, is a crude but visceral depiction of one of the pivotal events prior to the start of hostilities in 1775. A lack of artistic refinement is perhaps due to Revere's desire to bring his engraving to the public while memory of the event was still fresh and anger was still high; it was available for purchase less than three weeks after the deadly clash.

The text at the bottom of the engraving begins with a poem Revere likely composed, which opens: "Unhappy Boston! see thy Sons deplore, Thy hallowed Walks besmeared with guiltless Gore: While faithless P__n (Preston) and his savage Bands, With Murderous Rancour stretch their bloody Hands; Like fierce Barbarians grinning o'er their Prey, Approve the Carnage, and enjoy the Day." Also listed are the "unhappy Sufferers: Saml Gray, Saml Maverick, James Caldwell, Crispus Attucks, and Patrick Carr (killed)," and it is noted that there were "Six wounded; two of them (Christr Monk & John Clark) Mortally." These victims were counted among the earliest martyrs to the cause of American independence, with Attucks being the first known African American to be killed by the British.

Revere portrays the British as clearly the provokers, lined up and methodically delivering a volley of gunfire into the largely passive American protestors, the wounds of those struck by the Redcoats gushing to form red pools of blood. Captain Prescott, pictured on the far left holding his sword aloft, is shown directing the troops to fire point blank into the crowd, which eyewitnesses testified is not what happened. The image makes simple what had actually been a chaotic and complicated incident, and simplicity is what Boston's local resistance leaders wanted—a readily understandable symbol of British violence and subjugation. This takes the engraving from being more than merely a depiction of a dramatic event to a piece of propaganda intended to portray the British as villainous and the cause of independence as just.

Revere's engraving displays a clear attention to the architectural details of the city that would have been identifiable to most Bostonians. While it is unlikely that he was present at the event, Revere undoubtedly visited the site of event on King Street and drew a well-detailed sketch of the location that was used as evidence by the prosecution during the trial of the British soldiers held responsible for the deaths. The Old State House is positioned in the center of the background, in front of another landmark well known at the time, the First Church of England of Boston. The line of British troops on the right is positioned in front of the Custom House, identified by a sign, while a second sign labeled "Butcher's Hall" is just one example of artistic license that Revere took with his engraving, an indication of what he wanted his viewers to think of the British. A musket poking out of one of the windows of Butcher's Hall to fire on the crowd below alludes to the massacre being planned rather than spontaneous.

Another instance of Revere playing loose with the facts is the appearance of a woman among the colonists being fired upon, her clasped hands matching her anguished expression. Revere likely intended to reinforce the treachery of the British by having them disregard the presence of a woman. The rioters were undoubtedly overwhelmingly, if not all, male, but a woman named Jane Whitehouse was just a few feet from the soldiers when they opened fire and had been instructed to leave by a British sentry to avoid possible injury. She later testified on behalf of the British soldiers at their trial. Revere also took liberties in his depiction of the Americans as well-dressed in attire unlikely to have been worn by the protestors, who were primarily members of the city's working class.

Printed and copied in large numbers and distributed widely throughout Massachusetts and the other colonies, the engraving helped to convince many Americans that those responsible for the deaths were cold-blooded murderers killing with the official sanction of the British government. Although the soldiers were found guilty of manslaughter at their trial, justice hardly seemed to have been served. Helped immeasurably by Revere's ubiquitous engraving, the Boston Massacre crystallized in the minds of many colonists as an outrage that came to be commemorated annually with rousing speeches and demonstrations.

—Michael Carver

Questions for Further Study

1. What might have been the purpose of Revere including a small dog at the feet of one of the massacre's victims?

2. Patriot leaders in Boston produced a larger number of pamphlets describing the massacre in a way to generate sympathy for the victims and hatred for the British soldiers, but they had only a fraction of the impact that Revere's engraving did. Why might that have been?

3. Revere's engraving was one of many depictions of the Boston Massacre, including Henry Pelham's, which Revere arguably copied to a large extent. Why might Revere's be the one that achieved the greatest recognition and lasting fame?

Further Reading

Books

Hinderaker, Eric. *Boston's Massacre*. Cambridge, MA: Belknap Press, 2017.

Miller, Joel J. *The Revolutionary Paul Revere*. Nashville: Thomas Nelson, 2010.

Zabin, Serena. *The Boston Massacre: A Family History*. Boston: Houghton Mifflin Harcourt, 2020.

Websites

"Boston Massacre Engraving by Paul Revere." Paul Revere Heritage Project. http://www.paul-revere-heritage.com/boston-massacre-engraving.html.

"The Pamphlet War and the Boston Massacre." British Library. https://www.bl.uk/the-american-revolution/articles/the-pamphlet-war-and-the-boston-massacre.

Philip Dawe: "Tarring & Feathering" Satirical Print

Author/Creator
Philip Dawe, Robert Sayer, John Bennett

Date
1774

Image Type
Flyers

Significance
A British depiction of an attack on a customs official in Boston that became an important symbol of the violence suffered by Loyalists during the American Revolution

Overview

This document is an example of a satirical print of the type that became popular in the late eighteenth and early nineteenth centuries. Prints like these were produced on a single side of paper and often satirized contemporary events. The prints were designed to be visually striking to appeal to the general populace, and they would have been passed around and discussed in coffee houses and taverns. This print is a British depiction of the tarring and feathering of John Malcom, a customs official, in Boston in 1774. Tarring and feathering was a violent and traumatic ritual of public humiliation that became popular in New England in the mid-eighteenth century as a method of intimidating customs officials and punishing informers. The tarring and feathering of John Malcom was one of the most famous incidences of its kind. Malcom was a deeply unpopular figure in Boston, and on January 25, 1774, he inflamed the populace after a confrontation in which he struck a local shoemaker with his cane. When word spread of the assault, a crowd gathered, intent on punishing the official. Malcom was seized, covered in tar and feathers, paraded through the town, made to stand at the gallows with a noose around his neck, and forced to swallow large quantities of tea. Doctors feared that he would not survive the ordeal, evidence of the dangerous intensity of the mob.

This incident received extensive coverage in newspapers throughout Britain and was popularized by three satirical prints, including this one. The document offers an interpretation of events in Boston from the perspective of a British artist. It connects the attack on Malcom with other colonial protests and depicts the colonists as cruel and violent. The incident bolstered the British in their decision to impose punitive legislation on the town of Boston in early 1774. Meanwhile, the Patriot leadership took greater control of the crowds and ensured that Malcom was the last individual to be tarred and feathered in Boston.

About the Artist

Little is known about the artist, Philip Dawe. He was born around 1745 in London and was a pupil of the painter Henry Morland. Dawe was Morland's principal engraver. He used a technique called *mezzotint* to scratch lines onto a metal plate to create black and white prints. The process was widely used in eigh-

Document Image

The "Tarring & Feathering" print from 1774
(Gilder Lehrman Institute of American History)

teenth-century England to create reproductions of portraits and other paintings. In the 1770s he began to produce satirical prints on popular subjects, including politics, for Robert Sayer, who was one of the leading publishers in Europe. Sayer's books on geography, agriculture, and architecture were particularly popular with colonial markets, but he also sold large numbers of humorous mezzotints (like this one) known as drolls, which became popular in the 1770s and 1780s. In 1774, Sayer partnered with John Bennett, his former apprentice, and the pair increased their productivity. Sayer focused on the production of maps and sea charts, including a series of atlases of North America and the West Indies that catered to the colonial market, while Bennett began publishing a wider variety of small-scale prints on trendy political subjects.

This print has been attributed to Philip Dawe and was published by Sayer and Bennett in 1774. It was likely commissioned by Bennett following the success of similar prints such as "A New Method of Macaroni Making" (1774), which also depicted the tarring and feathering of John Malcom. Events in Boston, including the Boston Tea Party and the subsequent closure of the port (one of the Coercive or "Intolerable" Acts passed by Parliament to punish Massachusetts), were hot topics in the news at the time, and the publishers sought to capitalize on the trend. The print would have circulated widely in Britain and possibly the colonies too.

Bennett began to show signs of insanity in 1781 and was committed to an asylum in 1783. Sayer, by now a rich man, dissolved their partnership and retired shortly afterward. Dawe continued to produce mezzotints and other engravings until his death in 1809.

Context

This print was produced at a moment when Boston was once again at the center of the imperial dispute between Britain and its American colonies. Boston had emerged as the focal point of colonial resistance to imperial taxation, and in 1768, following an anti-customs riot, the British government decided to send troops into the town. The presence of soldiers hardly improved tensions, and in March 1770 frightened redcoats fired on a hostile crowd in an incident that was quickly dubbed the Boston Massacre. Britain responded by removing the soldiers from Boston and repealing most imperial taxes to ensure three years of relative calm. In 1773, however, tensions rose once again when the government passed the Tea Act. Unlike the Stamp Act and the Townshend Duties that had come before it, the Tea Act was not motivated by the need to raise money. Instead, the act was intended to bail out the British East India Company, which was on the verge of bankruptcy, by giving it a monopoly on the importation of tea to the colonies. In Boston, this justification made little difference: the Tea Act was viewed as yet another example of imperial oppression. Soon, a coalition of politicians, artisans, and merchants who now found themselves cut out of the tea trade organized a response. On December 16, 1773, some one hundred men, including merchants, artisans, and apprentices, boarded three ships that were docked at the harbor and threw forty-six tons of tea overboard.

A month after the Boston Tea Party, a fifty-one-year-old customs official, John Malcom, was attacked in what became the most publicized incident of tarring and feathering of the American Revolution. Malcom was a notorious figure in Boston who was known for his strong support of royal authority and his fiery temper. He had already been tarred and feathered once after he had informed on a vessel for petty smuggling. In November 1773, a crowd of thirty sailors had taken retribution in Portsmouth, New Hampshire, although they applied the tar over his clothes, which reduced the severity of their attack. Back in Boston, he was regularly jeered in the streets by passersby.

On January 25, 1774, Malcom was returning home from his office on Boston harbor when he was observed threatening a small boy who had apparently rammed into him on a sled. George Robert Twelves Hewes, a poor shoemaker who had been a bystander at the Boston Massacre and had participated in the Tea Party, intervened to protect the child. Malcom struck Hewes with his cane, briefly knocking him unconscious, before bystanders broke up the fight. Later that night a sizeable crowd gathered outside Malcom's house and dragged him outside. After he was thrown into a cart, his assailants poured scalding hot tar over his head and parts of his body. The crowd then covered him in feathers before pulling the cart through the streets of the town. They whipped him several times and then ordered him to curse the hated royal governor of Massachusetts. Malcom refused. He was then taken to the Liberty Tree, a famous elm tree near Boston Common, where he once again refused to curse the governor. Then he was dragged to the town gallows, where a rope was tied around his neck, and he was thrashed with clubs. Beaten and with tar covering his body, Malcom eventually cursed as ordered. In a final humiliation, the mob then forced him to swallow huge quantities of tea until he vomited. The attack left Malcom in a gruesome condition, although he did survive.

Explanation and Analysis of the Document

The tarring and feathering of John Malcom was covered extensively in newspapers in Britain and was popularized by satirical prints such as this one. In this print, a sailor, a tradesman, a minister, and two other Bostonians are portrayed with menacing faces as they compel the tarred and feathered customs official to drink tea. The artist has compressed the events of the day into one scene, including tar and feathers, a club, and a noose hanging from the Liberty Tree. A montage of visual clues reminds the audience of how the imperial dispute had evolved over the previous decade: the Stamp Act is posted upside down on the Liberty Tree to indicate its repeal in 1766, and men dressed as Native Americans are dumping boxes of tea labeled with Chinese characters into the harbor. The print would have been marketed as a commentary on contemporary political events and suggested to its audience that Boston had become a place of cruelty, violence, and anarchy.

The incident received further attention when Malcom traveled to England, where he campaigned for a pension and ran for election to the House of Commons in a highly symbolic campaign against John Wilkes, a staunch supporter of the Americans. Malcom took with him strips of his skin attached to tar, which he allegedly sent to members of Parliament as proof of his loyalty. Malcom claimed to be the first man in the colonies to have been tarred and feathered specifically for his political stance against the brewing rebellion. As the imperial crisis escalated over the subsequent months, similar stories of violence began to circulate in London. Victims were no longer just hated customs officials and informants like Malcom but also printers, clergymen, and increasingly ordinary people. Parliamentarians who advocated for harsher measures against the colonies could point to the volatile situation in Boston, where any political dissenter was at risk of tar and feathers.

The publicity around the incident bolstered the British government in its decision to impose punitive sanctions on Boston. In early 1774, it passed a series of Coercive Acts (the colonists called them the Intolerable Acts) that were intended to punish Boston and the colony of Massachusetts. The Boston Port Act closed the port of Boston to all trade until the damaged tea was paid for. The Massachusetts Government Act overhauled the colony's charter to weaken elected bodies and strengthen the power of the governor. Two further acts were designed to facilitate the deployment of troops in the town and made it clear that the government was prepared to use force. Prime Minister Lord North evoked the image of Malcom enduring "greater cruelty than any that went before" when he introduced the legislation to the House of Commons. The precarious situation of the Loyalists now began to receive attention at the highest levels of government. When, in August 1775, King George III finally declared the colonists to be in "open and avowed Rebellion," he specifically condemned their "Oppression of Our loyal Subjects." It was his self-proclaimed royal duty, he said, to shield Loyalists from the "Torrent of Violence" that was engulfing them.

—Jon Chandler

Questions for Further Study

1. Five men are depicted in this document as the perpetrators of the attack on John Malcom. Who do they represent, and why are they attacking the customs official?

2. How has the artist drawn connections between the attack and other events of the American Revolution?

3. Why could this document be considered an effective piece of propaganda?

Further Reading

Books

Hoock, Holger. *Scars of Independence: America's Violent Birth.* New York: Broadway Books, 2017.

Ingersoll, Thomas N. *The Loyalist Problem in Revolutionary New England.* New York: Cambridge University Press, 2016.

Young, Alfred F. *The Shoemaker and the Tea Party: Memory and the American Revolution.* Boston: Beacon Press, 1999.

Articles

Irvin, Benjamin H. "Tar, Feathers, and the Enemies of American Liberties, 1768–1776." *New England Quarterly* 76 (2003), 197–238.

Philbrick, Nathaniel. "The Worst Parade to Ever Hit the Streets of Boston." *Smithsonian Magazine*, March 31, 2013. https://www.smithsonianmag.com/history/the-worst-parade-to-ever-hit-the-streets-of-boston-12934258/.

Torbert, Amy. "Impressions of Tar and Feathers: The 'New American Suit' in Mezzotint, 1774–84." *Commonplace* 16, no. 1 (Fall 2015). http://commonplace.online/article/impressions-of-tar-and-feathers/.

Philip Dawe: *Edenton Tea Party* Satirical Print

Author/Creator
Philip Dawe

Date
1775

Image Type
Cartoons; Flyers

Significance
A political cartoon, drawn by a British artist prior to the American Revolution, mocking a group of colonial women in North Carolina who pledged to stop buying fabric or tea imported from Britain

Overview

This cartoon by a British artist was intended to mock a boycott led by colonial women. It was typical of the inexpensive prints showing figures and events of the day that were sold in large numbers during the late 1700s in England and its North American colonies. The growing push for the colonies' independence in the 1760s and 1770s inspired artists on both sides of the Atlantic to produce prints that either celebrated the cause (from the colonists' perspective) or ridiculed it (from the British perspective). With the British government seeking measures that would both limit colonial autonomy and extract more in taxes from the colonists after the French and Indian War, relations grew strained. The colonists sought ways of either avoiding or undermining London's attempts to impose duties on imported commodities such as textiles and tea. The most effective tactic proved to be boycotts, which were often organized by those traditionally responsible for the purchase of certain goods: colonial women.

Such boycotts began in the mid-1760s after Parliament passed the Townshend Acts and continued into the subsequent decade. Women refrained from purchasing British-made cloth and opted instead to sit at their own spinning wheels and looms to produce homespun cloth, the wearing of which came to be a mark of pride. They further committed themselves to no longer purchasing tea, one of the most popular and widely consumed beverages in the colonies and often served at formal events. The boycotting of tea took center stage after Parliament's Tea Act of 1773, which greatly reduced the price of tea for colonial consumers, led to anger among colonists who perceived the law as an attempt to encourage them to purchase taxed tea. The Sons of Liberty in Boston expressed their disdain by dumping of 90,000 pounds of tea from three ships into Boston Harbor on December 16, 1773. There were also less-theatrical efforts to discourage the purchase of tea from Britain, such as the group of women from the town of Edenton, North Carolina, who put their names on a resolution stating their objections to buying imported tea or textiles until all repressive laws had been repealed. News of the event elicited jeers in Britain, where such political activism by women was rare, and where the colonists' complaints about growing tyranny on the part of the British government seemed petty and unfounded, particularly because those living in the colonies paid far less in taxes than those in the British Isles.

Document Image

The Edenton Tea Party cartoon
(British Museum)

About the Artist

Philip Dawe, the likely artist of this drawing, was born to George Dawe, a London merchant, in the 1730s or 1740s. He studied under the famed British satirist William Hogarth and produced works on behalf of Sayer & Bennett, one of London's largest publishers of prints and maps. During the 1770s, in response to growing tensions in the colonies, Sayer & Bennett produced a series of prints completed by Dawe commenting on such recent events as the Boston Tea Party. Some of his prints came to be closely associated with the leadup to the American Revolution, most famously "Bostonian's Paying the Excise Man, or Tarring & Feathering," but Dawe's talent extended well beyond his prints deriding colonists who challenged the British government. A skilled practitioner in the mezzotint engraving technique, a printmaking process that emphasizes delicate lines and shading, Dawe also produced stirring battle scenes and sensitive portraits of woman from various social classes. He and his wife, Jane, had six children, three of whom became noted artists in their own right. Dawe likely died in 1832.

Context

All-male political groups such as the Sons of Liberty, which sought to advance the cause of American freedom in the years leading up to the revolution, have long overshadowed similar contributions made by organizations such as the Daughters of Liberty, whose members were all women. While some colonial women actively participated in anti-British protests and riots during the 1760s, most seeking to strike a blow for American independence tended to favor less-aggressive tactics than those employed by their male counterparts, whose activities included tarring and feathering customs officials and burning King George III in effigy. Women instead devoted their energies to writing scathing pamphlets and satirical plays and organizing boycotts intended to send a message to the British while reducing the revenue they made through their trade with the colonies.

Colonists first boycotted British goods in the late 1760s in response to Britain's chief financial minister, Charles Townshend, deciding to raise taxes to cover war debts and the costs of keeping British troops in the colonies. The Revenue Act of 1767 placed taxes on such imported items as lead, paper, glass, and tea. Although comparatively light, the trade duties embodied yet another instance of taxation without the colonists' consent coming two years after the much-hated Stamp Act.

As was often the case when it came to colonial resistance, Boston led the way, its residents organizing a boycott of British-made imports that several other colonial cities and villages emulated. The colonists hoped that drastic reductions in the purchase of imported goods would compel British merchants to press London to cancel the duties to restore their lost profits. Because many of the British goods were household items, boycott organizers fully understood that their success depended largely upon women's participation. Women across the colonies leapt at the chance to play a key role in the boycott movement by signing petitions pledging to refrain from drinking tea and to produce homespun cloth rather than purchase textiles made in British mills. The boycotts proved largely successful: Parliament, caving into pressure from merchants, repealed all the duties in 1770—except for the one on tea. The tea tax most famously resulted in the Boston Tea Party of 1773, but it also motivated women to organize boycotts as shown in this print.

Explanation and Analysis of the Document

Unjustly overlooked by generations of American historians, women proved indispensable to the cause of independence in colonial America in the years leading up to the revolution and during the war years, even as they received scorn from those who asserted that their gender precluded their being political actors. While not participating in such notable events as the Boston Tea Party, women were undeterred in their commitment to supporting boycotts of tea and other British goods, such as the one organized in Edenton, North Carolina, on October 25, 1774.

The Edenton boycott was an extension of preexisting dissent the community's residents had for the British, inflamed by Parliament's passage of the Tea Act of 1773, which allowed the British East India Company to bypass American merchants and sell directly to the colonists. In late August of 1774, the rector of St. Paul's Church, Daniel Earle, delivered a stirring address at a mass meeting held in the courthouse in which he proclaimed support for the beleaguered people of Boston, who were subjected to a closure of the city's harbor following the Boston Tea Party. Two months later, several women from Edenton (some accounts state fifty-one) met at the home of Mrs. Elizabeth King as members of the newly created Edenton Ladies' Patriotic Guild. The women decided to make clear their shared rejection of British tea and textiles and sign a petition, shown in the print, that reads: "We the Ladys of Edenton do hereby solemnly Engage not to Conform to that Pernicious Custom of Drinking Tea, or that we the aforesaid Ladys will not promote ye wear of any Manufacture from England untill such time that all Acts which tend to Enslave this our Native Country shall be Repealed."

The women subsequently sent the resolution to London, where it gained notoriety and coverage in both the *Morning Chronicle* and *London Advertiser* in January 1775. The "Edenton Tea Party" was met largely with derision in Britain, where women organizing for a political cause was a rarity. The very fact that women organized the meeting robbed it of any seriousness. Although some women in other colonial communities drew inspiration from this early public act on behalf of colonial independence, the resolution went largely unnoticed in North Carolina and remained forgotten for several decades.

The print is dated March 25, 1775, less than a month before the first battles of the American Revolution, a time when relations between England and the thirteen colonies reached a boiling point. It is the fifth in a series of satirical prints published by Sayer & Bennett, a London-based printer/publisher, ridiculing those in support of American freedom from Great Britain. Obviously directed at an English audience, all five images depict the colonists as grotesque, occasionally animalistic figures. This image is captioned "A Society of Patriotic Ladies, at Edenton in North Carolina." The heavily caricatured figures are clearly intended to depict the women of Edenton, and by extension all women who supported colonial resistance, in a negative light. Obvious care went into representing most of the women in as homely and unrefined a manner as possible. The two women in the back standing in front of a window appear to be taking turns drinking from a bowl; the younger woman seated at the table, quill pen in hand, seems to welcome the indiscreet attentions of a man who is likely not her husband. Two other men, both smallish in stature, stand in the doorway on the left, allowing women to pour canisters of tea into their hats. A matronly woman sits at the head of the table ready to bring down her gavel to restore order. Behind her appears an enslaved Black woman bearing a tray with an inkwell and quill.

The women appear to come from a range of social classes, although probably only women from the upper classes attended the meeting in Edenton; Mrs. Penelope Barker, the leader of the group, was married to Thomas Barker, the treasurer of the Province of North Carolina. As tea tended to be a rather expensive item, the custom of drinking it daily was largely limited to the well-to-do.

An unattended infant sits on the floor, amusing itself by tossing a small pitcher that belongs to the tea set the child is playing with, a none-too-subtle allusion to the colonists' apparent immature stance on the sale of tea. The child, neglected by all except a dog unsubtly urinating on a canister of tea, also provides criticism of the women's political activism as unnatural and a threat to their traditional roles as wives and mothers. Social norms of the era drew clear distinctions between the bold, masculine actions undertaken by groups like the Sons of Liberty and the less dramatic but no less important women's weaving of cloth and abstinence from purchasing British tea.

—Michael Carver

Questions for Further Study

1. Do the women in the cartoon seem to be serious about the endeavor they are undertaking? Why or why not?

2. What would be the purpose of producing this sort of satirical images for a British audience? What impact might such images end up having?

3. Why might this form of political protest have been tolerated and even celebrated in the colonies while it was ridiculed and discouraged in Great Britain?

Further Reading

Books

Berkin, Carol. *Revolutionary Mothers: Women in the Struggle for America's Independence*. New York: Vintage, 2005.

Norton, Mary Beth, *Liberty's Daughters: The Revolutionary Experience of American Women, 1750–1800*. Ithaca, NY: Cornell University Press, 1996.

Oberg, Barbara B., ed. *Women in the American Revolution: Gender, Politics and the Domestic World*. Charlottesville: University of Virginia Press, 2019.

Websites

"How the Daughters of Liberty Fought for Independence." New England Historical Society. https://www.newenglandhistoricalsociety.com/daughters-liberty-fought-independence/.

"Ten Facts: Women during the Revolutionary War." American Battlefield Trust. https://www.battlefields.org/learn/articles/ten-facts-women-during-revolutionary-war.

THE OLD PLANTATION PAINTING

AUTHOR/CREATOR
John Rose

DATE
1785–90

IMAGE TYPE
PAINTINGS

SIGNIFICANCE
The Old Plantation offers a unique insight into the social lives of enslaved African Americans in the eighteenth century, although historians continue to debate its origin and meaning

Overview

The Old Plantation is possibly the most famous illustration of African American life during the eighteenth century. This small watercolor (12 inches by 18 inches) has long been the subject of intense investigation and speculation. Historians, art historians, curators, and the wider public have studied the painting for decades in an attempt to understand when it was made, by whom, and why. The painting depicts what appears to be a complex of plantation buildings that are probably quarters for enslaved workers. The plantation is situated on a broad river, and in the foreground twelve adults are dancing and playing music. The people depicted are almost certainly enslaved laborers. No other painting is known to exist that shows so many individuals engaging in a relatively private activity on a mainland plantation in such an early period.

The Old Planation is an important source that can help us understand the private lives and cultural practices of enslaved people in the late eighteenth century. Planation slavery invariably stripped enslaved people of their cultural memory as well as their freedom, but this painting demonstrates how it was possible to preserve traditions alongside the development of new practices. The musical instruments, clothing, and dance movements suggest cultural connections with West Africa, although it is impossible to identify specific ethnic identities or influences. The painting provides a unique glimpse into the lives of enslaved plantation laborers, albeit an idyllic one that obscures the brutality of the colonial plantation.

About the Artist

This small watercolor painting is unsigned and undated, and it has no given provenance. The artist did not name the painting, but former owners gave it the title *The Old Plantation*, by which it is now generally known. A chemical analysis of the paper's watermark revealed that it had been manufactured between 1777 and 1794. Historians are not exactly certain where and when the painting was produced, but a probable date is 1785 to 1790.

For decades the identity of the artist was unknown. However, new research strongly suggests that the artist was John Rose (1752–1820), a watercolorist and government official who owned a plantation on the

Document Image

***The Old Plantation* painting**
(Abby Aldrich Rockefeller Folk Art Museum)

Coosaw River in Beaufort County, South Carolina, which is probably the setting of the painting. Rose owned dozens of enslaved workers but left no diaries, nor is there any contemporary documentation about the painting, so it is impossible to know for certain.

Context

In the period in which the painting was likely produced, more than 100,000 enslaved people lived in South Carolina. Over half of these enslaved people lived on large plantations like that belonging to John Rose, with fifty or more slaves. Most of the enslaved people in South Carolina in the late eighteenth century had been born in America, but about one-third had been born in Africa. Historians estimate that between 1760 and 1790 around 53,000 captives were imported into South Carolina from Africa, although the actual figure was likely much larger. There is no demographic information available about the enslaved people featured in this painting, but Charleston newspapers carried weekly advertisements offering slaves for sale from Angola, Gambia, Nigeria, and the Gold Coast. New arrivals from many different ethnic and linguistic backgrounds no doubt found themselves working alongside second- or third-generation enslaved laborers who had no personal memory of Africa and had greater exposure to spoken English. These differences in language were an obstacle to verbal communication among enslaved workers and encouraged nonverbal alternatives, such as music and dance.

Whether born in Africa or America, their legal status as slaves ensured that they would be regarded simply as chattel property and nothing more. This reduced status from free human beings to property is reflected in the historical record, which usually ignores slaves unless they are mentioned in newspaper advertisements, property transactions, criminal records, or occasionally church registers. The same attitudes were true in the world of art. Enslaved plantation workers, if represented at all, were often depicted as finely dressed and engaging cheerfully in benign labor. The most common visual image of slavery in the eighteenth century comes from the stylized portraits of wealthy owners in which a single Black slave waits in attendance in the background to reflect the white owners' power and prosperity. Sometimes the enslaved workers are dressed extravagantly to demonstrate that their owners had the means to purchase them lavish clothing. Other eighteenth-century images of enslaved humans appeared as decorative woodcuts in newspaper advertisements for slave sales or fugitives, or in atlases as stylized symbols of North America. Nowhere were enslaved people represented as individuals at this time.

The Old Plantation, in contrast, is distinctive as the earliest representation of multiple African American slaves in a moment of free time, away from the rigors of life on the plantation. The painting captures a personal and relatively private event that reflects their own distinct cultural practices. Plantation slavery, both intentionally and unintentionally, deprived enslaved people of their cultural traditions as well as their freedom. Language, dress, music, and religion were gradually lost over the course of transportation to and enslavement in the Americas. This painting illustrates how enslaved people were able to preserve cultural memory in a new world and demonstrates the connections between cultural practice of African Americans and their heritage in Africa.

Explanation and Analysis of the Document

The Old Plantation depicts twelve people, who are almost certainly enslaved plantation workers, dancing and playing music. A central male figure is holding a long stick or staff. The two women in the center are dancing with what appear to be scarves, but they are in fact probably each holding a *shegureh*, a rattle of West African origin that was made of a gourd enclosed inside a net into which hard objects such as bones or shells were woven. When shaken, these objects would strike against the gourd to create a percussive sound. The man on the right plays a banjo, which was the most popular musical instrument among enslaved peoples during the late eighteenth century. Another male musician plays a small drum held between his thighs. Some scholars have identified it as the *gudugudu*, a particular type of drum also originating in West Africa, but it is possible that the object being struck was a substitute such as a pot or a pan.

The women in *The Old Plantation* wear headscarves, fitted gowns, and long skirts. Several of the men also seem to be wearing headscarves, while the banjo player wears a round flat-brimmed hat. Except for the headscarves and their bare feet, the male and female clothing conforms to the style of ordinary late eighteenth-century laborers, both enslaved and free. It is possible that the people in the painting are wearing their "best" clothes rather than everyday wear or that the artist has deliberately "sanitized" their clothing, which was more likely to have been worn and ragged. Alternatively, the people depicted may have been household slaves or artisans who had access to finer clothing than fieldhands. Some of the men are depicted with earrings, which were common items of jewelry among enslaved South Carolinians, and several are drawn with beards.

There are three containers in the lower right foreground of the painting: a brown jug, a glass bottle, and a white jug that was probably manufactured in England. These may demonstrate artistic license as it is not certain that these items would have been found at an actual dance and positioned in this way. The background depicts a large river, possibly the Coosaw River, that is being traversed by two canoes, which were a common mode of transport between plantations in South Carolina. The buildings include the plantation house and several outbuildings, including stables and what appears to be a row of cabins for enslaved workers. The cabins may have chimneys made from wood or clay, which sometimes featured on enslaved workers' houses on larger plantations in South Carolina. Two cabins are also shown in the foreground, which suggests that the painting may represent a dance in the laborers' quarter.

It is impossible to know for certain the artist's intention when he painted this scene. Historians disagree about what the painting is supposed to represent, with suggestions including a customary weekend dance, a secular festival, or a dance with unknown spiritual significance. A common but unlikely interpretation is that it represents a wedding in a ceremony known as "jumping the broom" due to the prominence of the man bent forward holding a stick. However, this interpretation ignores the fact that sticks were a common element in dances from West Africa. Instead, it is most likely that the scene depicts a combination of objects, behaviors, and activities that the artist had witnessed over a period of time.

Although the musical instruments, clothing, and dance movements suggest the cultural influence of West Africa, it is impossible to tell if the people in this painting were born in Africa or not. Nor is it possible to identify specific ethnic identities or influences. Instead, what is depicted probably reflects a fusion of a variety of musical cultures that occurred in Black societies throughout the Americas. The painting provides a unique glimpse into life among enslaved workers, but one that appears serene and idyllic and masks the harsh life of enslaved plantation laborers in late eighteenth century South Carolina.

—Jon Chandler

Questions for Further Study

1. Historians disagree about what the scene is supposed to represent. What activity you think is depicted in this painting, and why?

2. To what extent does the painting depict connections between the cultural practices of enslaved African Americans and their heritage in Africa?

3. This painting is one of the earliest visual representations of a plantation in mainland North America. Do you think it is an accurate depiction of plantation life? Why or why not?

Further Reading

Books

Morgan, Philip D. *Slave Counterpoint: Black Culture in the Eighteenth-Century Chesapeake & Lowcountry*. Chapel Hill: University of North Carolina Press, 1998.

Shames, Susan P. *The Old Plantation: The Artist Revealed*. Williamsburg: Colonial Williamsburg Foundation, 2010.

Articles

Handler, Jerome S. "The Old Plantation Painting at Colonial Williamsburg: New Findings and Some Observations." *African Diaspora Archaeology Newsletter* 13, no. 4 (2010).

Websites

"The Trans-Atlantic Slave Trade Database." *Slave Voyages*. https://www.slavevoyages.org/.

Slavery Images: A Visual Record of the African Slave Trade and Slave Life in the Early African Diaspora. http://www.slavery-images.org/.

"The Times, A Political Portrait" Cartoon

Author/Creator
Unknown

Date
1795–97

Image Type
Cartoons

Significance
A pro-Federalist political cartoon of the mid-1790s using the French Revolution as means of underscoring the supposed radicalism of the Democratic-Republicans

Overview

This political cartoon depicts one of the most important areas of disagreement in post-revolutionary America. There exists a tendency among many to believe that the Founding Fathers fundamentally agreed about the nature of the new government they had created; in reality, the first decade after the ratification of the Constitution, which was the product of numerous compromises, was one of the most divisive and bitter in the history of American politics. Two groups dominated the political landscape by the 1790s. One favored a strong federal government committed to global trade and developing into a world power, and the other remained suspicious of a powerful central government and was committed to a largely agrarian economy. The former group, the Federalists, was initially the larger and more powerful of the two, which enabled it to dominate the federal government during the first twelve years of the nation's existence. But the latter group, the Democratic-Republicans, proved resilient and grew in numbers by ridiculing the Federalists as the party of the commercial elites while they represented independent farmers.

What the size of the federal government and the extent of its power should be was arguably the central debate of both lawmakers and everyday citizens in the earliest years of the young American republic. The Federalists fervently believed that the Unites States should join the ranks of such world powers as Great Britain and could do so only with a centralized government consisting of the nation's most brilliant minds who, in turn, would be voted into office only by those who were literate or met property ownership qualifications. Unlike the Federalists, who feared too much democracy, the Democratic-Republicans generally welcomed broader involvement in American government, arguing that the Federalist platform potentially threatened to turn the nation into a monarchy. The Democratic-Republicans also resisted the Federalists' economic program and wanted the United States to seek closer ties with France, whose involvement had enabled the Americans to secure their independence, instead of Great Britain, with whom the Federalists hoped to establish stronger bonds of trade and diplomacy. When the French Revolution became increasingly bloody and destructive, the two sides once again took different positions: the Democratic-Republicans used the Federalists' criticism of the revolutionaries in France as proof of their disdain for democracy, while the Federalists claimed that the Democratic-Republicans

Document Image

"The Times, a Political Portrait"
(American Historical Print Collectors Society)

would plunge the United States into similar turmoil if ever allowed to take power, which is the message of the cartoon.

About the Artist

The artist who created this drawing is unknown.

Context

In his farewell address to the American people given on September 17, 1796, after serving two terms as president, George Washington left his audience with a warning about political parties: that while they "may now and then answer popular ends, they are likely in the course of time and things, to become potent engines, by which cunning, ambitious, and unprincipled men will be enabled to subvert the power of the people and to usurp for themselves the reins of government, destroying afterwards the very engines which have lifted them to unjust dominion." Washington had watched with considerable concern over the previous eight years how two factions, the Democratic-Republican Party and the Federalist Party, which Washington reluctantly aligned with, emerged and increasingly quarreled over the future of the young republic. He feared that lawmakers might come to be more loyal to their political parties than to the Constitution and the people who had elected them to office, which might bring about the end of the fragile republic.

But Washington's words of warning seemed to have little impact in the years that followed. The Federalists rallied around the newly elected president, John Adams, and the Democratic-Republicans supported Vice President Thomas Jefferson, each side accusing the other of failing to abide by their respective interpretations of the Constitution. It was a continuation and intensification of a debate that had taken shape even before the ink signatures had dried on America's most important founding document. Out of the debate arose the first two political parties that clashed for power in the formative years of the United States, setting the stage for similar such struggles that persist to the present day.

Secretary of the Treasury Alexander Hamilton came to be the Federalists' foremost advocate and de facto leader. While Washington generally supported the Federalist vision of a strong national government, he believed a president should avoid formal association with any political faction; he feared that organized parties would prove detrimental to the nation's health. Washington scrupulously avoiding becoming involved in any of the debates that raged in Congress during his two terms, but it was widely understood that he worked behind the scenes to advance the Federalists' agenda of a national bank, tariffs on imported goods, and a federal government dominated by an enlightened ruling class that made informed decisions on behalf of the masses.

Hamilton's views were opposed by those who feared a Federalist-dominated government would implement policies not dissimilar from those imposed by the British that had justified the American Revolution. Thomas Jefferson emerged as the most vocal of Hamilton's critics, insisting that the Federalists used government appointments and awarded special privileges to gain allies and consolidate their control over the federal government. He further fumed over the Federalists' efforts to create a national network as a means of improving their chances of winning local and state elections. Jefferson, James Madison (at the time a representative from Virginia), and other like-minded individuals believed in the concept of the United States as an agrarian republic of farmer-citizens who worked their own land and did not bend to the will of a monied elite.

The Federalists and Democratic-Republicans found themselves on opposite side of numerous issues pertaining to both domestic and foreign issues. Such was the case when the French Revolution, in part inspired by the American Revolution, transformed into an uncontrollable event that plunged Europe into more than two decades of war. The Federalists and the Democratic-Republicans viewed events in France through contrary lenses, a difference in viewpoints referenced in the cartoon.

Explanation and Analysis of the Document

The French Revolution shook Europe to its very foundation, setting into motion the gradual disappearance of monarchies that had ruled for centuries, replaced by liberal governments and expanded voting rights. Its effects could be felt across the Atlantic as it illuminated the fundamental differences between the social philosophies of the Federalists and the Democratic-

Republicans. Both sides initially greeted the start of the 1789 uprising in France with considerable jubilation, which they celebrated as another blow against unjust rule. But the revolution's increasing radicalism during the early 1790s terrified the Federalists; the elimination of the Catholic Church and the brutal executions of the French king and queen confirmed to them what could happen when enlightened elites lose control of the government and mob rule takes their place. In stark contrast to the Federalists' feelings of horror, the Democratic-Republicans held up the French Revolution as a prime example of a democratic takeover that swept aside any vestiges of elitism. Some Democratic-Republicans went so far as to emulate the French revolutionaries by adopting their short hairstyles and fashion sense, wearing distinctive trousers called *sans culottes*.

This cartoon, labeled "The Times, a Political Portrait," encapsulates the deepening political divisions as they existed at the close of the eighteenth century and clearly draws upon the divisive influence of the French Revolution on politics in the mid-1790s. The Federalists painted the Democratic-Republicans as aristocratic elites and accused them of nurturing the sort of radicalism that had brought chaos and bloodshed to France. Democratic-Republicans lobbed their own accusations at their rivals, whose condemnations of the French revolutionaries they equated with their desire to maintain control over the federal government, smothering the spirit of democracy. If the Democratic-Republicans viewed the French Revolution as a continuation and perhaps a purer form of the revolution that had enabled the thirteen colonies to gain their independence, the Federalists saw it as a corrupted and deeply flawed form of popular unrest.

Attempting to champion the Federalist position, the cartoon centers on a horse-drawn carriage carrying the uniformed figure of President George Washington commanding a column of troops symbolizing the relentless advance of federalism. The cartoon's caption reads: "Triumph Government: perish all its enemies. Traitors, be warned: justice, though slow, is sure." Thomas Jefferson, the era's foremost advocate for a modestly sized federal government with minimal power, can be seen gripping the spoke of one of Washington's coach's rear wheels, desperately trying to disrupt its progress toward federalism. Aiding Jefferson with an oversize pen lodged in front of the same wheel is fellow Democratic-Republican leader James Madison, while a third figure stands at the reach of the coach, vainly trying to hold it back. This is likely Edmond-Charles Genêt, a French envoy to the United States in 1793, who criticized the Washington administration's decision to remain neutral when revolutionary France went to war with several European states, including England, in the early 1790s. Benjamin Franklin Bache, the editor for the Philadelphia *Aurora*, which frequently attacked the Federalist Party and its leaders, finds himself being trampled by the troops and horses drawing Washington's coach as a dog relieves itself on a copy of his newspaper.

The orderly progress of Washington's "Federal Chariot" stands in stark contrast to the figures depicted in the left background of the image: frenzied French revolutionaries, in the midst of an invasion of the United States, torture execute innocent civilians with the caption "The Cannibals are landing" below them. The revolutionaries, one prominently shown displaying a severed head on a pike, perhaps symbolize the Democratic-Republicans or the presence of the radical concepts of personal liberty that inspired the increasingly violent French Revolution and were espoused by Jefferson and fellow Democratic-Republicans. From overhead descends an eagle enwreathed by storm clouds, brandishing a shield, and discharging lightning bolts at the oblivious "Cannibals" below.

The negative depiction of Jefferson, one of several produced during the time period, reveals the depth of enmity that existed between the Federalists and the Democratic-Republicans. But the Federalists' dominance in the federal government proved short-lived; after the election of John Adams in 1796, they never won another election and gradually disappeared from the scene. Washington's retirement from politics left the Federalists without a unifying source of leadership, and the party quickly split between supporters of President Adams, who was comparatively moderate and open to compromise with the Democratic-Republicans, and Alexander Hamilton, who was generally not.

—Michael Carver

Questions for Further Study

1. What is the possible significance of President George Washington being depicted in a military uniform rather than civilian attire? What is the possible message of the artist?

2. Is such a cartoon an effective way of condemning an opposing political view? Why would these sorts of political cartoons have been so popular in the late 1700s?

3. In what ways might this cartoon appear to take issue with what most Americans consider to be essential rights? Why might the artist think it was necessary to limit such rights?

Further Reading

Books

Cost, Jay. *The Price of Greatness: Alexander Hamilton, James Madison, and the Creation of American Oligarchy*. New York: Basic Books, 2018.

Elkins, Stanley, and Eric McKitrick. *The Age of Federalism: The Early American Republic, 1788–1800*. New York: Oxford University Press, 1993.

Wood, Gordon S. *Empire of Liberty: A History of the Early Republic, 1789–1815*. New York: Oxford University Press, 2009.

Websites

"Dividing into Parties: Then and Now: Federalists v. Democratic-Republicans." Digital Exhibits, Utah State University. http://exhibits.usu.edu/exhibits/show/politicalparties/polarized.

"The Federalist and the Republican Party." American Experience, PBS. https://www.pbs.org/wgbh/americanexperience/features/duel-federalist-and-republican-party/.

Colonial Cloth Makers Illustration

Author/Creator Unknown	**Image Type** Illustrations
Date 1800s	**Significance** A depiction of women in early America producing homespun cotton cloth, a multi-step process that was a key responsibility before the rise of textile mills

Overview

This illustration depicts one of the key contributions of women in the early republic. The upheaval of the American Revolution (1775–84) thrust women into a variety of roles and responsibilities that opened when their fathers, brothers, and husbands went to war. Many women, despite a lack of formal education or training, rose to the occasion of running family farms and businesses with great success. Others, through no fault of their own, did not. But by war's end, there was a general sense among women, including future First Lady Abigail Adams, and more than a few men that the question of specific rights for women should be addressed. There were some successes for American women, such as easier access to divorces and short-lived voting rights in New Jersey, but society in the new nation remained overwhelmingly dominated by men.

If women were not yet welcome to be full participants in the public sphere, the American Revolution did inspire many to find ways of asserting themselves in their homes and insisting upon greater recognition of the importance of their domestic duties. Americans prided themselves on being at the vanguard of a new, more equitable nation that prized liberty above all else; a more equitable household did not seem much of a jump to take. American women would take on the responsibility of instructing the children in the values of the American republic, using their sense of duty to keep their families clean, fed, and clothed as an example of one's duty to the nation. This new outlook gave such female-centric tasks a new significance, all the more so for weaving due to the continued absence of English textiles in the late 1700s. As they had both before and during the revolution, women turned to their spinning wheels and looms to make homespun cloth in large enough quantities that the country never again depended upon foreign sources of cloth. While textile mills eventually outproduced homespun producers, the wheel and loom remained powerful symbols of female empowerment.

About the Artist

The artist is unknown.

Context

During the colonial era, weaving fabric was not extensively done; colonists tended to purchase textiles from

Document Image

Depiction of colonial cloth makers
(Granger)

Great Britain rather than produce them themselves. This began to change in the 1760s when British tariffs on imported textiles compelled many colonial women to stop buying it and begin producing homespun cloth, both out of economic necessity and as a form of political protest. When the war for American independence began in 1775, many women contributed to the war effort by producing uniforms and bandages. In the years of the Early Republic, after the American Revolution, manufactured cloth from England remained difficult to procure and prohibitively expensive for many American families. This necessitated the household production of fabric, a time and labor-intensive process performed largely by women.

Women's household duties took on a new symbolic character with the advent of the republican motherhood movement. Champions of the ideology argued that American mothers needed to acquire a fuller education to better instill a sense of civic virtue in their children. While this most obviously manifested itself in teaching their sons and daughters about government and history, republican motherhood extended to respect for the ability with which women ran their households and mastered such skills as weaving, thus setting an example of self-sacrifice for young girls to follow and both husbands and sons to draw inspiration from in their service to the new nation.

Weaving became more widely practiced in the northeastern states, where a variety of spinning wheels and looms came to be adopted. Hemp and wool, both of which were widely available across most of country, were initially the most popular materials for weaving cloth. But cotton, while initially deemed to challenging to spin, became the widely used material for the making of cloth soon after Eli Whitney invented the cotton gin in 1793. Whitney's invention in turn boosted the production of cotton in the South and thread in New England.

While textile mills located mainly in New England spun large quantities of yarn and thread, before 1814 individual families using handlooms were responsible for weaving nearly all the cloth produced in the United States, which was considered to be equal in quality to British textiles, if not better. Women weavers mastered a range of techniques to produce tablecloths, items of clothing, towels, blankets, rugs, and other household items.

The textile industry grew in size and economic importance in the first decades of the nineteenth century in response to the Embargo of 1807 and the War of 1812, which eliminated textile imports and necessitated an increase in domestic production. Between the embargo and the end of the war, the number of cotton spindles rose from 8,000 to 130,000. As textile production shifted increasingly toward factories, more and more fabric came to be manufactured in the New England mills rather than local producers, although many families relocating to western homesteads continued to rely on homespun cloth.

Explanation and Analysis of the Document

This image shows the process of converting sheared wool into cloth. Some stages of the textile-making process are not shown in the image, including shearing, which involved the removal of wool from sheep using a pair of hand shears; separating useable wool from undesirable pieces; repeatedly washing the sheared wool in hot water in order to remove such impurities as lanolin oil; and then picking, which entailed separating the wool fibers by hand in order remove any remaining bits of dirt or grass. Children three or four years old often performed the task of picking, their first assigned chore.

The woman seated on the left is engaged in carding the sheared wool piled next to her, the first stage in production, which dates back to France in the late 1200s. She is using a pair of wooden carders: large rectangular, handled combs made from wood into which hundreds of tiny metal hooks are inserted. A small tuft of wool is placed between the carders, one balanced on the woman's knee while the other is pulled across it repeatedly, allowing the hooks to arrange the wool fibers in a uniform direction and with consistent density while also removing any lingering debris. After an adequate number of strokes, the carded wool forms a sheet that is rolled into a cylindrical-shaped rolag. Completed rolags are piled in a basket at the woman's feet, to be used in the second phase of the process, spinning.

Seated behind her spinning wheel on the right side of the image, another woman is taking the rolags and using them to produce the woolen yarn that will be woven together to produce cloth. The history of spinning dates back thousands of years in regions around the world, and spinning wheels likely first appeared in China and India before being adopted by Europeans in the thirteenth century, replacing the smaller and portable drop spinners due to their higher production rates.

Although not depicted in the image, it was not uncommon in early America for the spun yarn to be dyed in a solution derived from natural sources such as onion skins, bark, flowers, and nuts. Those who could afford it might have used a comparatively expensive dye made from indigo plants grown in the West Indies and later South Carolina that gave the yarn a distinctive blue color.

The final and most complicated stage of cloth production, weaving, is represented by the woman seated at the large machine positioned left of center, a loom. The yarn produced during the spinning process was attached to the loom using a device called the warp to create a series of lengthwise sets of yarns. It was necessary to carefully measure and thread the yarn onto the loom before using an instrument called the shuttle, which the woman is holding in her right hand, to interweave the warp yarns with a series of crosswise weft yarns. The completed fabric consisted of tightly woven warp and weft yarns.

As made clear by the image, cloth production in early America was a task often performed by women, but this was not the case before this, during the colonial era, when men did the weaving and women did the spinning. Other domestic duties expected of women in the late eighteenth and early nineteenth centuries are represented by the presence of two young children and a fourth woman bearing a tray with a kettle and perhaps some food on it. The only male figure, the man entering through the door carrying firewood that he most likely chopped, symbolizes the clear distinction between the expected responsibilities to be completed by the two genders.

The production of fabric both assisted in providing a family with such essential items as clothing and could potentially provide additional income for the household if it was sold on the local or regional market. President Thomas Jefferson's decision to place an embargo on foreign goods in 1807 deprived the United States of British textiles for a number of years, which incentivized domestic fabric production in New England mills and, by aggregating production in the mills, reduced the number of local fabric producers.

—Michael Carver

Questions for Further Study

1. What would have been the advantage of having children close by while cloth making was taking place?

2. Women often organized and participated in "spinning bees," which enabled them to produce large quantities of thread or cloth as a group. What might they have discussed?

3. It was far more likely that a woman who was a professional spinner of thread was unmarried (hence the term "spinster") than married. Why might this have been?

Further Reading

Books

Boydston, Jeanne. *Home and Work: Housework, Wages, and the Ideology of Labor in the Early Republic.* New York: Oxford University Press, 1994.

McMahon, Lucia. *Mere Equals: The Paradox of Educated Women in the Early American Republic.* Ithaca: Cornell University Press, 2012.

Ulrich, Laurel Thatcher. *The Age of Homespun: Objects and Stories in the Creation of an American Myth.* New York: Knopf, 2001.

Zagarri, Rosemarie. *Revolutionary Backlash: Women and Politics in the Early American Republic.* Philadelphia: University of Pennsylvania Press, 2008.

Painting Of A Newly Cleared Small Farm Site

Author/Creator
Unknown

Date
c. 1800

Image Type
Paintings; Illustrations

Significance
Illustrates some of the challenges those who traveled to the western United States in the late eighteenth and early nineteenth centuries needed to overcome to establish a homestead farm

Overview

This image depicts a newly cleared farm site from the early eighteenth century. Land ownership became an increasingly tricky prospect for men living in western Europe and the British Isles by the sixteenth century, driven in large part by the region's rapidly expanding population and the growing demand for food. The rising cost of wheat incentivized the purchase of land for production, which increased its value and made it nearly impossible for a landless man of limited financial means to compete with wealthy investors. But for those willing to face any number of challenges in a largely unknown, far-off location, land ownership seemed possible in the English colonies of North America. Colonial proprietors, desperate to increase the colonies' populations, began to offer land grants to those willing to undertake the arduous journey. The seemingly limitless acreage of the North American colonies and the relative ease with which it could be acquired cemented the area's reputation as a land of opportunity and advancement.

After the American Revolution, the newly established state governments faced a similar dilemma as their colonial predecessors: increasing the size of their populations and encouraging movement away from the densely populated eastern communities to the far less inhabited western reaches. State governments continued to offer land grants, although this led to occasional disputes between states, such as Virginia and Connecticut, over where their western borders existed, a situation that the federal government resolved by assuming control over the western lands. Once the legal kinks had been worked out, which included negotiated settlements with Native American tribes, a steady exodus of settlers left their eastern homes and began to move west, many in the Northwest Territory, the location of much of the present-day Midwestern United States.

Most individuals and families who relocated west sought to establish farms on land that tended to be heavily forested. Clearing the acres necessary to construct a home and begin the planting process was arduous and time-consuming. Those who could do so looked to their neighbors to help complete major tasks more efficiently and quickly, which promoted a sense of community that helped settlers endure any number of challenges and dangers. Many families in isolated locations, in fact, had no choice but to look to one another to survive. This image offers some insight into

Document Image

Illustration of a newly cleared small farm site
(Sarin Images / GRANGER)

the sorts of undertakings newly arrived settlers needed to complete if they wished to realize their dream of becoming independent farmers.

About the Artist

The artist is unknown.

Context

The American victory over the British in the American Revolution resulted in the ratification of the Treaty of Paris in 1783. One of the ten terms in the treaty was the formal recognition of the United States' boundaries extending past the Allegheny Mountains to the Mississippi River, a vast area that included the Ohio Valley. The colonists before the American Revolution had been anxious to expand into this area but were barred from doing so by the British government, which sought to protect the land rights of the Native American tribes. The U.S. government brokered treaties with the Iroquois Confederacy, the Shawnee, and other Indigenous groups, often after bloody conflicts, that obligated them to relocate westward, a process that would continue in the decades that followed as treaty after treaty was broken.

Many of those who went west from the eastern states were veterans of the American Revolution who had been promised bounty land warrants by the Continental Congress as a sign of appreciation. The newly established U.S. Congress made good on the pledge by passing an act in 1788 that provided free land in the public domain to soldiers and officers who had served during the conflict or the heirs of those who had lost their lives. Privates and noncommissioned officers were to receive 100 acres of bounty land, and officers were entitled to larger allotments based on their rank: the higher the rank, the greater the acreage. Congress set aside a tract of 4,000 square miles in the Northwest Territory for those possessing the land warrants, nearly 14,000 of which had been issued by 1803, the same year that Congress passed another act officially opening the area, now designated the U.S. military District of Ohio, for settlement.

Another factor influencing Easterners to journey west was the young nation's rapidly expanding population, which roughly doubled from 5.3 million to 9.6 million from 1800 to 1820. Many of these new Americans, including immigrants, resided in rapidly growing cities, but those wishing to farm had little choice but to head for the West. Eastern farmlands were either already owned or nearing exhaustion after decades of cultivation, and in the South, where the plantation system reigned supreme, only those of means could afford to buy new land.

Eastern migrants usually reached the "Old Northwest" by traveling by flatboat down the Ohio and Monongahela Rivers before reaching a riverfront community, often Cincinnati, before resuming the journey in horse or oxen-drawn wagons or on foot. Upon arriving at their claim, ideally in the spring or summer months, the settlers set about constructing crude cabins or lean-tos and beginning the arduous process of clearing out wooded areas in time to plant crops, usually corn. Men and boys hunted game for food while women and girls prepared meals and took care of the laundry. The demands of starting and tending a homestead left little time for leisure, and it was not uncommon for members of a family to have no interaction with outsiders for a period of months.

Communities gradually formed, thanks in part to groups of families migrating together and clustering in the same general area. They established local governments, churches, schools, and businesses and helped one another complete arduous tasks. But families often pulled up stakes and sold their homesteads when new regions opened for settlement, fueled by a hope that greater opportunities awaited them.

Explanation and Analysis of the Document

Dense woods along the top and right side of the image reflect how forested the area is and the challenge of clearing it to make way for new farms on the western frontier with just the use of hand tools and livestock. Settler families going west typically contended with thick forests of massive trees. Most settlers thought it was better to establish a farm on land that had previously been forested rather than grasslands because the soil was thought to be more productive. The process of a family clearing enough acreage to keep them fed—ten to fifteen acres—required four to five years to complete. First underbrush and then needed to be removed, often by using the process of "slashing," which involved chopping the trees down and then burning them after they had dried or killing the trees by cutting away the bark in strips, a practice known as "girdling." Those with the financial means of doing so might hire "choppers," often newly arrived immigrants, to assist the family or clear the land themselves. A more common method of pooling labor involved the organization of a "logging bee," which involved settler families living ten to twenty miles from one another combining tools and teams of oxen to clear land together. Due to the difficulty involved in removing stumps, it was not uncommon for the first year's crops to be planted between them until removal could be completed and increase the amount of acreage for plowing and planting.

In the image, some of the felled timber, likely that of the highest quality, has been utilized for the construction of a modestly sized log cabin and an outbuilding, as well as the distinct worm fencing cordoning off part of the property. First appearing in the colonies during the mid-1600s, worm, snake, or zig-zag fences grew in popularity due to their effectiveness and the relative ease with which they could be constructed from split wood rails. Worm fences required far more timber to be built compared to other types, which was certainly not an issue in forested western areas. Log houses on the frontier tended to be sparsely furnished, the result of the limited carrying capacities of settlers' wagons. A cabin might have a table, one or two benches, and a wooden bunk or "sleeping shelf" made from planks of wood held up by pegs or boards so that the sleeper did not make contact with the floor.

In addition to clearing the land and constructing shelters, a key task for homesteaders was the digging of wells. Families who reached an open territory first usually staked their claims near rivers or streams, but most had little choice but to dig wells and hope for the best. Ideally, a well could be dug relatively close to the house, but a well situated near a barn or outhouse could easily become contaminated, causing illness among the homesteaders and their livestock. If a well provided little water, families might resort to strict conservation efforts that included collecting rainwater or melted snow and limiting the frequency of baths, each family member using the same tub of water.

The well-defined gender roles as they existed on early American homesteads can be detected in the image. A group of four men tackles the physically demanding task of clearing the land, using a team of oxen to assist them in their effort, while a woman carries a pail to the well, presumably to complete such domestic chores as laundry or cooking. Women also saw to the decorating of the cabins, weaving rugs from scraps of cloth and sewing curtains and tablecloths. While men and women of the early nineteenth century adhered to strict notions of the acceptable roles for their respective genders, there existed an understanding that the labors of both were indispensable to the survival of the family. And women frequently performed taxing outdoor labor that included planting, nurturing, and harvesting crops, as well as looking after such livestock as cows and chickens. Women also helped to provide additional financial support by producing textiles to be sold. Both genders fully understood that surviving the daily challenges and threats posed by the wilderness, be they droughts, fires, blizzards, or disease, necessitated everyone doing their part to sustain the family. The emergence of separate "spheres" based on gender, with women overseeing household (the "domestic sphere") and men asserting their dominance in society (the "public sphere") did not occur until the processes of industrialization and urbanization transformed America.

—Michael Carver

Questions for Further Study

1. Why might the U.S. government have been so willing to adopt policies intended to encourage families to relocate to the western part of the country? What did it stand to gain?

2. Beyond growing crops for sustenance, why did so many Americans seek to own land in the decades after the American Revolution?

3. How might the communities that formed from the sort of homestead in the picture have acquired characteristics different from established communities that already existed in the east?

Further Reading

Books

Brown, Dee. *Wondrous Times on the Frontier: America during the 1880s.* Little Rock: August House Publishers, 1991.

Hurt, R. Douglas. *The Ohio Frontier: Crucible of the Old Northwest, 1720–1830.* Bloomington: Indiana University Press, 1996.

McCullough, David. *The Pioneers: The Heroic Story of the Settlers Who Brought the American Ideal West.* New York: Simon & Schuster, 2019.

Rohrbough, Malcolm J. *Trans-Appalachian Frontier: People, Societies, and Institutions, 1775–1850.* Bloomington: Indiana University Press, 2007.

Elkanah Tisdale: "The Gerry-mander" Cartoon

Author/Creator Elkanah Tisdale	**Significance** Popularized the term "gerrymander" by illustrating Federalist opposition to the Massachusetts state senate districts created by the Jeffersonian Republicans to favor their own party
Date 1812	
Image Type Cartoons	

Overview

This cartoon, first printed in the March 26, 1812, edition of *Boston Gazette*, introduced and popularized the term "gerrymander." Most newspapers in the early republic were highly partisan—essentially extensions of political parties. Rather than provide objective reporting of facts or a balance of contrasting views, the partisan press sought to inflame its base's passions and provide the party's perspective on issues of the day. In addition to motivating party members, this reporting communicated the party's message to the faithful so they could present unified positions in public discourse and convince others to support the party. Cartoons played a critical role in this process. They could easily be understood, even by those with minimal literacy, and often, like this one, contained very effective and biting satire. This particular example was so effective that the word "gerrymander" entered America's political lexicon as a term for manipulating legislative district boundaries to favor one party or group.

The gerrymander cartoon was created in response to the redistricting of 1811. Massachusetts's constitution gave the legislature wide latitude in drawing state senate districts. It specified that there be a minimum of thirteen districts for the forty seats in the state senate, allowing more populous districts to elect multiple senators. Control of the Massachusetts senate had gone back and forth between Federalists and Jeffersonian Republicans for the previous decade. Jeffersonian Republicans had gained control of the Massachusetts senate and governorship just in time to receive the data from the 1810 Census, which they promptly used to redistrict the state in a way that favored them heavily in the state senate. The gerrymander proved effective. Despite narrowly defeating incumbent governor Elbridge Gerry, a Jeffersonian Republican, for the governorship, the Federalists won only eleven of the state's forty state senate seats.

About the Artist

While there is some uncertainty about who created the cartoon, most scholars accept the evidence presented by John W. Dean in an 1892 journal article that Elkanah Tisdale drew the cartoon as originally published. The basic image was reproduced countless times in newspapers and broadsides, hardly any of which used the *Boston Gazette*'s engraving of Tisdale's

Document Image

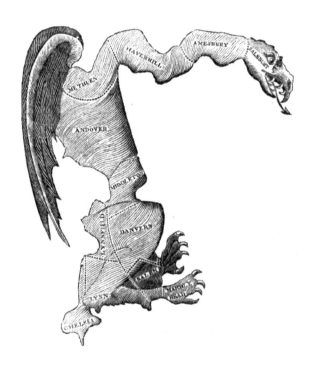

"The Gerry-mander" Cartoon from 1812
(Library of Congress)

cartoon, so there are slight differences in other versions. Tisdale was born in Connecticut, most likely in 1768. As an adult, he moved frequently throughout New England and New York. His personal associations with well-known Federalists and the content of this cartoon in particular suggest he was sympathetic to the Federalist Party. The cartoon itself stemmed from conversations at a dinner party hosted by a prominent Boston Federalist. His other noteworthy published engraved images are full-page illustrations in a 1795 reprint of John Tumball's epic satire *M'Fingal*, a lampooning of British Loyalists during the American Revolution, and his depiction of the U.S. Constitutional Convention in the 1823 edition of Charles Goodrich's *A History of the United States*. Art critics and historians conclude that his design work was better than his engravings. He was most successful as a painter of miniatures. Two of his miniature portraits were exhibited at the prestigious American Academy of the Fine Arts in 1818, and he was known as an influential teacher of other miniature painters. Tisdale died in 1823.

Context

The drawing of districts is of paramount importance in a district-based election system. Depending on the criteria used, it can radically affect whether the population is represented fairly. The framers of the Constitution felt that the British Parliament, against whom they had successfully rebelled, did not fairly represent the population. A notable example of unfair representation in Parliament was the existence of "rotten boroughs," districts with an equal vote in Parliament but vastly lower numbers of potential voters. In structuring the government of the new United States, as well as those of its constituent states, the framers sought to ensure that, at least in the lower house of legislatures, representation would be divided so that the population was represented fairly. The U.S. Constitution mandated an "enumeration" of the population every ten years to provide the information needed for this task. This is the basis for the decennial census and reapportionment that have become hallmarks of American political structure. The Constitution of Massachusetts defined fair representation in the state's senate somewhat differently, by proportion of taxes paid rather than by head count of the population. It called for the Massachusetts senate to have forty seats that were to come from at least thirteen districts, with no district selecting more than six of the forty senators. The apportionment satirized in the "gerrymander" cartoon created eighteen districts.

Partisan rivalry between Federalists and Jeffersonian Republicans was bitter and intense from its the beginning in the election of 1800. It was so extreme that defeated president John Adams, a Federalist, refused to attend his victorious rival Thomas Jefferson's inauguration. The division was just as intense in 1812. The election that year was held under recently redrawn districts that heavily favored Jeffersonian Republican candidates. Federalists such as Tisdale seized upon the contorted-looking shape of the Essex South district to highlight the perceived injustice of the redistricting. Noting that it resembled a salamander, Tisdale's cartoon depicted the Essex South district as a sharp-beaked birdlike "monster" he named the "gerrymander," after the state's Jeffersonian Republican governor, Elbridge Gerry. Election day validated the Federalists' fears of the highly partisan nature of the new districts. They won only eleven of the forty state senate seats, despite taking the governorship from the Jeffersonians by a slim majority of 50.6 percent to 49.4 percent. All three of the seats elected from the Essex South district went to Jeffersonian Republicans.

Explanation and Analysis of the Document

The image itself is a somewhat elongated map of the Essex South state senate district, created by the redistricting of 1812, modified to appear as a vicious, perhaps even mythical, monstrous bird of prey. The town districts of Salem and Marblehead in the lower southeast quadrant are modified to appear as talons. Tisdale attached wings to the town districts of Andover and Methuen on the map's western edge. To finish off the image, he depicted the shape of the Salsbury town district in the northeast corner of the map as the profile of a beaked, serpent-like creature with an open mouth, bared fangs, and menacing tongue sticking out. A title above the cartoon labels it "The Gerry-mander" with the subtitle elaboration of "A new species of *Monster*, which appeared in *Essex South District* in Jan. 1812." The exaggerated geography and frightening appearance of the image suggest an unnatural and dangerous malevolence in the creation of the district, reflective of the bitter intensity of the partisan rivalry between Federalists and Jeffersonian Republicans.

The cartoon is meant to highlight Federalists' feeling of injustice at the 1811 redistricting by the Massachusetts legislature. It uses the Essex South district as an example to indict the entire redistricting process. Analysis of voting data confirms the Federalist perceptions that the redistricting process skewed election results to deny them representation proportionate to their support among the voting public. Every state senate seat was a contested race in 1812. Added together, Federalist state senate candidates received backing from 51,759 voters, compared to only 49,801 voters for the Jeffersonian Republicans; yet the more-popular Federalists won only eleven of the forty seats. The results from the governor's race held the same year reinforce this conclusion, with the Jeffersonian Republican Gerry losing to Federalist Caleb Strong by 1,380 votes.

The two districts created for Essex County, Essex South and Essex North, illustrate how the Jeffersonian Republicans manipulated boundaries in the redistricting process to win many more seats than their standing with the voting public warranted. Essex South, the subject of the cartoon, was allocated three of the forty state senate seats. Jeffersonian Republicans won all of those. The rest of the county, in the Essex North district, only had two seats, both won by Federalists. In a multi-member district, voters can cast a number of votes equal to the number of seats in the district. If a district has three seats, each voter can vote for three candidates for that office. A candidate must receive votes from a majority of voters to be awarded one of the district's seats. The two winners in Essex North both received a little under 3,600 votes each from the 4,848 people who voted. The three Jeffersonian Republicans in Essex South only received around 3,000 from the 5,834 voters in that district. Countywide, Federalists received votes from about 6,400 voters, compared with a little over 4,300 for the Jeffersonian Republicans. If Essex County had been a single district, as it had been the previous ten years, instead of two districts, Federalist candidates would have won all seats allocated to Essex County, as they had in the previous ten years. Splitting Essex County the way they did gave Jeffersonian Republicans three seats they would not have won under a configuration that did not split the county. A similar dynamic existed in Worchester and Hampshire Counties. Worchester was split into two districts of two seats each. Each party won the seats of one of the districts; however, the countywide vote heavily favored the Federalists, 6,427 to 4,160. Hampshire's two districts were each just single seats, one going to each party; however, the countywide vote favored Federalists 5,256 to 2,955.

The use of Governor Gerry's name in the cartoon forever tarnished his reputation for later generations. This is quite ironic. Although he was complicit in the redistricting by signing it into law, he seemed to have little to do with devising the districts. Prior to that time, he was a distinguished member of the revolutionary generation. He was one of the signers of the Declaration of Independence and a delegate to the U.S. Constitutional Convention. Like several other notable figures of the American Revolution, such as Patrick Henry and Samuel Adams, he was an anti-Federalist and refused to endorse the new Constitution. The pinnacle of his career was only a few months after his loss of the governorship when he was elected vice president on the Jeffersonian Republican ticket with President James Madison. Despite those achievements, his name has come down to Americans not as a notable member of the revolutionary generation but as the namesake of a shady practice used by self-serving politicians to promote their own partisan objectives.

—G. David Price

Questions for Further Study

1. How ruthless was competition between American political parties in the early republic? What forms did this competition take?

2. What message is the artist trying to convey in the cartoon? Is there a discernible tone that the author is trying to use in conveying his message? On what features of the image are you basing your conclusions of the cartoon's message and tone?

3. Toward what audience is the artist aiming his cartoon? How does the cartoon play to the emotions of that audience?

4. Given the context in which the cartoon was created, the cartoon's message, its tone, and the emotions it seeks to invoke, how effective do you think the cartoon was?

Further Reading

Books

Buel, Richard. *America on the Brink: How the Political Struggle over the War of 1812 Almost Destroyed the Young Republic.* Palgrave Macmillan, 2005.

Cox, Gary W., and Jonathan N. Katz. *Elbridge Gerry's Salamander: The Electoral Consequences of the Reapportionment Revolution.* Cambridge University Press, 2002.

Daniel, Marcus Leonard. *Scandal & Civility: Journalism and the Birth of American Democracy.* Oxford University Press, 2009.

Dawson, Matthew Q. *Partisanship and the Birth of America's Second Party, 1796–1800.* Praeger, 2000.

Ferling, John. *Adams vs. Jefferson: The Tumultuous Election of 1800.* Oxford University Press, 2005.

Foletta, Marshall. *Coming to Terms with Democracy: Federalist Intellectuals and the Shaping of an American Culture.* University Press of Virginia, 2001.

Pasley, Jeffrey L. *"The Tyranny of Printers": Newspaper Politics in the Early American Republic.* University Press of Virginia, 2001.

THE PLANTATION PAINTING

AUTHOR/CREATOR Unknown	IMAGE TYPE PAINTINGS
DATE c. 1825	SIGNIFICANCE Example of American folk art of the nineteenth century, a popular style of art created by those not formally trained

Overview

The Plantation, by an unknown artist, is an example of American folk art. During the nineteenth century, American folk art became popular in the rural parts of the American colonies. The art form flourished and grew into one of the most important subsets of American art. Folk art is often self-taught and encompasses a wide variety of art, including painting, pottery, textiles (particularly quilts), metalwork, and sculpture. American folk paintings often depict the everyday life of their subjects. Because it showcases ordinary life, folk art is important to historians' understanding of cultural history, particularly that of the "common folk." In addition, folk art is extremely diverse, which allows for the study of different social structures that influenced the America of the nineteenth century. American folk artists were deeply influenced by traditions and regional differences and often express a vibrancy that makes the pieces unique and tells the complicated story of American history.

This particular painting depicts a large planation house and the landscape surrounding it. The period following the Revolutionary War saw a growth in the planting of cash crops. As a result, the practice of forcing enslaved Africans to tend the crops grew within American society, particularly in the Southern states. This painting idealizes the plantation and does not showcase any of the harsh realities faced by those enslaved.

About the Creator

The Plantation was painted by an unknown artist but has been dated to around 1825. The painting is owned and housed at the Metropolitan Museum of Art in New York City as part of the museum's extensive folk art collection.

Context

Nineteenth-century America experienced many sweeping changes that went on to have lasting effects on the nation and its people. Several facets of life changed dramatically, including culture, politics, religion, and industry. The early part of the nineteenth century saw national expansion and reforms set to make America more prosperous. In 1803 the Louisiana Purchase was finalized, doubling the size of the country. New American expansion opened questions about

Document Image

The Plantation
(Metropolitan Museum of Art)

the practice of enslavement, including whether it would be allowed in the country's new territory.

The changes of the nineteenth century would have affected the artist who created *The Plantation*. By the time this painting was created, the Atlantic slave trade would have been banned, although the domestic slave trade was still flourishing. The plantation culture was born prior to the American Revolution when America went from, as some have described it, a "society with slaves" to a "slave society"—that is, a society whose social, political, and commercial institutions relied on the practice. Slavery became the dominant form of labor in certain states, thereby shaping all aspects of life. The plantation culture was an extremely complex one, and many tried to ignore the brutal aspects of this form of labor, instead idealizing the plantation as a sort of benign and prosperous family farm.

The plantation system was introduced following the creation of the British American colonies in the 1600s. From the start, it was clear that the system flourished on inequality and brutality, particularly with England's participation in the slave trade. The focus of the plantation system was to cultivate and make a profit from cash crops sold on the international market. The early system focused on labor completed by indentured servants, but then it shifted to enslaving African and Indigenous people to work on the plantations. Indentured servants were primarily from the British Isles and were contracted to work for four to seven years in return for room, board, and passage. The system implemented a rigid class structure. The first enslaved Africans were forcibly brought to Virginia in 1619 and gradually became the primary source of labor for the plantation system until the Civil War (1861–65).

Explanation and Analysis of the Document

The painting *The Plantation* showcases a romanticized view of an unknown plantation. Rural landscapes such as this were a popular subject for early folk artists. Some art historians have suggested that *The Plantation* may have been based on a plantation in Virginia. Because of its idealized view and for other factors, some have speculated that the painting was based on the artist's imagination. *The Plantation* is fairly symmetrical, with the use of trees to frame the scene depicted. This symmetry is fairly unique and leads to further questions concerning the slightly distorted aspects of the painting. It appears that the plantation is staked on a rather large hill, lending the appearance of a sort of conceptual map.

The plantation house at the top of the hill is exceptionally grand and is flanked on either side by what could possibly be the quarters of those enslaved on the plantation. The painting also depicts several work buildings, warehouses, and a water mill. The plantation house is quite large, even out of proportion with the rest of the picture. The style of the house is also fairly unique for the period. Surrounding the home is a fence and what appear to be flowerbeds filled with pink flowers. The artist chose to highlight lush foliage and vegetation within the painting. Grapevines and trees add a rural aspect to the painting. One important item that appears to be missing from the image is the crop or crops that the planation would produce. The sole purpose of a plantation was to produce vast quantities of crops, and it is fascinating that the artist did not highlight this. However, the abundance of other vegetation illustrates prosperity. The water mill may be the only clue to the question surrounding the crops. Water mills were traditionally used for grinding grain, which was most likely produced on the plantation through the labor of those enslaved there.

One of the more complicated aspects is the inclusion of a large naval vessel. The vessel itself is highly detailed, with the inclusion of twelve canons and the American flag. The inclusion of the ship can help to pinpoint a possible location of the plantation either on the Atlantic coast or a large river. Most large sea vessels could not navigate river travel, but it is possible that smaller ships could make such a journey. Typically in this period, flatboats were used for river travel. In the lower right-hand corner, the artist includes a man fishing in the reeds by the water. His style of clothing appears to be humble in design.

Art historians have noted that the painter's style, reminiscent of stitches in embroidery, suggests that the painting was based on a piece of needlework. Furthermore, the painting appears to have been made by someone self-taught rather than someone educated in the art schools that would have existed in America and Europe.

The idea and image of the plantation have been romanticized widely in art and literature. *The Plantation* showcases this romanticized view in a complected art piece. This painting is an excellent example of American folk art because it illustrates a significant part of American culture during the nineteenth century: the plantation. The artist's attention to detail, notable for what is missing as much as for what is included, highlights the denial of cruelty inherent in the idealization of the subject matter. In one aspect, the painting is idyllic, and in the other, it begs complicated questions about the artist and how they saw this facet of American life.

—Antoinette Bettasso

Questions for Further Study

1. Briefly summarize what this image depicts of the American plantation system in the nineteenth century. Then, explain the details that stand out the most.

2. What do you believe the artist is trying to showcase in this painting?

3. What is the significance of showcasing a ship in this painting? Does it illustrate anything significant about the plantation culture?

4. How does the study of art contribute to the understanding of history and historical people?

Further Reading

Books

Anderson, Brook Davis, Stacy C. Hollander, and Gerard C. Wertkin. *American Anthem: Masterworks from the American Folk Art Museum.* Harry N. Abrams, 2001.

Wertkin, Gerard C., editor. *Encyclopedia of American Folk Art.* Routledge, 2004.

Websites

American Folk Art Museum website. https://folkartmuseum.org.

Barratt, Carrie Rebora. "Nineteenth-Century American Folk Art." American Wing, Metropolitan Museum of Art. 2004. https://www.metmuseum.org/toah/hd/afkp/hd_afkp.htm.

Laney, James D. "19th Century American and British Folk Art: Workshop and Home Tour." https://olli.unt.edu/sites/default/files/Documents/Fall2019/Handouts/folk_art_w_photos_03.pdf.

Noyes, Chandra. "How Folk Art Tells the American Story." Art & Object. 2020. https://www.artandobject.com/news/how-folk-art-tells-american-story.

Carl Rakeman: "The Iron Horse Wins—1830" Painting

Author/Creator Carl Rakeman	**Image Type** Paintings
Date 1939	**Significance** Depiction of the famed 1830 race between a small steam locomotive, the "Tom Thumb," and a horse, which hinted at the future possibilities of railroads

Overview

This painting is one of more than 100 completed by Carl Rakeman starting in the 1920s on behalf of the Bureau of Public Roads, the forerunner of the Federal Highway Administration, to commemorate notable events in the development of transportation in the United States. Rakeman's work adorned the walls of government buildings across the country.

One of Rakeman's many commissioned works with a transportation theme is of an impromptu race held on August 28, 1830, that pitted an early steam locomotive designed and built by Peter Cooper against a gray horse, each pulling a train wagon. The contest took place during a round trip from Baltimore to Ellicott's Mills that Cooper organized, hoping to persuade the Baltimore & Ohio (B&O) Railroad Company to use steam-powered locomotives to replace the horses and mules the company used to pull railroad cars carrying goods and passengers. Railroads had yet to prove their effectiveness as a viable form of transportation in 1830; the combination of rivers and canals, such as the Erie Canal, completed just five years prior, held great promise in transporting goods across great distances at comparatively low cost. But waterways, both natural and constructed, had limitations when it came to the reliable transport of goods and passengers year-round due to such factors as floods and wintertime freezes. Whether or not the race actually took place is up for debate, but B&O did agree to explore the use of Cooper's locomotives.

The painting is notable as a commemoration of an event that helped to vindicate the potential usefulness of steam-powered trains, and as an example of American pride in the nation's rapid modernization.

About the Artist

Born in Washington, D.C., in 1878 to Joseph and Eva Rakeman, Carl Rakeman studied art in Paris and Munich before embarking on a long and distinguished career in the United States as an artist who produced works depicting historic figures and events, most notably murals in the Senate Building and the Ohio State House. For thirty years he worked for the Bureau of Public Roads, part of the U.S. Department of Agriculture, for which he completed more than 100 paintings of American roadways and events in transportation history. Rakeman's first notable commission came in 1913 when E. F. Andrews, the director of the Corcoran

Document Image

"The Iron Horse Wins—1830"
(Carl Rakeman / Alamy)

Institute in Washington, D.C., recommended the young artist to the Rutherford B. Hayes Center to produce copies of the official portraits of the late president and his wife. Rakeman died in Fremont, Ohio, in 1965.

Context

Americans of the 1820s and 1830s generally viewed railroads as taking a supplementary role in the development of a national transportation system; the future of America's economic growth and westward expansion seemed intertwined with the building of canals. Linking together key waterways and lakes, canals enabled farmers and entrepreneurs from New York to Illinois to transport shipments of goods on horse-drawn barges with greater speed and larger volumes compared to wagons traveling on turnpikes. With the opening of the Erie Canal in 1825, the most impressive engineering feat yet completed in the United States, New York City seemed poised to outpace New Orleans as the nation's preeminent destination for western-produced goods intended for export.

But there existed obvious limits to canals, starting with the immense expense required for their construction, a cost usually covered by state governments hoping to replicate the sort of recent economic expansion enjoyed by New York. Geography proved an even more difficult obstacle for some states; neither Pennsylvania nor Maryland could complete their ambitious canal-building plans due to the challenging terrain of the Allegheny Mountains. And other factors beyond anyone's control, such as flooding and freezing, further limited canals' year-round accessibility.

Given the obvious drawbacks to canals, inventors sought to develop a new form of transportation to link trade centers and allow for the movement of passengers and goods with greater reliability and speed. By the first decade of the nineteenth century, engineers in both the United States and Great Britain had begun experimenting with the use of steam engines for the purpose of overland travel. In 1825 inventor John Stevens drew upon his previous work on steamships to construct a locomotive that he ran on a small section of track on his estate in Hoboken, New Jersey. Stevens, as a partner in the Camden & Amboy Railroad, already co-owned the nation's first railroad charter, which provided the company with an exclusive monopoly on railroads in New Jersey. Then in 1830 the Baltimore and Ohio Railroad was the first to complete and operate a thirteen-mile stretch of track linking Baltimore to Ellicott's Mills. It was on this line that Peter Cooper successfully tested his invention, the "Tom Thumb," the first steam locomotive engineers built in the United States and the subject of this painting.

The earliest railroads, most of which linked water routes rather than each other, hardly seemed capable of dethroning canals as the nation's primary form of transportation. The first steam locomotives were underpowered and often broke down, and the tracks laid down by different companies varied in width, making it impossible for cars built for one line to travel on another. It would take several innovations and improvements throughout the 1830s and 1840s, including stronger iron rails, more powerful locomotives, and standard track gauges, before railroads came to be viewed as a viable alternative to canals rather than as a novelty. Nearly 3,000 miles of railroad track crisscrossed the United States in 1840, and more than 9,000 miles existed by 1850, with the tempo of construction increasing in the years that followed. Railroads proved a decisive factor in the Union winning the Civil War. By committing to railroads, the more industrialized northern states possessed twice as many miles of track (over 20,000 miles), which generally adhered to a standard gauge, as the largely agrarian South.

Explanation and Analysis of the Document

Construction on the Baltimore & Ohio (B&O) Railroad formally got underway on February 4, 1828, far earlier than the traditional July 4 start of new canal construction projects. Within two years, B&O had completed a 1.5-mile line of standard-gauge track just outside Baltimore, Maryland. Another segment of track, thirteen miles long, opened in May 1830, stretching from Baltimore to the town of Ellicott's Mills, ready to carry goods and passengers. The line depended exclusively on horses and mules to pull the cars, just like the canals the railroad operators hoped to compete with and ultimately replace.

The situation changed considerably when in August an inventor, developer, and entrepreneur from New York named Peter Cooper requested permission to test a small steam locomotive he had recently cobbled together from a variety of accumulated parts, including old steam engines and musket barrels. His plan was to so impress B&O officials with his locomotive that they would agree to use it and purchase iron rails from the struggling ironworks that he had recently founded in Baltimore. Cooper received permission to begin his testing, initiating the era of steam-powered locomotives in the United States.

Curious onlookers assembled along the track that linked Baltimore to Ellicott's Mills on August 28, 1830, to witness the inaugural trip of the "Tom Thumb" on the B&O Railroad. The diminutive, coal-burning locomotive—thirteen feet long, less than three feet wide—pushed an open car carrying eighteen passengers, including B&O's directors, the full distance of thirteen miles in roughly two hours. According to some accounts of the exhibition, a portion of the return trip from Ellicott's Mills to Baltimore involved a race between the "Tom Thumb" and a horse-drawn passenger train riding on a parallel track. If the potentially fictional accounts are to be believed, the steamer at first appeared to be chugging toward an easy victory, traveling at speeds of ten to fifteen miles an hour until its blower belt broke, robbing the locomotive of steam pressure and speed. The horse-powered train managed to pull ahead and win the race. Whether or not the contest took place, the B&O officials were enthused about the prospect of testing Cooper's engine on their line, and B&O decided to cease the use of horses in July 1831.

Rakeman's painting exudes a palpable sense of excitement in its depiction of an event that combines elements of American history with American mythology; many scholars contend that the contest never actually took place. Factual or not, a race pitting an "iron horse" against one of flesh and blood symbolizes the larger competition between industry and agriculture in the northern United States, with the former fully dominating by the close of the nineteenth century.

The painting's setting is one of bucolic openness, suggesting a United States still largely untouched by the forces of industrialization and urbanization. The trail of dark-colored smoke pouring from the locomotive's stack contrasts against the bright blue sky peppered with fluffy, white clouds.

The slapdash appearance of Cooper's modest engine conveys some sense of how he managed to assemble it from a collection of whatever parts he was able to track down. One can also gain a sense of Cooper's design, which deviated significantly from earlier locomotives built in Great Britain, most notably in terms of its use of a vertical boiler as opposed to the horizontal boilers used by British designers like Richard Trevithick and George Stephenson. The "Tom Thumb" also powered only one of its axles, unlike the British engines that powered both axles. These features did not appear in later American locomotives, making the "Tom Thumb" all the more unique.

Neither Cooper nor the B&O seemed to recognize how historically significant the "Tom Thumb" would prove to be; in 1834, the locomotive was scrapped for parts. At the time, railroad's preeminent position in the American economy was not yet guaranteed. By the time Carl Rakeman completed his painting, a reappraisal of Cooper and his engine's importance to the development of the nation had taken place, ensuring both a well-deserved place in American history.

—Michael Carver

Questions for Further Study

1. Despite its historical significance, neither Cooper nor B&O thought it was necessary to preserve the "Tom Thumb." Why might that have been?

2. How might stories like the 1830 race, which may not have occurred, come to be accepted as fact? What other such examples can you think of?

3. What elements of the painting seem to promote a vision of the event that is uniquely American in nature?

Further Reading

Books

Holbrook, Stewart H. *The Story of American Railroads: From the Iron Horse to the Diesel Locomotive.* Mineola, NY: Dover, 2016.

Stover, John F. *History of the Baltimore and Ohio Railroad.* West Lafayette, IN: Purdue University Press, 1987.

Wolmar, Christian. *The Great Railroad Revolution: The History of Trains in America.* New York: PublicAffairs, 2012.

Websites

"Roads, Canals, and Rails in the 1800s." Resource Library, National Geographic. https://education.nationalgeographic.org/resource/early-transportation.

"Camp-Meeting" Lithograph

Author/Creator Hugh Bridport, Alexander Rider	**Image Type** Illustrations
Date c. 1832	**Significance** Depicts the impact of popular religious revivalism on the American public in the early nineteenth century

Overview

This print, issued by the Philadelphia firm Kennedy & Lucas Lithography, shows a religious revival meeting, or camp-meeting, of the early nineteenth century. It shows an enthusiastic preacher speaking from a rough wooden pulpit to an audience of both rapt worshippers and uninvolved observers. The work depicts the revival as both a religious celebration and a social gathering. The original artist is identified in the bottom left-hand corner of the print by the phrase "A. Rider pinxit." Hugh Bridport is identified as the lithographic artist in the bottom right-hand corner with the phrase "Drawn on Stone by H. Bridport."

The print is a lithograph, meaning "writing on stone." Lithography was a relatively new technique in the early nineteenth century. It had been developed in 1798 in Germany and spread rapidly around Europe; by 1803 it had been introduced into England. The process was introduced in the United States as early as 1819, but it was only in 1822 that Barnett and Doolittle, the first commercial lithography house in the country, opened. By 1832, the time this print is believed to have been made, there were lithography firms in many American cities—including Philadelphia, the home of Kennedy & Lucas Lithography. Lithographs became enormously popular in the mid-nineteenth century because lithography made art prints like this one cheap and easy to produce.

The firm of Kennedy & Lucas was Philadelphia's first commercial lithographic studio, established by David Kennedy and William Lucas in 1828. In addition to scenes like this one, the business also printed advertisements, book illustrations, and covers for sheet music. William Lucas died in 1833, the year after this print appeared, and in 1834 the company's lithographic equipment was sold at a public auction. Lucas had been a gilder, a person who works with gold leaf, before entering into lithography. Kennedy was also a guilder, and he owned and operated a glass and picture store. Hugh Bridport, the artist who created the final product, regularly worked for the company during its six years in business.

About the Artist

The lithograph reproduced here was the work of two artists: Alexander Rider, a trained artist and engraver from Austria, and Hugh Bridport, an English portrait painter trained at the Royal Academy, who also worked as an architect and engraver. According to the information on the print itself, Rider made the original

Document Image

The "Camp-Meeting" lithograph
(National Museum of American History)

drawing of "Camp-Meeting," while Bridport translated Rider's work onto the lithographic stone.

Alexander Rider was a skilled painter who may have come to the United States as an artist in the employ of the emperor of Austria. Existing records show that he was working as a book illustrator through most of the 1810s and into the 1820s. His work in that genre includes the illustrations for Alexander Wilson's *American Ornithology* (1825–1833) and John D. Godman's *American Natural History* (1846). By 1830 he was working as a delineator—a type of sketch artist—for the firms Kennedy & Lucas and Childs & Lehman. It was apparently at that time that he visited a revival meeting and made the sketches on which the lithograph was based.

In addition to his lithographic work, Hugh Bridport (1794–1870) also had a career as a portrait painter, a drawing instructor, and an architect. Hugh and his brother George, another artist, immigrated from England to Philadelphia in 1816. By 1822 the brothers were working as architectural drawing instructors, and in 1824 Hugh became a founding member of the Franklin Institute, where he taught architectural drawing classes.

Bridport was responsible for some of Kennedy & Lucas's earliest prints, especially those that required a background in architecture. Two of his major works besides "Camp-Meeting" were the prints "Cowell as Crack in 'The Turnpike Gate'" (1828) and "The Pagoda and Labyrinth Gardens, Near Fairmount" (1828). He also created a famous early print of Niagara Falls.

After Kennedy & Lucas closed in 1833, Bridport moved away from lithography into portrait painting, at which he was quite successful. He had several exhibits at the Pennsylvania Academy of Fine Arts and the Artists' Fund Society, and by the time of the Civil War his estate was valued at $15,000 (almost $500,000 today).

Context

The revival depicted in "Camp-Meeting" was typical of the new emergence of religious feeling that swept through the United States in the early decades of the nineteenth century. Sometimes called the "Second Great Awakening" and sometimes the "Great Revival," the movement began in the backwoods of Virginia and Kentucky at the end of the eighteenth century.

Revivalism emerged in the United States at a time when the country was undergoing a series of crises in politics, economics, and religion. Politics in the new nation was dominated by an elite group of people who saw themselves as the country's rightful leaders because of their wealth, birth, and education. That began to change in the generation after the Revolutionary War. By the late 1790s, Americans on the frontier began to discard political ideas that had dominated discourse during the Revolution. People who moved westward over the Appalachian mountains into the new lands of Kentucky, Tennessee, or Ohio learned to deal with the wilderness without the support on which people further east relied. That independence revolutionized politics in the period following the War of 1812.

The people who were moving to the West were doing so for economic reasons rather than political ones. Some of them were seeking new or better lands. Others sought to exploit the newly opened lands, not by farming them but by speculating in them, buying lands at low prices and then reselling them to latecomers at a significant profit. Still others wanted to trade with the local Native Americans, as the British and French had done for decades. All of them saw the West as a place where they might be able to achieve the success they had not found in the East.

At the same time, new ideas about religious practice began to take root in these frontier areas. Seventeenth-century Puritans in New England were strict Calvinists; they believed that salvation was strictly limited to a small number of people, known as the Elect. Admission to heaven was based solely upon divine grace; believers who were not among the saved were doomed to eternal damnation. By the end of the eighteenth century, however, many Protestants had rejected that idea in favor of a more democratic vision of the afterlife. In this new concept, salvation was potentially achievable by anyone, although it was still dependent on divine grace. This democratization of salvation begin to spread widely across the American colonies even before the Revolutionary War.

The key characteristic that set revivalism off from other forms of Protestant worship was the new converts' public displays of emotion. Traveling missionaries and circuit riders, mainly from sects like the Methodists and Baptists, moved between frontier communities, preaching the need for public repentance to win salvation. In 1799, for instance, Methodist minister James McGready traveled into southwestern Kentucky to preach salvation to the people of the Red River settlement in what is now Logan County. McGready's services were among the first backwoods revival meetings in the American West.

The revivals were characterized by ecstatic conversion experiences, in which both men and women became emotionally overcome by the sense of their sin. They reacted by shouting, weeping, singing, and even fainting. Sometimes, said spectators, the newly converted lay on the open ground overnight, too overcome to seek shelter.

These revivals may have begun in the backwoods of the American West, but they were not limited to the region. By the 1820s, itinerant preachers begin crisscrossing upstate New York, finding new believers and converts wherever they spoke. By the end of the 1820s, the fires of revivalism had passed over upstate New York so often that it became known popularly as "the burned-over district." The religious revivals in this region helped give birth to new forms of spiritual practice that would help define American beliefs for the next century.

Explanation and Analysis of the Document

Alexander Rider's drawing and the lithograph Hugh Bridport made from it show a revival meeting typical of the late 1820s and early 1830s, We can see a rudimentary pulpit made out of wood in which a preacher, hatless and throwing his hands in the air, is speaking to a crowd of potential converts. Other figures are seated on the pulpit behind the speaker; these might be preachers waiting to take their turn speaking. Many converts in the congregation are women reacting ecstatically to the preacher's words. In the foreground at the right, one man appears to be having a conversion experience; he is shown weeping, one hand over his face and the other raised toward heaven.

Just as numerous as the converts are other people who, by the way they are dressed, appear to be spectators. They pay little or no attention to what the speaker is saying but seem to be enjoying the spectacle as if it were carnival. Some of them are accompanied by dogs.

Rider likely based his illustration on a recent meeting somewhere in upstate New York or Pennsylvania. Both groups, converts and spectators alike, are dressed in fashionable clothes, and none of the characters wear buckskins or other frontier clothing. In the background, the revival scene is surrounded by a number of tents, as well as wagons and horses or oxen; revivals were often multiday affairs, and spectators and participants alike traveled for miles to be part of the celebration. "Camp-Meeting" graphically depicts both the fervor and the spectacle of this type of nineteenth-century evangelical practice.

—Kenneth R. Shepherd

Questions for Further Study

1. Out of all the people who are paying attention to the preacher, how many appear to be undergoing a conversion experience?

2. How many and what kinds of animals can you see in the print? What do you think their presence in the print signifies?

3. Based on what the artist chooses to show in this scene, is he primarily interested in the scene as a religious experience or as an entertaining spectacle? Please explain.

Further Reading

Books

Howe, Daniel Walker. *What Hath God Wrought: The Transformation of America, 1815–1848*. New York: Oxford University Press, 2009.

Johnson, Paul E. *A Shopkeeper's Millennium: Society and Revivals in Rochester, New York, 1815–1837*. New York: Hill and Wang, 1978.

Tyler, Alice Felt. *Freedom's Ferment: Phases of American Social History from the Colonial Period to the Outbreak of the Civil War*. New York: Harper & Row, 1980.

Wood, Gordon S. *Empire of Liberty: A History of the Early Republic, 1789–1815*. New York: Oxford University Press, 2009.

Articles

Craven, Wayne. "Hugh Bridport, Philadelphia Miniaturist, Engraver, and Lithographer." *Antiques*, April 1966: 248–52.

Websites

"Religion and the Founding of the American Republic." Library of Congress Exhibitions. https://www.loc.gov/exhibits/religion/rel07.html.

"Rider, Alexander." Library Company of Philadelphia. https://digital.librarycompany.org/.

"KING ANDREW THE FIRST" CARTOON

AUTHOR/CREATOR Unknown	**IMAGE TYPE** CARTOONS
DATE c. 1833	**SIGNIFICANCE** Demonstrates the Whigs' reaction in opposition to Jackson's veto of the charter of the Second Bank of the United States

Overview

"King Andrew the First" is a political cartoon dating from approximately 1833. It shows a caricature of President Andrew Jackson in the guise of a royal figure. The image is packed with symbols of royal or imperial authority. Jackson wears an elaborate crown and a heavy, fur-lined cloak over a robe. He carries a mace in his right hand and wears a sword at his hip. He is clad in elaborate shoes and is standing on tattered copies of the Constitution of the United States and bills for internal improvements and the chartering of the U.S. Bank. Behind him is a throne surrounded by large velvet curtains, with an image of an imperial eagle to its right. In front of him lies a tattered book with its cover torn and leaves ripped out, bearing the title "Judiciary of the U. States."

Four mottos surround Jackson's picture. At the top is "Born to Commitment." At the right-hand side is the phrase "Had I Been Consulted." On the left-hand side is "Of Veto Memory," and at the bottom is the image's title, "King Andrew the First."

The image signifies Jackson's significant changes to the American presidency during his first term in office. Before that time, American presidents had, as often as not, deferred to Congress over questions of policy. But Jackson, used to command, set policy during his administration and expected Congress to follow his instructions. The result of this was a breakup of the American political system that had existed since the end of the War of 1812, more than a decade before. Out of it came the construction of a new two-party system in the United States, one that would last up to the start of the American Civil War.

About the Artist

Although "King Andrew the First" is one of the most famous examples of political cartooning in American history, the name of the artist who drew it is unknown. The historian Frank Weitenkampf, who was for years the curator of prints at the New York Public Library, dates the print to the year 1833 and says that it first appeared in the form of a broadside—a large sheet of paper printed only on one side, so that it could be mounted on a flat surface like a poster.

It seems likely that the artist, whoever he or she was, was a political opponent of President Jackson. Weitenkampf says that this picture also appears in a variant form that contains several lines of print, con-

Document Image

The "King Andrew the First" Cartoon
(Library of Congress)

demning Jackson for what the printmaker calls "putting himself above the law."

Context

Andrew Jackson (1767–1845) was unlike any man who had been president before him. He was born a poor farmer's son on the fringes of the American frontier immediately before the American War for Independence. Both his parents and his only brother died before he became an adult. He had little formal education, but he became a prominent frontier lawyer and a circuit court judge in Tennessee. Jackson based his political philosophy on one great overriding idea: the obligation of the national government to defend ordinary people against the tyranny of the wealthy.

During the War of 1812, Jackson commanded volunteer forces in raids against the Creek Indians. He eventually forced them to sign a treaty that stripped them of their lands, comprising most of what is now Alabama and Mississippi and parts of Georgia and Tennessee. During his presidency Jackson favored the forcible removal of Native Americans from their lands and their relocation westward to reservations on the western side of the Mississippi River. Using a combination of harassment and bribery, Jackson's administrators forced many of the Native American nations on a long and deadly march now known as the Trail of Tears. In 1815 Jackson led American forces against the British in New Orleans. He won a victory in a battle that later proved to have been fought after the peace treaty ending the war had been signed.

Jackson suffered from the mudslinging of his political opponents. His wife Rachel's divorce was not final when he married her, and the two had to be remarried two years after their original marriage date. In addition, Jackson was keenly sensitive to personal slights and fought several duels before becoming widely known throughout the country. He also valued personal commitment to him over any party ideology.

Despite his fierce temper and imperious nature, Jackson supported increasing popular participation in government: the democratization of American politics. By the time Jackson became president, people began to notice this process. One of these was a Frenchman called Alexis de Toqueville, who wrote an account of the months he spent in the United States called *Democracy in America* (1831). *Democracy in America* is still considered both a classic study of the process of democratization and a history of the political development of the United States.

Besides his expulsion of Native Americans from their lands, Jackson is best remembered for his veto of the Second Bank of the United States. The veto had a catastrophic effect on the American economy. It removed many of the restraints the bank had put on bad economic practices, and the results were dramatic. State banks promptly issued large amounts of paper money without having gold to give that money value. State indebtedness soared to about $170 million by the end of Jackson's second term.

Jackson even took steps that made it easier for state banks to get further into debt. Sales of public land had mushroomed, amounting to about twenty million acres by 1836, five times what sales had been in 1832. Then, in an executive order called the Specie Circular of July 11, 1836, the president called for all land sales to be made in gold or silver. The result was that an already scarce hard-money supply became even scarcer.

The end result of Jackson's war on the Second Bank of the United States was the economic depression known to history as the Panic of 1837. Jackson had left office by the time the Panic became severe, and his successor, Martin Van Buren, proved unequal to the challenges of the economy. As a result, the country slipped even further into recession until the 1890s.

If there was one event that truly spelled the end of the period of relative prosperity that followed the War of 1812, it was this Panic. It upended the politics of the previous four decades, spurred immigration westward, and steered the American economy further in the direction of capitalism. The election of 1840 marked the first time in forty years that a non-Democrat was elected president.

Explanation and Analysis of the Document

The print "King Andrew the First" appeared just after Andrew Jackson was inaugurated for a second term in office. Its imagery is significant. It shows Jackson as a king because, at the time, the president was pulling power into his own hands that previously had been held only by Congress.

The proximate cause of the conflict between Jackson and Congress was what to do about the Second Bank of the United States. Jackson believed that the directors of the bank, in particular its president, Nicholas Biddle, were trying to undermine his authority. When members of Congress brought the bank's charter—a bill passed by Congress that permitted the bank to do business—for renewal, Jackson vetoed the measure.

The key to understanding this image is the scroll labeled "Veto" in Jackson's left hand. The president's opponents made the point in this print that Jackson was acting in a monarchical fashion because he was abusing the veto. This was not the first time, nor would it be the only time, that Jackson used the veto to stop legislation that he objected to. He had already used the veto more than any of his predecessors.

During his first term in office, Jackson had killed a bill known as the Maysville Road Bill, effectively ending federal support for internal improvements. The Maysville Road was a proposed route from Lexington, Kentucky, to Maysville, Kentucky, on the Ohio River. It was designed to meet a segment of the National Road, a military and trade route that ran through the Cumberland Pass in the Appalachian Mountains. Congress passed the Maysville Road Bill in 1830, providing funding from the federal government to help complete the road's construction. However, when the Bill came before Jackson for his signature at the end of May, 1830, Jackson vetoed the measure.

Jackson objected to the Maysville Road project for several different reasons. First was because it was not national in scope; it fell entirely within the borders of Kentucky. Therefore, he argued, it ought to be paid for by Kentucky rather than by the federal government. In addition, as far as Jackson was concerned, funding construction projects, or "internal improvements," prevented the federal government from paying off the national debt. Jackson may have had a hidden motive as well: the bill benefited Senator Henry Clay's home state, and Jackson saw Clay as a political enemy.

Jackson's rivalry with Clay may have led to the second great veto of his two terms in office: the veto of the Second Bank of the United States. Jackson did not like the bank on principle. He felt it was benefiting monied interests at the expense of ordinary Americans. At the same time, however, he recognized that it was performing an important function: paying down the national debt, which Jackson wished to accomplish at all costs. So, when Louis McLane, Jackson's secretary of the treasury and a friend of bank president Nicholas Biddle, recommended a recharter of the Second Bank, Jackson initially did not object. When the National Republicans nominated Henry Clay for the presidency in 1832, Clay worked with Biddle to call for a recharter of the bank. Jackson saw this as an attempt to strike at his power base.

Congress passed the recharter of the Second Bank of the United States on July 3, 1832, about four months before the presidential election. Jackson's opponents in Congress saw the bill's passage as a repudiation of the president's policies during his first term in office. They believed that Jackson would veto the measure. Still, they thought the bank was popular enough to undermine the president's campaign for reelection. Jackson's opponents were wrong. Only a week after the recharter's passage, Jackson issued his veto.

Jackson's veto was unlike any veto that any previous president had used. Most of his predecessors used the veto power sparingly, usually only in cases where they felt strongly that a bill violated the terms of the Constitution. Jackson pointed out why he felt the bank's recharter was unconstitutional. He also listed several political, social, and economic reasons. As far as Jackson was concerned, the bank was a monopoly, and that alone was enough to end it. In addition, the president said, the bank's use of stock served as a funnel to remove money from the pockets of ordinary Americans and put it in the those of the rich. The president also alleged that $8 million of the Bank's shares were held by foreigners, suggesting that American money was going to enrich non-Americans. Jackson indicated that the bank enforced social inequalities on Americans and therefore threatened the very basis of American life.

—Kenneth R. Shepherd

Questions for Further Study

1. Look at all the things that surround the figure of Andrew Jackson. Does the overall effect support the idea that Jackson was acting more like a king than a president?

2. What role does the veto play in the iconography of Jackson's image?

3. Jackson was in poor health at the time this print was issued. (He was in great pain from being shot in a duel decades earlier—the bullet was still in his body—and he had been very sick with influenza.) Does the caricaturist hint at Jackson's illness? If so, does that increase or detract from the point the caricaturist is trying to make?

Further Reading

Books

Brown, David S. *The First Populist: The Defiant Life of Andrew Jackson*. New York: Scribner, 2022.

Cheathem, Mark Renfred. *Andrew Jackson and the Rise of the Democratic Party*. Knoxville: University of Tennessee Press, 2018.

Howe, Daniel Walker. *What Hath God Wrought: The Transformation of America, 1815–1848*. New York: Oxford University Press, 2009.

Remini, Robert Vincent. *Andrew Jackson and the Course of American Democracy: 1833–1845*. New York: Harper & Row, 1984.

Sellers, Charles. *The Market Revolution: Jacksonian America 1815–1846*. New York: Oxford University Press, 1994.

William Henry Bartlett: Erie Canal, Lockport Illustration

Author/Creator William Henry Bartlett	**Image Type** Illustrations
Date 1838	**Significance** Documents a key element in the rapid development of U.S. transportation networks in the early nineteenth century

Overview

The appropriately named Lockport is a city in New York State located about twenty miles east of Niagara Falls. During his 1838 trip to Canada, the artist Willian Henry Bartlett would have passed through Lockport on his way to visit an author, Nathaniel Parker Willis, whose book he was illustrating. In Lockport, he would have made a sketch of an Erie Canal lock. The sketch was later converted into a steel engraving for publication in Willis's *American Scenery; or Land, Lake, and River: Illustrations of Transatlantic Nature*. This iconic and widely reproduced image provides a snapshot of the transportation revolution the young United States was undergoing as it was pushing its boundaries westward during the early decades of the nineteenth century. A key part of that revolution was the Erie Canal connecting New York City with Lake Erie. The illustration depicts one of the so-called Flight of Five locks in Lockport, a staircase lock that lifted or lowered canal boats over the Niagara Escarpment in five stages.

The text that accompanied this illustration when it was originally published read: "This town, so suddenly sprung into existence, is about thirty miles from Lake Erie, and exhibits one of those wonders of enterprise which astonish calculation. The waters of Lake Erie, which have come thus far without much descent, are here let down sixty feet by five double locks, and thence pursue a perfectly level course, sixty-five miles, to Rochester. The remarkable thing at Lockport, however, is a deep cut from here to the (Tonawanda) Creek, seven miles in length, and partly through solid rock, at an average depth of twenty feet. The canal boat glides through this flinty bed, with jagged precipices on each side; and the whole route has very much the effect of passing through an immense cavern."

About the Artist

William Henry Bartlett was born in 1809 in London, England. In 1822 he was apprenticed to a London architect, John Britton, at whose office he studied and copied architectural drawings to learn the trade. In 1829, he began working as a journeyman for Britton while also providing sketches for London publishers. Among his early works was a series of sketches for an 1836 book by William Beattie, *Switzerland Illustrated*. In ensuing years, he traveled widely, creating illustrations in Syria, the Middle East, Asia Minor, the Mediterranean coast, Italy, western Europe, the British Isles, the United States, and Canada.

Document Image

Willian Henry Bartlett's illustration of the Erie Canal in Lockport, New York
(Sarin Images / GRANGER)

Bartlett visited North America four times: 1836–37, 1838, 1841, and 1852. On his first trip, he provided illustrations that were included in Nathaniel Parker Willis's *American Scenery*. In 1838 he was in Canada sketching for Willis's *Canadian Scenery Illustrated*. During that trip, he traveled from Quebec City to Niagara Falls and then by way of the Erie Canal to visit Willis in Owego, New York, stopping along the way in Lockport, where he created a sketch of one of the locks that was the basis for this image. Bartlett was widely known and respected for his attention to architectural detail and for his ability to capture the picturesque in his landscapes. Most of his sketches, and the engravings that were made from them, emphasized light and shadow, rough and irregular features, mountains, stretches of rivers, towering crags, and, often, ruined buildings. Many of his sketches have historical value because they are tied to a specific geographical location, giving modern viewers an accurate rendering of how the scene would have appeared at the time. Bartlett went on to become the author and illustrator for a number of works, including two books about the United States: *The Pilgrim Fathers* and *The History of the United States*. From 1849 to 1852 he was the editor of *Sharp's London Magazine*. He died on September 13, 1854, and was buried at sea while he was returning to England from a sketching trip in Turkey and Greece.

Context

In the early nineteenth century, recognition among the nation's leaders was growing that without improvements in transportation, the United States would remain fragmented, its western territories would remain essentially foreign nations, and the abundant raw materials of these regions—timber, minerals, metals, ores—would remain untapped. Under President Thomas Jefferson, Secretary of the Treasury Albert Gallatin (1761–1849) developed a plan for a system of "internal improvements" that would alter this state of affairs. In 1808 he released a report that called for a massive federal investment in a network of roads and canals that would link every part of the growing country. One of his proposals was for the construction of four major roads, including the National Road (or Cumberland Road) running from Baltimore to Illinois. He also called for a canal system that would link New York and all of New England to the West. What ensued in the wake of his proposals was a debate about the role of the federal government in sponsoring and paying for the "internal improvements." Ironically, in the Northeast and along the central coast, merchants and manufacturers tended to favor the construction of highways, for they could already ship goods by sea if necessary. Support for canals and development of waterways was firmer in the South, which relied on water transportation to move agricultural goods.

The idea of a canal to link the Atlantic to the Great Lakes had been proposed as early as 1724. Americans had observed that barge canals were part of the landscape in England and on the continent and were being used to speed the flow of commerce and innovation. Proposals to build such a canal through New York were delayed by local, state, and national political wrangling, as well as by the War of 1812. Ultimately, however, in such states as New York, Pennsylvania, Delaware, and Maryland, the proponents of canal building won out, leading to a near frenzy of canal building in those states and beyond so that by 1840, some 3,000 miles of canals had been built. The crown jewel of the canal system was the Erie Canal, which linked the Hudson River to Lake Erie at a cost of just under $8 million (about $140 million in 2021 dollars). Construction began in 1817, and the canal opened in its entirety in 1825 as one of the engineering marvels of the century. The federal government had concluded that the project was too expensive, so the State of New York assumed the cost of carving the 363 miles of the canal through what at the time was a wilderness. One of the immediate problems the builders faced was the shortage of labor. That problem was solved by an influx of Irish immigrants who, because they were Catholic, encountered suspicion, hostility, and often an inability to find jobs. Many were willing to take on the arduous task of felling trees in the virgin forest, digging the soil with shovels, and hauling away rock and debris.

At the time, the Erie Canal was dubbed "Clinton's Folly," referring to New York Governor DeWitt Clinton, who used his political clout to promote the project. He defended his vision of the impact of the canal on New York City, stating: "The city will, in the course of time, become the granary of the world, the emporium of commerce, the seat of manufactures, the focus of great moneyed operations. And before the revolution of a century, the whole island of Manhattan, covered with inhabitants and replenished with a dense population, will constitute one vast city." The first section of the Erie Canal, from Brockport to Albany, opened in 1823. When the project was completed in 1825, some 40,000 people attended a grand opening ceremony. From a nearby hilltop, fifty-four cannon rounds were fired, representing the number of counties in the state. A ceremonial flotilla was headed by a boat carrying state and local officials. A bottle of sea water from New York Harbor was poured into Lake Erie. The canal whose opening was being celebrated was forty feet wide at the top and twenty-eight feet wide at the bottom. It passed over eighteen aqueducts and through eighty-three locks, with a combined up-and-down range of 675 feet, overcoming the 568-foot rise between the Hudson River and Lake Erie.

Almost immediately, the canal was an overwhelming success. It redefined settlement patterns. Cities such as Buffalo, Syracuse, Albany, and Utica grew exponentially. It turned New York City into a world financial capital. It would later provide supply lines that helped the North win the Civil War. The canal could offer freight rates that were 10 percent of the cost of shipping goods by land. Because of the canal, wheat shipments to East Coast ports, for example, grew from about 3,600 bushels in 1829 to half a million by 1837 and a million by 1841.

The success of the Erie Canal triggered a craze for canal building in other states. From 1825 to 1832, Ohio constructed the Ohio and Erie Canal linking Lake Erie with the Ohio River at a cost of $1.2 million in federal, state, and private funds. Indiana passed a bill that earmarked a sixth of the state's total wealth for internal improvements, including the Wabash and Erie Canal. By 1860, nearly every state north of Virginia had built canals. Although the railroads were beginning to overtake canals as a preferred transportation mode, the social and economic impact of canals such as the Erie Canal in the first half of the century was enormous. They opened the western states to settlement and agriculture. Most importantly, the canals contributed to the forging of bonds of national unity. The Erie Canal also gave rise to a popular 1912 song, "Fifteen Years on the Erie Canal," also known as "Low Bridge, Everybody Down" or "Mule Named Sal," which memorialized the years from 1825 to 1880 when the mule barges passed back and forth on the Erie Canal before steam power took over.

Explanation and Analysis of the Document

The image, in muted browns and greens with touches of red, depicts one of the locks on the Erie Canal as it passes through Lockport, New York. The canal itself is flanked by rocky cliffs and a number of buildings, walkways, and stairways. Several men are included in the scene. The two at the bottom right appear to be handling a barrel, which would likely have been filled by a commodity such as flour. One man is sitting on the lock itself, while another is leaning with one arm on the lock. Two men are standing on a level embankment, while another man is perched aboard a canal boat with the words "Ohio of Rome BUFFALO" on the side. Rome was the name of the New York town where construction on the canal began. The man on the canal boat is holding a pole he would most likely have used to help guide the boat and prevent it from bumping into the sides of the canal. Overall, the image creates a sense of bustling industry as the United States expanded westward by opening transportation routes.

—Michael J. O'Neal

Questions for Further Study

1. What perception of the United States might this illustration have produced in England at the time?

2. What details in the image contribute to its realism?

3. What was Bartlett's purpose in including the figures of the eight men in the illustration?

Further Reading

Books

Andrist, Ralph K. *The Erie Canal.* Rockville, MD: New Word City, 2018.

Bernstein, Peter L. *Wedding of the Waters: The Erie Canal and the Making of a Great Nation.* New York: Norton, 2005.

Koeppel, Gerard. *Bond of Union: Building the Erie Canal and the American Empire.* Boston: Da Capo Press, 2009.

Morganstein, Martin, and Joan H. Cregg. *Erie Canal (Images of America).* Charleston, SC: Arcadia Publishing, 2001.

Sheriff, Carol. *The Artificial River: The Erie Canal and the Paradox of Progress, 1817–1862.* New York: Hill and Wang, 1996.

Stack, Debbie Daino, and Ronald S. Marquisee. *Cruising America's Waterways: The Erie Canal.* Manlius, NY: Media Artists, 2001.

Articles

Linnabery, Ann Marie. "Niagara Discoveries: Bartlett's Prints Brought Niagara to the World." *Lockport Union-Sun and Journal*, June 24, 2017. https://www.lockportjournal.com/news/lifestyles/niagara-discoveries-bartlett-s-prints-brought-niagara-to-the-world/article_8d81fe70-0b6c-5f63-82d3-8e8c010545d7.html.

Whitford, Noble E. "Effects of the Erie Canal on New York History." *Quarterly Journal of the New York State Historical Association* 7, no. 2 (April 1926): 84–95.

Websites

"Canal History." New York State Canal Corporation. https://www.canals.ny.gov/history/history.html.

Erie Canal Museum. https://eriecanalmuseum.org/.

Erie Canalway National Heritage Corridor. https://eriecanalway.org/.

Documentaries

"200 Years on the Erie Canal." *CBS Sunday Morning*, CBS, July 9, 2017. https://www.youtube.com/watch?v=iLfGSXuHu5g.

ROBERT CRUIKSHANK: "PRESIDENT'S LEVEE" ILLUSTRATION

AUTHOR/CREATOR Robert Cruikshank	**IMAGE TYPE** ILLUSTRATIONS
DATE 1841	**SIGNIFICANCE** A popular view of the first inauguration of President Andrew Jackson

Overview

"President's Levee, or All Creation Going to the White House" is an aquatint produced by the British artist Robert Cruikshank. It was originally published as the frontispiece to Volume II of a book of travel stories, *The Playfair Papers, or Brother Jonathan, the Smartest Nation in All Creation*, by Hugo Playfair, published in London in 1841. Cruikshank established his reputation as a caricaturist, and it is not certain whether the book was intended to be taken seriously. It is not even clear if the author was a real person or if the name Playfair was a pseudonym used by the man believed to be the book's editor, Paul Paterson.

Cruikshank's illustration is described as an aquatint, a term used to describe a type of picture made by inscribing a metal plate with acid. The acid eats into the metal of the plate, forming ridges and depressions. After the picture is completed, the artist washes the acid off and coats the plate with ink in a process known as intaglio. The ink settles into the depressions of the plate, and the artist wipes the excess ink off the ridges. He can then make multiple impressions of the print. Each print can then be colored by hand, giving an effect like a watercolor painting—as shown in this copy of Cruikshank's print.

Aquatinting has some advantages and disadvantages over other types of printing that came into common use during the nineteenth century. It allows the artist a great range of expression. The artist can vary the texture of the depressions, and that in turn can produce a highly complex impression. The downside is that aquatint plates wear out relatively quickly—as compared to, say, lithographic stone—and the resolution of the image becomes impaired. Later impressions degrade in quality relatively quickly.

About the Artist

Isaac Robert Cruikshank (1789–1856), more frequently known as Robert Cruikshank, was the eldest son of caricaturist Isaac Cruikshank (1764–1811) and elder brother of the illustrator George Cruikshank (1792–1878). Isaac Cruikshank was one of the leading caricaturists in Great Britain at the time of the French Revolution, and his work became famous for graphic satire. George Cruikshank later won a reputation for his illustrations of Charles Dickens's characters, and his best-known work appeared in *Oliver Twist* (1838).

Document Image

"President's Levee, or All Creation Going to the White House"
(Library of Congress)

Although Cruikshank had an active life growing up (his parents purchased him a midshipman commission in the British East India Company's ship *Perseverance*), there is no evidence that he ever traveled to the United States, much less was present at Andrew Jackson's 1829 inauguration. So the illustration is not itself an eyewitness account.

In fact, during the early 1820s Cruikshank honed his skills as a portraitist. In 1818 and 1819 he made many illustrations of Regency dandies, particularly ones riding bicycles, and satirized the men's hypocrisy and superficiality. Between 1820 and 1827 Cruikshank produced hundreds of images, satirizing such events as the estrangement between George IV and his wife, Caroline. In 1816 he married, and in 1817 his first son was born. A year and a half later, he fathered a second son. Much of his work between the late 1820s and the early 1830s concentrated on caricatures and lampoons of upper-class people in the Royal Court around London.

By 1841 Robert Cruikshank had begun a decline that lasted for the rest of his life. He had suffered a closed-head injury in a riding accident when he was young, and that—combined with his penchant for drinking—may have played a role. Although he continued working as an illustrator, his commissions became fewer and fewer. In March of 1856 he succumbed to a bronchial infection and died. He was buried in Highgate Cemetery, London.

Context

"President's Levee, or All Creation Going to the White House" depicts the situation in Washington, D.C., during the first inauguration of Andrew Jackson on March 4, 1829. It purports to show the situation described by several eyewitnesses: an enormous crowd of Jackson supporters descending on the White House. Some sources say that the crowd was made up mostly of backwoodsman and people from the West who mobbed the White House, drank the beer, liquor, and punch provided, and ended of the day with a riot that smashed furnishings and caused hundreds of dollars' worth of damage. Other sources suggest that the crowd, although made up of people from all levels of society, did much less damage than was reported. Modern historians believe that both accounts have some truth, but both are also colored by the politics of the day.

To understand why Jackson's inauguration was such an emotional occasion, we need to look at the politics that surrounded Jackson's election to the presidency. Andrew Jackson had made his reputation as a war hero, first during the Creek War of 1814 and then as the victor in the Battle of New Orleans in January 1815, at the end of the War of 1812. He then went on to fight the Seminole Indians in Florida, driving them out of their lands and setting processes in motion that would admit Florida as a state.

Jackson's reputation suffered from some of the things he did during these wars. When the treaty ending the Creek War was signed in July of 1814, Jackson negotiated terms confiscating twenty-three million acres of Creek land and demanding submission by the Creek nation to the authority of the U.S. government. The victory at New Orleans was due as much to luck and mistakes on the part of the British as to any expertise on Jackson's part. The war against the Seminoles, which was meant to encourage the Spanish to cede Florida to the United States, instead provoked international incidents with both Spain and Great Britain. Jackson led an invasion of Florida and, not waiting for a declaration of war from the United States, seized two British subjects who he believed had been inciting the Seminoles to fight, and executed them.

By 1824, then, Jackson was an influential and controversial figure, known across the nation. In the presidential election of that year—the first widely contested presidential election in a generation—he quickly became one of the most favored candidates. the election of 1824 was one of the most fraught in American history. The two-party system that had governed the Republic during its early years had broken down after the War of 1812. In theory, this meant that everyone belonged to the same party and agreed on major points. In practice, that was increasingly not the case. In 1824 voters nominated five candidates, all of whom had different ideas on how the country should be run and who should be running it. After the ballots had been cast, however, no single candidate had enough electoral votes to win. Intense negotiations ensued; in the end, only three candidates remained: Jackson himself; John Quincy Adams, the most experienced politician of the age; and Henry Clay, a planter and senator from Kentucky, a master politician able to muster the voting power of the western frontier.

Although Jackson won the majority of the popular vote, he did not have enough electoral votes to take the presidency (a situation familiar to American voters in recent years). Instead, Henry Clay, who finished third, urged his supporters to cast their ballots for Adams rather than see Jackson (whom he disliked intensely) win the presidency. Soon after, Adams asked Clay to become his secretary of state, and Jackson's supporters went wild with anger. They claimed that Adams and Clay had made a corrupt bargain and that the election should have gone to Jackson, who was the frontrunner in the popular vote.

Adams was inaugurated without incident, but Jackson's friends kept agitating for the military hero to run again in 1828. In that election, Jackson won the presidency handily. His supporters saw his victory as a triumph for democracy over privilege. At Jackson's inauguration in March of 1829, thousands of voters from all over the nation watched their candidate become president of the United States.

Explanation and Analysis of the Document

Robert Cruikshank's "President's Levee, or All Creation Going to the White House" shows a crowd moving from the scene of Andrew Jackson's inauguration ceremony at the Capitol to the President's House—it would not be called the White House for another generation—for a reception that was open to all attendees. Jackson himself does not appear in the print, for the artist's focus is on the crowd attending the ceremony. In general, Cruikshank's print follows most contemporary accounts of the event closely.

Nonetheless, Cruikshank's work poses some challenges as a historical source. The artist produced the print more than a decade after the event it depicts, so it is not easy to think of it as a primary source. In addition, "President's Levee" was created to serve as the frontispiece to a literary work, one that a modern critic has termed "a semi-fictitious account" of visiting the United States in the mid-nineteenth century. Cruikshank's print reveals some mid-nineteenth-century ideas about Jackson's inauguration (which gained legendary status almost immediately), but for a fuller context historians have to consider the book in which the print initially appeared.

Cruikshank's print follows the contemporary descriptions of Jackson's inauguration reasonably closely. Margaret Bayard Smith, a member of the upper levels of Washingtonian society—her husband was a friend of Thomas Jefferson—described the scene in 1829 as an "impenetrable" mass of humanity. People from around the country and from all levels of society came to see Jackson as president. She described the scene at the Capitol as "a perfect levee," consisting of about a hundred couples. Soon, however, Smith noted, the order broke down as the mob of people headed from the inaugural ceremony held in front of the Capitol to the President's House, where the ceremony was to take place. "Country men, farmers, gentlemen, mounted and dismounted, boys, women and children, Black and white. . . . The *Majesty of the People* had disappeared, and a rabble, a mob, of boys, negros, women, children, scrambling, fighting, romping." Smith estimated that some 20,000 people were trying to get to the President's House for the celebration. She compared the crush to the Parisian mobs that stormed the Tuileries and Versailles during the French Revolution.

"President's Levee" depicts this portion of the celebration by the White House as it might have looked when the disturbance Smith describes started. He shows people dressed in costumes from all walks of life. Some are ladies and gentlemen dressed in the latest style; others are frontiersmen, wearing broad-brimmed hats, work boots, and rolled-up trousers. At the center of the print a horse has broken free from its traces and is bucking, threatening the people in the carriage behind it. The print also demonstrates that the "Presidential Levee" is a celebration; some people have brought their dogs and little children. At the moment depicted, the violence that Smith describes has not begun, but based on the action in the middle of the scene, it appears to be about to start.

There is, however, another level to Cruikshank's print. Margaret Bayard Smith described the party at the President's House following the inauguration as a "levee"—a term that, to contemporaries, meant an intimate ceremony conducted by a king. "Levee" had been used to describe public receptions that had been held by Presidents George Washington and John Adams but had fallen out of favor under Thomas Jefferson. The fact that Smith refers to Jackson's reception as a "levee" is ironic, given the extent to which Jackson embraced an image of democratic fellowship in his campaign.

In addition, the work in which Cruikshank's print appears takes a somewhat ironic look at the United States' reputation for freedom and liberty. The book's subtitle, *Brother Jonathan, the Smartest Nation in All Creation*, is significant. "Brother Jonathan" is a precursor to the figure we now call Uncle Sam. In the early nineteenth century, before Uncle Sam's depiction became common, cartoonists used Brother Jonathan as a symbol of the New England Yankee. Outwardly Brother Jonathan looked like Uncle Sam, but while the latter was a symbol of pride for the American people, Brother Jonathan was a figure of fun, a kind of country bumpkin whose lack of social graces commentators played up for comic effect.

—Kenneth R. Shepherd

Questions for Further Study

1. Even though this image is meant to show the "President's Levee," Andrew Jackson is nowhere in sight. What do you think this means?

2. We can see the faces of only a few of the people in the picture. Why might the artist have chosen not to show the faces of individuals? What point might he be making by doing this?

3. Look closely at the crowd outside the President's House. Do you see any figures that look like Brother Jonathan or possibly Uncle Sam? What message might those figures be conveying about the artist's intent?

Further Reading

Books

Brown, David S. *The First Populist: The Defiant Life of Andrew Jackson*. New York: Scribner, 2022.

Cheathem, Mark Renfred. *Andrew Jackson and the Rise of the Democratic Party*. Knoxville: University of Tennessee Press, 2018.

Howe, Daniel Walker. *What Hath God Wrought: The Transformation of America, 1815–1848*. New York: Oxford University Press, 2009.

Remini, Robert Vincent. *Andrew Jackson: The Course of American Freedom, 1822–1832*. New York: Harper & Row, 1984.

Sellers, Charles. *The Market Revolution: Jacksonian America 1815–1846*. New York: Oxford University Press, 1994.

Lowell Offering Masthead

Author/Creator
Unknown

Date
1845

Image Type
Illustrations

Significance
The cover illustration for a publication featuring the writings of women who worked for the Lowell mills, one of the few companies that employed women in the early 1800s, portraying the factory setting as idyllic

Overview

The magazine represented by this masthead was one of the few in the early 1800s that featured writings by women. Textile production in cotton mills, specifically those in New England, in the early 1800s marked a new chapter of industrialization in the United States, which was moving increasingly away from being a nation of small independent farmers that Thomas Jefferson championed. Cloth production in textile mills, the first American factories, soon outpaced production by hand or loom by individuals at home, who could not produce cloth quickly enough to meet the growing demand or make use of the large quantities of short staple cotton being produce in the South. Initially powered by water wheels, textile mills housed a growing array of ever-larger and more complicated machinery that spun the thread and wove it into rolls of cloth. A sizeable human workforce was also needed to monitor the machines and to perform tasks automation had not yet replaced.

The textile mills in Lowell, Massachusetts, broke new ground by using a vastly improved power loom and employing mainly young women, or "mill girls," as they called themselves, to perform various tasks. Early factory owners often found it difficult to attract male workers, particularly among those who were skilled workers or sought to be farmers. At the Lowell mills, the solution was to offer employment to women with the promise of good pay and accommodations in boardinghouses, where the mill girls would be looked after and well protected. Although the highest-paid mill girls, those with specialized skills, made less than the least-skilled male workers, and women were barred from holding any managerial positions, thousands of young women were drawn to the opportunity to make regular wages in an environment where they would be looked after. By the mid-1830s, more than five thousand mill girls worked at the eight Lowell mills, earning between two and three dollars per week while working seventy hours or more. Many of the mill girls sent what they earned back home to help support their families; others saved as much as they could, hoping to be able to live more comfortably once they married and had children—which continued to be expected of them even as they asserted some degree of autonomy. At the end of the workday and on days off, the mill girls were encouraged to seek out forms of self-improvement, including writing poems and essays, some of which were featured in a magazine, the *Lowell Offering*.

Document Image

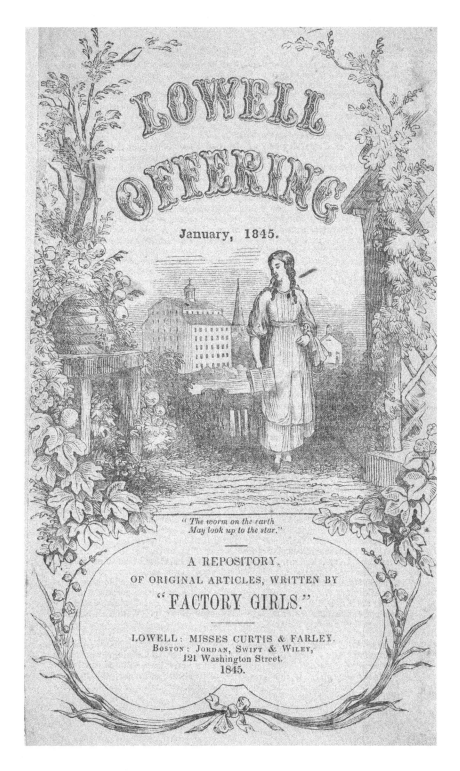

The Lowell Offering masthead from 1845
(American Antiquarian Society)

About the Artist

The artist is unknown. The image was used for the cover of the *Lowell Offering* for several years.

Context

The small Massachusetts town of East Chelmsford in the early nineteenth century resembled many in New England, its open fields providing for grazing sheep and cattle while a modest textile mile located next to a stream produced thread used by women of the community to produce textiles. But East Chelmsford was transformed by the mid-1820s, its largely agrarian character replaced by that of a manufacturing hub dominated by textile mills and connected to an expanding network of canals. It was renamed Lowell in 1826, the name of the family who owned and operated the mills, which brought them enormous wealth and influence.

While some textile mills, particularly those in the mid-Atlantic states, employed entire families, including young children, to work in the mills, the Lowell mills hired young women, most in their late teens and early twenties, from farming communities. They lived in well-maintained dormitories and boarding houses located close to the mills and were kept under a watchful eye both on the job and off. It was generally expected that the women in the employ of the mills, after some years of working, would eventually marry and therefore no longer require employment.

Women in the employ of the Lowell mills received comparatively high wages for the era, which consequently attracted a great many applicants from New England. They also had opportunities to better themselves by attending evening classes and lectures and had books available to them courtesy of Lowell's circulating libraries. Mill employees frequently took part in women's literacy clubs that enabled them to discuss books they had read and improve their writing and share it with one another. One such club's members, led by Harriot F. Curtis, decided to publish their writings in an annual review called *The Garland of the Mills* before taking a more ambitious route and producing a monthly magazine, the *Lowell Offering*.

Many of essays, articles, poems, and short stories featured in the roughly thirty-page magazines placed a heavy emphasis on "mutual improvement." This concept first developed in England during the mid-1820s among working-class men seeking to gain an education they had not yet been able to attain. The magazine's content also stressed the importance of community rather than individualism to promote a general sense of contentedness among the mill girls and discourage questioning of the long work shifts and working conditions. Only rarely did the *Lowell Offering* make any mention of conditions at the mills, which worsened by the mid-1840s, and the magazine's editors rejected any submissions judged too critical of the mills' owners and managers. The fact that contributing authors were only identified by first name further underscores the magazine producers' commitment to discouraging notions of individuality.

But the idealized message of the *Lowell Offering* became increasingly discordant with the harsh realities of the mill girls' workdays, particularly when it came to the long workdays, which averaged between twelve and fourteen hours by 1845. Many of the mill workers complained that the long hours impacted both their physical and mental health, making them more susceptible to illness and premature aging while subjecting them to endless drudgery in the mills that they found tedious. There seemed little point in the Lowell mills offering opportunities for person betterment if the girls were too exhausted to participate. Leaders in the burgeoning labor union movement in New England, just beginning to take shape in the 1840s, accused the *Lowell Offering* of presenting an idyllic vision of life for the mill girls that was wholly inconsistent with the much harsher reality. The magazine ceased publication in 1849.

Explanation and Analysis of the Document

The cover of the *Lowell Offering* portrays a serene-looking young woman out for a stroll, her right hand holding an open book, perhaps a bible or a book of prose. To the left of the girl stands a beehive nestled among a group of flowering bushes and trees bearing fruit, an obvious symbol of the textile mills and the bounty they provide. Just below the girl reads the *Offering*'s motto: "The worm of the earth / May look up to the star," an expression of the view that the mill girls could rise above their humble backgrounds through thrift and hard work. Text below that identifies the magazine as "A Repository of Original Articles, Written by 'Factory Girls,'" a change from the initial volumes that identified the authors as "Females Actively Employed in the Mills."

The background of the image features, from left to right, a mill, the steeple of a church, and a schoolhouse: structures symbolizing the supposed benefits the Lowell mills provided their young female employees. The mills offered a sense of structure and paid good wages for women in a comparatively safe work environment. To deflect the widely held views of many in New England that it was immoral for women to work outside the home, the mill owners insisted their employees attend church services regularly, a policy represented by the church steeple. Finally, the schoolhouse signifies the educational opportunities the mills provided for their workers, provided they weren't too exhausted at the end of a workday to take advantage of them. Not pictured, but of no less importance, is a company boardinghouse, a refuge intended to guard the young residents from possible "immoral influences" with a watchful "housemother" making sure they adhered to the moral codes, attended church, and did not interact with unsavory visitors, particularly after curfew. It was in the boardinghouses where the young women were able to enjoy their precious little free time, singing, reading to one another, and writing poems or essays for possible publication in the *Offering*.

The overall mood conveyed by the cover image is one of serenity and leisure, but this is far removed from the reality of what life was like for the factory girls, which was one of strict regimentation and little free time. A system of factory bells rang over the course of the workday, waking the girls between 4:30 and 5:40 in the morning, marking the start and end of shifts, announcing mealtimes, and tolling at curfew, which was no later than 7:30 in the evening. Making the transition from life on a farm to life at the mill proved difficult if not distressful for many of the new employees, both in terms of surroundings and the type of labor performed. Most had never ventured far from their homes and families; now they found themselves friendless in an alien environment, a recipe for an acute sense of isolation. Performing a limited, redundant, and unchanging series of tasks in a noisy, airless factory was yet another challenge for the mill girls to overcome. Factory girls suspected of engaging in any improper behavior faced the prospect of immediate dismissal. But for young women who wanted to work or had no option but to seek employment, few options existed outside of the mills, especially if they had to compete directly with men.

Frustration among the Lowell mill workers over a wage reduction of 25 percent led to the creation of a union, the Factory Girls Association, in 1834. It carried out a strike in 1834 and another in 1836 over lowered wages, neither of which was successful, and the group disbanded shortly thereafter. A new union representing the Lowell workers, the Female Labor Reform Association, formed in 1845 under the leadership of Sarah Bagley to advocate for a workday shortened to ten hours and improved working conditions. Its influence proved to be limited as mill owners came to recognize that they could draw upon a more complaint source of workers, immigrants, and American-born women increasingly sought employment as teachers and domestic servants. Factory work continued to be largely associated with and made available to women until the late 1800s, when the increasingly mechanized nature of agriculture forced a growing number of men to seek jobs in industry, forcing women out and cultivating a perception of factories as unsuitable workspaces for women.

While short-lived, the *Lowell Offering* represented some meaningful advancements by American women because of industrialization. It gave voice to young women getting the opportunity to work outside the home for the first time and to enjoy some measure of financial independence and freedom from the dominance of a male authority figure. Women proving themselves on the factory floor promoted the belief that they could do likewise in the realm of politics, boosting the women's rights movement.

—Michael Carver

Questions for Further Study

1. Why might the artist of the cover have decided to place so much emphasis on nature, with the inclusion of flowers, trees, and other forms of plant life?

2. Beyond the women who worked at the Lowell mills, who might have found reading the *Lowell Offering* interesting? Why?

3. In what respects does the young woman on the cover challenge notions of female identity as they existed in the mid-1800s? In what ways does she reflect them?

Further Reading

Books

Eisler, Benita, ed. *The Lowell Offering: Writings by New England Mill Women (1840–1845)*. Philadelphia: Lippincott, 1977.

Levinson, Jeff, ed. *Mill Girls of Lowell*. Boston: History Compass, 2007.

Moran, William. *The Belles of New England: The Women of the Textile Mills and the Families Whose Wealth They Wove*. New York: St. Martin's Griffin, 2004.

Robinson, Harriet H. *Loom and Spindle: or, Life among the Early Mill Girls*. Carlisle, MA: Applewood Books, 2011.

Nathaniel Currier: "The Drunkard's Progress" Cartoon

Author/Creator	Image Type
Nathaniel Currier	Cartoons; Flyers
Date	**Significance**
1846	Supported the temperance movement in the nineteenth century, which eventually led to Prohibition in the twentieth century

Overview

This document is an example of an American political or societal cartoon, produced as a lithograph. Lithographic prints or flyers were used during the nineteenth century as a means of mass communication to highlight events, portray images and scenes, or convey a message, whether it be political or social. Lithographs had been around for centuries, especially in Europe, but modern lithography was new in the 1800s, invented in the Kingdom of Bavaria in 1796. Lithography uses simple chemical processes to create an image and can be used to print text or images onto paper or other material.

This cartoon is a warning to Americans of the dangers of alcohol and supports the temperance movement of the mid-nineteenth century. As early as the 1820s, with a new influx of immigration from Ireland (mainly Catholics), a small temperance movement emerged in the United States that tended to link alcohol consumption with Irish or Catholic immigrants, and images began to appear that highlighted the supposed dangers of drinking. As with "The Drunkard's Progress" in 1846, these images and the movement in general focused on the supposed downfall of American society, mostly men and the tearing apart of families because of alcohol abuse.

The American Temperance Society formed in 1826 and benefited from a renewed interest in religion and morality. Within twelve years it claimed more than 8,000 local groups and over 1,250,000 members. By 1839, eighteen temperance journals were published. At the same time, some Protestant and Catholic church leaders were beginning to promote temperance to their congregations. In the 1840s, several states passed laws allowing voters to determine whether liquor licenses would be issued. In the 1850s, thirteen states and territories passed laws prohibiting alcohol. This coincided with the rise of nativism in the United States before the Civil War, an ideology that opposed immigration, Catholicism, and anyone who was not born in the United States. Nativists often linked alcoholism with immigration and Catholicism.

About the Artist

This document was created by Nathaniel Currier (1813–1888), an American lithographer from Massachusetts. Currier was born in Roxbury, Massachusetts, in 1813 and became apprenticed to the Boston printing firm of William and John Pendleton in 1828. The

Document Image

Nathaniel Currier's *"Drunkard's Progress"* Cartoon
(Library of Congress)

Pendletons ran the first successful lithograph firm in the United States. It was a new practice, having been invented only recently in Europe. Currier worked in their shop for five years, learning the trade, before moving to the shop of M.E.D. Brown, where he worked for a year before opening a shop with John Pendleton in New York City. Pendleton backed out of the venture, but Currier would open his own successful business in 1835 and make a name for himself in the industry.

His own business focused at first on the standard practice of printing sheet music, letterheads, handbills, and other items but eventually switched to addressing more societal issues and current events. In 1835 he printed "Ruins of the Merchant's Exchange N.Y. after the Destructive Conflagration of Decbr 16 & 17, 1835," depicting a fire in New York, which was published in the *New York Sun*. In 1840 he printed a response to another disaster, "Awful Conflagration of the Steam Boat 'Lexington' in Long Island Sound on Monday Eveg Jany 13th 1840, by Which Melancholy Occurrence Over 100 Persons Perished," a steamboat accident. That same year, he was joined by James Ives (1824–1895), whose skills as bookkeeper grew the firm immensely. It was during this period that he created "The Drunkard's Progress: From the First Glass to the Grave."

In 1857, the firm Currier and Ives was formed, and with Ives's contributions, Currier's work was able to be marketed and sold to thousands. Currier and Ives were famous for landscape scenes, Christmas scenes, and other popular depictions of Victorian-era society. They also ventured into political imagery and produced political cartoons, banners, significant historical scenes, and illustrations of current events, such as "The Drunkard's Progress."

Currier, who was a volunteer firefighter in New York City and whose lithographs often portrayed his work, turned the business over to his son Edward in 1880. He died at his home in Massachusetts in 1888.

Context

During the 1820s, immigration doubled, with many of the immigrants coming from Catholic Ireland. Between 1831 and 1840, immigration more than quadrupled to a total of 599,000, with one-third being Irish and another 150,000 German, many of them Catholic as well. Immigration tripled in the 1850s, reaching close to two million, half from Ireland and the German states. Nativism took the form of political anti-Catholicism directed mostly at the Irish but also at Germans. It became prominent in particular in the mid-1850s with the rise of the Know Nothing Party.

Tying alcoholism or drunkenness to immigration became a common practice in the mid-1800s to demonize the immigrant population, especially Catholics, as well as to contribute to the temperance movement. Native-born Protestants were portrayed as true Americans, family men (usually men) who were the fabric that bound society. Anything else was the dreaded "other" and should be feared.

The nineteenth-century images of drunkenness and addiction that arose from the temperance movement were largely grounded in Christian moralizing, but the movement also had roots in what was then a new vision of medicine that emphasized the physical action of drugs on the body and mind. It was a radical break from the thinking of earlier generations, who saw intoxication as a product of the intervention of deities or spirits.

Concerns about alcohol abuse also took on a new urgency because of the large amount that was consumed in the late eighteenth and early nineteenth centuries. Stimulated by higher wages and the increased availability of drinks such as whiskey and gin, in 1830 the average American was consuming an estimated 7.1 gallons of alcohol per year. That is more than three times the average today, and more than five times what it had been a century earlier in Great Britain. Many who saw a problem in this trend blamed immigrants, mostly those from Ireland and the Catholic German states.

What the adherents to the temperance movement saw as the "epidemic" of alcoholism in nineteenth century America stemmed from a convergence of several factors in antebellum America. One was economic changes resulting from industrialization, which led to a rapid urbanization of the country and the severing of older ties to family, profession, and societal place. Another was a so-called breakdown of morality and societal norms.

Alcohol use and temperance clashed in the mid-1800s and led to a heightened sense of fear amongst a segment of the population before the Civil War. Newspapers, flyers, and cartoons added to the growing tension and stoked fears while helping to grow both the nativist and the temperance movements. The convergence of these beliefs and events, illustrated by images such as "The Drunkard's Progress," highlight how society could be swayed by mass media at the time.

Explanation and Analysis of the Document

One of the first aspects of this document that likely strikes a modern reader is the gendered aspects used to shock the target audience. The person who becomes the "Drunkard" is a man, which aligns with the belief (and mostly reality) at the time that men were responsible for providing for their families in the United States. A woman and child are also present, but they are the ones affected by the decisions (drinking) of the man. Again, this is consistent with nineteenth-century life in the United States.

At the first two stages of drink, "A Glass with a Friend" and "A Glass to Keep the Cold Out," the drinks are social and there are women present, but once the man begins his transformation into the "Drunkard," he is at first surrounded by other men and later alone. The man is clearly dressed like a gentleman at first and comports himself as such until step four, when he becomes "Drunk and Riotous." This was a fear tactic used by nativists: the charge that immigrants and Catholics were ruining the fabric of American society because they were "Drunk and Riotous."

After reaching the so-called "summit" at stage five, the "Drunkard," now shown with tattered clothes and in a clearly inebriated state, slowly deteriorates as he progresses down the symbolic archway. Step six is titled "Poverty and Disease" and shows that his gentlemanly walking stick has become a cane to lean on. By step seven, he has become "Forsaken by his Friends" and looks forlorn and weary. His hair now appears to be unruly and even matted, and the colors, which were once bright, have darkened as he descends into the depths of alcoholism.

By step eight, the now-distraught man has almost reached the end of the journey, having entered "Desperation and Crime." He is shown robbing another man, which again links crime to alcohol, another fear tactic used by both the nativists and the temperance movement. By the ninth and final step, the transformation from respectable gentleman to degenerate has been completed, and this message is clear to anyone viewing the lithograph. This image is the most striking of all, showing the man committing suicide by shooting himself in the head, with the step called "Death by Suicide." The implications are clear. If you drink, this is the path that is before you. There is no such thing as a casual or social drinker. You are placed on a path, the "Drunkard's Progress," which culminates in death and, more importantly, the destruction of Protestant working-class society.

The fact that immigrants, even Western Europeans, clung to their culture, religion, traditions, and language, is what drove many nativists to fear them and to drive that fear into the rest of society. Alcohol was often a tool used to widen the divide. The portrayal of a devastated woman (presumably the "Drunkard's" wife) and child under the arch can be seen as the real focal point of the lithograph. This is what the adherents of the temperance movement wanted to portray: the destruction of morality and society. The viewer also notices in the image homes in disrepair, highlighting how alcohol and the decline of the man lead to the overall downfall of society.

—Seth A. Weitz

Questions for Further Study

1. As the population in America grew in the 1800s, so did the need for mass communication. Why would this lithograph have been an effective way to reach a large number of people in America?

2. What is the outcome of drinking as depicted in each of the illustrations? Analyze the panels and be specific in your response.

3. What does this lithograph tell us about gender roles in the nineteenth century?

Further Reading

Books

Gusfield, J. R. *Symbolic Crusade: Status Politics and the American Temperance Movement*, 2nd ed. Urbana: University of Illinois Press, 1986.

Tyrell, I. R. *Sobering Up: From Temperance to Prohibition in Antebellum America, 1800–1860*. Westport, CT: Greenwood, 1979.

Documentaries

Temperance and Prohibition. Shanelle Sotilleo and Jewell Lavalas, directors. 2012. http://www.youtube.com/watch?v=7IOjkbUvTpI.

Richard Doyle: "The Land of Liberty" Cartoon

Author/Creator Richard Doyle **Date** 1847	**Significance** Illustrated the hypocrisy demonstrated by the so-called Land of Liberty in the 1840s, referring to the practice of slavery, the prevalence of lynching, and the U.S. War with Mexico **Image Type** Cartoons

Overview

This cartoon was published in England in 1847 during the middle of the U.S. war with Mexico, and it relies on irony to depict what the British saw as the hypocrisy of the United States in general and President James K. Polk in particular. The English had abolished slavery in 1807 and often expressed a sense of moral superiority over Americans, who continued to maintain slavery as an institution despite growing opposition to the practice, and who often enforced the slave system through lynching. However, it is important to mention that at this point, even though there was no slavery in England, British textile mills were almost completely dependent on cotton produced by enslaved workers in the United States. In the meantime, the United States was presumably extending the fruits of liberty by expanding rapidly into western territories such as Oregon, Washington, and particularly Texas, which the United States annexed from Mexico in 1845 in the nation's quest for territorial expansion.

About the Artist

British illustrator Richard Doyle (1824–1883) was one the founders of the magazine *Punch, or The London Charivari*, a weekly humor magazine that was first published in England in 1841. The magazine was incredibly influential in its time and is credited with coining the term "cartoon" from the Italian *cartone*, which originally referred to a sketch on a piece of cardboard.

Doyle drew the cover of the first issue of the magazine and designed the masthead. Apart from his work at *Punch*, he also published illustrations for books on a variety of subjects, including fairy tales, fantasy stories, a humorous book about the Middle Ages, and other works of fiction. On a side note, Richard was the uncle of Arthur Conan Doyle, creator of the famous fictional detective Sherlock Holmes.

Context

The nineteenth century was a tumultuous time for the United States as major economic, cultural, and political changes swept through the nation. However, it was the central issue of slavery that dominated the political and economic landscape. Growing numbers of people were becoming not only very vocal in their opposition to the institution of slavery but were waging

Document Image

Richard Doyle's "Land of Liberty" cartoon
(Sarin Images / GRANGER)

a major political battle against the practice that would reach a critical point in the coming decades.

The march to the Civil War (1861–65) and the eventual abolition of slavery can be seen by looking at the major political headlines of the era. While there were protests about slavery going all the way back to the Constitutional Convention, the territorial expansion of the nation began to erode the political power of the wealthy southern slave owners as more and more states decided to outlaw slavery. In an effort to maintain a political equilibrium, the Missouri Compromise was drafted in 1820, establishing the Mason-Dixon Line: every new state to the south of this new arbitrary boundary would be a slave state, and those to the north would be free states. While this was not an optimal solution, as it divided the country and would eventually draw the battle lines of the Civil War, it did provide a balance between the two factions.

That is not to say that either side gave up its cause. In 1826 New Jersey and Pennsylvania passed "personal liberty laws" that stated that anyone accused of escaping slavery had the right to a hearing before they could be returned to the South. In retaliation, in 1830 North Carolina courts declared that the slave owner's power over the people they enslaved was "absolute," legally making them property in an effort to circumvent the liberty laws and prevent those they'd enslaved from being granted freedom by the northern courts.

In 1831 Nat Turner led a rebellion of enslaved people in Virginia. It was suppressed after only a few days, but the retaliation in the wake of the rebellion was devastating. Virginia and other southern states enacted draconian laws further limiting the rights of Black people in the region. It also led to the lynching of over 120 enslaved people and free African Americans, and the legal execution of 56 more who were accused of aiding the rebellion. While lynching had long been a tool of slave owners, in the wake of southern panic, the use of the practice accelerated, and it became a standard part of the southern experience, much to the horror and disgust of many in the free states.

In 1839 the *Amistad* case further fanned the flames. The *Amistad* was a ship transporting fifty-three Africans from Sierra Leone who had been captured and was in violation of all international treaties of the time. The captives rebelled, killing the crew and taking the ship, and they drifted until they were picked up by a U.S. Navy ship in American waters. The Africans were held and would have been transported back to Cuba and a life of slavery if a group of abolitionists had not come to their defense in court. The case highlighted the evils of slavery and was taken all the way to the Supreme Court, where, after a vigorous eight-and-a-half-hour argument by former president John Quincy Adams, the court sided with the Africans, declaring that they had never been slaves. This decision sent shockwaves through the South, feeding increasing fears that the era of slavery was under threat.

Unfortunately, in 1842 the Supreme Court reversed course and issued a ruling that declared the personal liberty laws of Pennsylvania and New Jersey to be unconstitutional by declaring that enslaved people officially were property. However, the courts were not the only place where these issues were playing out. The Baptist Church had maintained an uneasy peace between its northern and southern congregations by carefully avoiding all mention of slavery. This came to an end in 1844 when the Baptist leadership refused to grant missionary status to slaveholders. This caused a major rift in the church, with many southern members advocating that the Bible justified slavery, and culminated with the creation of the Southern Baptist Church in 1845. Such a split also occurred in the Presbyterian and Methodist denominations.

In 1845 a conflict over the annexation of Texas devolved into war. The Independent Republic of Texas was seeking entry into the United States, an act favored by both sides. However, Mexico still considered Texas part of its territory. President James K. Polk, who ran on a platform of territorial expansion, made monetary offers to the Mexican government for not only Texas but California as well. The Mexican government considered the offer to be an insult, and the tension between the two nations escalated, with Polk determined to follow through on the belief that it was the "manifest destiny" of the United States to own all the land from the Atlantic to the Pacific coast.

As a result, U.S. military forces were stationed specifically to antagonize Mexican forces and initiate a conflict. The U.S. War with Mexico (1846–48) was a relatively brief one, lasting only a year and nine months. Casualties in Mexico were severe, and the country's defeat heralded a loss of prestige and an economic collapse. The consequences for the United States were wide ranging. The Treaty of Guadalupe Hidalgo, ending the war, gave the United States 500,000 square miles of land, effectively expanding the borders of the United

States by almost one-third and creating a power struggle for the disposition of those territories between the free and slave state movements, eventually leading to the Civil War.

Explanation and Analysis of the Document

The central figure of this piece is a caricature of Polk shown as "Brother Jonathan," a popular and often insulting symbol of the American public that predates "Uncle Sam." Brother Jonathan was a sly, unsophisticated, self-interested, lazy trickster who came to embody many of the negative traits the citizens of England saw in America. Here he reclines in the center of the picture, smugly secure since he holds both a whip and a gun. He is leaning on a box marked "dollars" and is apparently enjoying some wine while he lives a life of ease. He rests his feet on an overturned bust of George Washington, disrespecting the legacy of the founders. Enslaved people are bought and sold around him, led off in chains to an unenviable fate.

His pipe smoke swirls around the American flag, which prominently features a Phrygian cap, also known as a liberty cap, on the top of the flagpole. The Phrygian cap goes all the way back to the Roman empire and was widely used during the Revolutionary War to demonstrate how the colonists were throwing off the "slavery" of the British empire. All this is in contrast to the realistic images of the United States that swirl around the flag.

One scene is labeled "Slavery" and depicts the ruthlessness of the practice. The scene "Lynch Law" refers to the indiscriminate brutalization and murder of Black people throughout the South and the complete lack of legislative movement to stop the barbaric practice. Other scenes depict the brawls and gunfights that had become part of the popular image of American life. Hanging over it all is the U.S. War with Mexico, driven by a desire for territory to enhance American power at the expense of the Mexican people. The carnage is overseen by a flying demonic figure wielding a torch and a vague look of satisfaction at the efforts of the U.S. military.

These images combined create a damning depiction of U.S. policies at the time. While many Americans were clearly aware of the problems within their nation—in fact, by 1847 it was virtually impossible to ignore them—this cartoon demonstrates what the other nations were seeing from the outside looking in. The level of hypocrisy for a nation that called itself the Land of Liberty was plain to see for anyone who made the choice to look.

—David Adkins

Questions for Further Study

1. What does this illustration tell us about the international opinion of the United States in the 1840s?

2. How do you think attitudes toward slavery affected political decisions relating to the U.S. War with Mexico?

3. What is the significance of the "Brother Jonathan" figure resting his foot on the overturned bust of George Washington?

4. How did the outcome of the U.S. War with Mexico affect our societal views today?

Further Reading

Books

Baptist, Edward E. *The Half Has Never Been Told: Slavery and the Making of American Capitalism.* Basic Books, 2016.

Berlin, Ira. *Many Thousands Gone: The First Two Centuries of Slavery in North America.* Harvard University Press, 1998.

Davis, David Brion. *Inhuman Bondage: The Rise and Fall of Slavery in the New World.* Oxford University Press, 2008.

Doyle, Richard. *Richard Doyle's Journal, 1840.* Harper Collins, 1842.

Greenberg, Amy S. *A Wicked War: Polk, Clay, Lincoln, and the 1846 U.S. Invasion of Mexico.* Vintage Press, 2013.

Howe, Daniel Walker. *What Hath God Wrought: The Transformation of America, 1815–1848.* Oxford University Press, 2009.

Documentaries

Slavery and the Making of America (four-part series). PBS, 2005

Nathaniel Currier: "The Way They Go To California" Cartoon

Author/Creator
Nathaniel Currier

Date
1849

Image Type
Cartoons

Significance
Shows the popular enthusiasm aroused by the discovery of gold in California

Overview

"The Way They Go to California" is a lithograph produced by Nathaniel Currier, the senior partner of Currier & Ives, the best-known lithographic printmaker and distributor in nineteenth-century America. The company Nathaniel Currier formed in 1835 in New York City became one of the most successful art studios of the period. Its prints were found in homes across the country. Even today, Currier & Ives prints are reproduced and used on calendars for people who cherish the images they evoke of an earlier era.

"The Way They Go to California" was created through a process called lithography, which was invented by a German experimenter named Aloys Senefelder in 1798. Senefelder discovered that he could use a waxy soap to draw images on a flat stone, and then use an acid solution to dissolve away the parts of the stone not covered by wax. He then coated the stone's surface with ink. The ink stuck to the stone but not the wax-covered areas. The result proved to be a simple, quick, and most importantly, cheap way of reproducing image and text.

Although Senefelder quickly patented his means of producing images by lithography, the process spread out of his control. By 1801, independent lithographers were working in France. By 1803, another lithographer had set up shop in London. Some of the London prints included copies of works by the American artist Benjamin West, who had joined the Royal Academy as its president in 1792. In 1818, the first lithograph in the United States was printed in Philadelphia: a portrait of a clergyman meant to introduce a volume of his sermons.

The first American commercial lithographic press was established in New York in 1822. But the most successful early businesses were rooted in Boston, which by 1831 had become the center of lithography in the United States. The brothers William S. and John Pendleton ran the most successful Boston firm. The Pendleton brothers had taken on Nathaniel Currier as an apprentice in 1828. By 1834, Currier had relocated to Boston and opened his own business. In 1849, he issued the print reproduced above.

About the Artist

Nathaniel Currier (1813–1888) is today the best-known producer of Americana prints. A native of Roxbury, Massachusetts, he was apprenticed to

Document Image

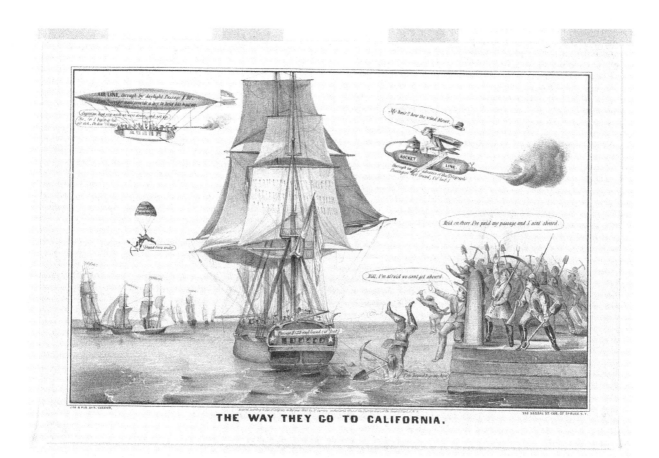

Nathaniel Currier's "Way They Go to California" cartoon
(Library of Congress)

William and John Pendleton that age of fifteen. In 1833 he moved to Philadelphia to work for M. E. D. Brown, and the following year he relocated to New York City. There he started a partnership called Currier & Stodart, his first lithographic business. The partnership lasted only a single year. By 1835 Currier was operating independently as a lithographer in an office on Wall Street.

Currier specialized in small-scale job printing, such as designing letterheads for local businesses or printing sheet music and handbills. Soon, however, he began creating prints for distribution depicting local news incidents. His "Ruins of the Merchant's Exchange N.Y. after the Destructive Conflagration of Decbr 16 & 17, 1835" was distributed by the *New York Sun* to accompany the newspaper's reporting on the fire. The company's future direction became plain when Courier issued a print commemorating a fire that destroyed the steamboat *Lexington* on January 13, 1840. One hundred people died in the disaster. (The *Lexington* fire is still ranked as the worst disaster to have taken place in Long Island Sound.) The event marked the start of his career as a creator of popular prints. The caricature "The Way They Go to California" appeared nine years later.

Currier was joined in business by New York native James Merritt Ives (1824–1895) in 1852. Ives was originally employed as a bookkeeper, but his successes on behalf of the lithographic firm led Currier to make him a partner in 1857. Ives was responsible for many of the prints for which the company is best remembered today: depictions of idealized rural life, sporting events, and other examples of Americana.

Currier's business became a success because he could produce multiple copies of pictures cheaply. He established a factory on Spruce Sreet and systematized the production of prints, bringing all aspects of production under one roof. He oversaw the grinding and polishing of the lithographic stones, hired staff artists (known as delineators), and paid them fifteen to eighteen dollars a week (between $504 and $598 today) to draw the pictures. At different times, important American artists such as Fanny Palmer (1812–1876), the landscape painter George Inness (1825–1894), Eastman Johnson (1824–1906), the cofounder of the Metropolitan Museum of Art, and George Catlin (1796–1872), the famous portraitist of Plains Indians, all worked for Currier & Ives.

Context

The discovery of gold in California—the event that inspired the Currier print reproduced above—was a transforming event in the history of the American West. It came as the climax of the movement known as manifest destiny, an imperialistic idea that asserted the United States' right to push its borders to the Pacific Ocean. It also attracted thousands of Americans, young and old, from the eastern half of the continent to the western half. One result of this was the admittance of California to the Union in 1850, which in turn sparked a crisis that ended only with the U.S. Civil War.

If there was a beginning to the crisis, it started with the emigration of citizens from U.S. territories to Texas, then part of Mexico, in the 1830s. At the time, the Mexican government was interested in attracting as many settlers as possible to its northern province of Texas and offered generous terms to Americans interested in immigrating. Many of them were slaveholders from the American South, interested in expanding cotton production into East Texas. Although Mexico outlawed slavery in 1829, enforcement of the ban proved difficult. Slavery as an institution soon became common among American settlers. By 1835, when Mexican authorities tried to enforce the antislavery provisions, the Americans launched a revolt known as the Texas revolution. In April of 1836, following the battle of San Jacinto, Texas won its independence and became a sovereign nation.

Part of the treaty establishing Texas independence stipulated that the new country would not join the United States. In 1845, however, the U.S. Congress declared its intention to annex the Republic of Texas. At the end of that year, Texas entered the Union as the twenty-eighth state. Soon, the United States was at war with Mexico over disputed territory between the two nations.

The impact of the U.S. War with Mexico (1846–48) spread far beyond the original territory of the former Mexican state of Texas. U.S. troops occupied the city of Santa Fe and the state of Alta California before launching an invasion of Mexico and eventually capturing Mexico City. In the Treaty of Guadalupe Hidalgo (1848), envoy Nicolas Trist negotiated what became known as the Mexican Cession, a large territory that included what is now Arizona, New Mexico, and California.

At about the same time that Trist was negotiating an end to the U.S. War with Mexico, an entrepreneur named Johann Sutter found gold particles in the millrace (the water that drives the wheel) of the sawmill he was building near the town of Coloma in the Sierra Nevada mountains. Although Sutter tried to keep the discovery a secret, news quickly got out, and it sparked a frenzy of immigration to the new territory. By July, men hungry for gold were moving into California from Hawaii and Baja Mexico. By the end of the summer, gold seekers had arrived from Oregon. Over the next six months, more came from as far away as South America, Australia, and China. Stories about the discovery spread in the East when President James K. Polk mentioned it in his annual message to Congress in December 1848.

President Polk was interested in gold partly because it promised to improve the status of the American currency. With encouragement from the president, a new mint was established in San Francisco to turn gold bullion into American cash. The abundance of new American gold coins meant that Andrew Jackson's hard-money policies, which had led to the depression known as the Panic of 1837, got the solid backing they needed to succeed.

The gold rush of 1848 sparked a massive migration to California. Very quickly, California's population ballooned, and in just a few months it far exceeded that of other territories. Although most of the gold seekers chose to return home, enough of the migrants stayed on the West Coast to give the territory a population of 93,000 in the census of 1850. In September of that year, California became the thirty-first state of the United States of America. But this brought up a question: should slavery be permitted in California? Resolving that issue would lead to a series of bills collectively known as the Compromise of 1850 and a political philosophy called popular sovereignty. But the questions those issues raised would only be resolved at the end of the U.S. Civil War.

Explanation and Analysis of the Document

"The Way They Go to California" is a satiric print that shows the fever that swept through the United States following the discovery of gold at Sutter's Mill in January 1848. Most of the gold seekers are shown on board ships; many others have been left behind and are falling off the pier waving picks and shovels in their eagerness to start for California and the gold fields. A few have chosen distinctly unorthodox means of travel: one man is riding a rocket. In contrast, many others are in the cabin of an airship propelled by what looks like a steam engine. One figure is even suspended from a parachute.

"The Way They Go to California" was only one of a number of prints that Courier released around the time of the California gold rush. In 1851 or 1852, they published a print titled "Miners in the Sierras," which showed hard-working miners exploiting their claim. Other prints echoed the satirical bent of "The Way They Go to California." "The Way They Cross the Isthmus" and "The Way They Wait for 'The Steamer' at Panama" depicts a band of immigrants making their way across the isthmus of Panama. "The Way They Raise a California Outfit" shows the costs of preparing for life as a miner, while "The Way They Came from California" shows the immigrants on their way back east.

It is clear that the main thrust of "The Way They Go to California" is aimed at the mob of travelers seized by the gold fever who tried to get to California between 1848 and 1850. One interesting way the print stands out, even today, lies in its depiction of travel and travel technology. In the mid-nineteenth century, technology was expanding American horizons in ways that had never happened in human history.

Chief among these was the electric telegraph. Its practicality had been demonstrated in May of 1844 by Professor Samuel Morse, who sent an instantaneous message from the chambers of the U.S. Supreme Court in Washington to a receiver in Baltimore, Maryland, about forty miles away. Morse's device did something that had never been done before: it allowed fast and accurate communication across long distances. Although the first telegraph line would not reach San Francisco until October 1861, the miracle of instant communication helped make the trip seem shorter than it was.

Even air travel seemed accessible in the period that saw the advent of the telegraph. In 1849, when gold fever was reaching its highest pitch, Rufus Porter, the founder *Scientific American* magazine, placed an advertisement for an airship, consisting of a balloon with a cabin suspended below. It was powered by an engine with a long exhaust pipe extending out its rear. Porter's Aerial Transport, as he called the device, was supposed to move at speeds between sixty and one hundred miles per hour. Its promoter said that it could make the trip to California and back to the East Coast in seven days. Porter also said the device could carry more than 300 passengers, and he sent the fare at $200 per person. The design of Porter's device looked very much like the airship appearing in the Nathaniel Currier print, and its method of propulsion resembles that of the sausage-shaped rocket in the image.

Although the depictions of air travel in "The Way They Go to California" are fanciful, the United States was nevertheless at the cusp of a real revolution in travel, known as the Transportation Revolution. Canals had already been constructed to link the country by water, improving the nation's ability to move freight and people across long distances. Steamboats had been moving up and down American waters for decades. Railroad passenger service began in 1830, and when the English writer Charles Dickens visited America on a lecture tour in 1842, he was able to travel around the country quite easily by rail. By 1850, the United States boasted 9,000 miles of track, and nineteen years later the country would complete the first transcontinental railroad, linking the gold fields of California with the East Coast. Currier's picture of air travel may have been naïve or ahead of its time, but—despite its comedic design—it accurately reflects a mid-nineteenth century fascination with speedy long-distance travel.

—Kenneth R. Shepherd

Questions for Further Study

1. Do the people in the picture seem poor, middle-class, or wealthy? Pay attention to what their clothes and boots indicate about their economic status.

2. One of the major issues facing the gold seekers heading to California was the question of preparedness. Many would-be miners had no idea how they were going to survive long enough to extract Californian gold. What signs of that lack of preparation do you see in the print?

3. Currier's print uses speech balloons to give some of the figures a voice. Speech balloons have become commonplace in modern comics and graphic novels. How effective are Currier's speech balloons in getting his point across?

Further Reading

Books

Howe, Daniel Walker. *What Hath God Wrought: The Transformation of America, 1815–1848*. New York: Oxford University Press, 2009.

Le Beau, Brian F. *Currier & Ives: America Imagined*. Washington, DC: Smithsonian Institution Press, 2001.

Sleeper-Smith, Susan, et al., eds. *Why You Can't Teach United States History without American Indians*. Chapel Hill: University of North Carolina Press, 2015.

Taylor, Alan. *American Republics: A Continental History of the United States, 1783–1850*. New York: Norton, 2022.

Currier & Ives: "Congressional Scales" Cartoon

Author/Creator Currier & Ives	**Image Type** Cartoons
Date 1850	**Significance** Satirically depicts the efforts of President Zachary Taylor to balance the interests of the North and the South over the slavery question in 1850

Overview

This cartoon, produced by the New York firm Currier & Ives, satirized President Zachary Taylor's efforts to balance the competing interests of the North and South over the issue of slavery in 1850. Taylor (1784–1850) is one of the nation's "forgotten" presidents, largely for two reasons. One is that he was not a politician but rather a general, earning the nickname "Old Rough and Ready" for his success in the Seminole Wars and in the U.S. War with Mexico of 1846–1848. Indeed he was the first U.S. president to have been elected without having previously served in political office. He expressed little interest in politics and kept his distance from Congress and even his own Cabinet. During his brief time in office, his major concern was preserving the Union. The other reason he tends to be forgotten is the brevity of his tenure as president. He took office in March 1849 but died just sixteen months later of a stomach ailment. Whatever importance attaches to him stems from his occupation of the White House at a time of national crisis.

Taylor was a slave owner. His plantations in Mississippi and Louisiana were worked by enslaved people, and he is believed to have been the last president to bring enslaved servants with him to the White House. Despite being a slave owner, he opposed the spread of slavery, and during his presidency, he attempted to balance the concerns of the slaveholding southern states with those of abolitionists, primarily in the North, as depicted in the Currier & Ives cartoon. Events, however, complicated his efforts. Under the terms of the Treaty of Guadalupe Hidalgo, which ended the U.S. War with Mexico, territory in what would become the American Southwest was ceded to the United States, and the bitterly debated question that arose was whether states formed out of that territory would be slave states or free states. Already, the specter of disunion and civil war was hovering over the country.

About the Artist

It is unknown who, specifically, produced "Congressional Scales," but the firm that produced it was Currier & Ives, the well-known lithography firm in New York City. The brainchild of the company was Nathaniel Currier, who was born in Roxbury, Massachusetts, in 1813. By the age of twenty, "Nat" was an accomplished lithographer. He moved to Philadelphia, where he produced lithographic stones of scientific

Document Image

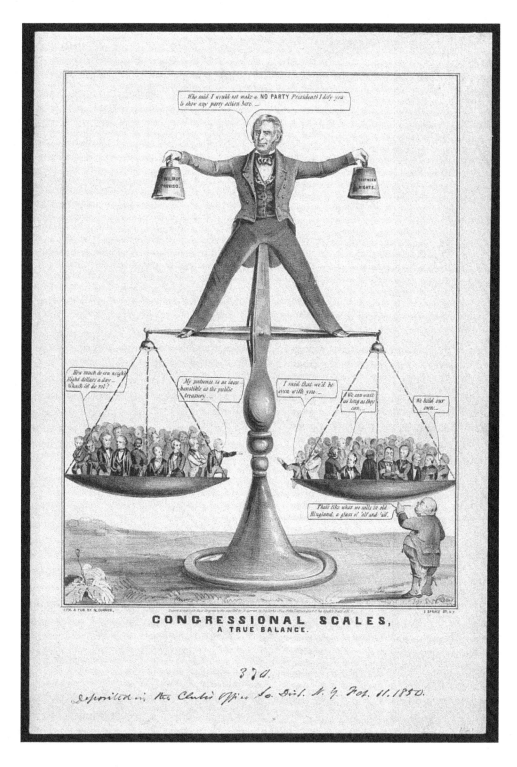

The "Congressional Scales" cartoon
(Library of Congress)

images. In 1834 he moved to New York City, where he purchased a print shop, found a partner, and created the firm Currier and Stodart, although Stodart left the business just a year later. Currier set up shop for himself and soon found that the public had an appetite for pictures of newsworthy events, which were not to be found in newspapers of the day. He caught the attention of the *New York Sun*, which contracted with him to produce an illustrated sheet for the paper, making the *Sun* the first illustrated newspaper published in the United States. In the years that followed, Currier hired his artistically inclined brothers to provide illustrations; one was Charles, who invented a new type of lithographic crayon that he patented and named Crayola.

In 1852, Charles introduced Currier to a friend, James Merritt Ives. Ives joined the business as a bookkeeper, straightened out its books, reorganized the business operations, and streamlined the production process. In 1857, Currier offered Ives a full partnership and made him general manager of the firm Currier & Ives, which the pair described as "Publishers of Cheap and Popular Pictures." Currier & Ives produced prints in many categories: disaster scenes, sentimental images, sports, humor, hunting scenes, religion, city and rural scenes, trains, ships, racehorses, historical portraits, and politics. After Currier's death in 1888, the business was taken over by his son. In all, until the business closed in 1907, the firm produced more than 7,500 titles and more than a million prints.

Context

The year 1850 was one of crisis for the United States. Since the nation's founding, the issue of slavery had been a thorny one. It was a sticking point at the Constitutional Convention, and in the decades that followed it threatened to tear the fledgling nation apart. Free states were those in the North; as of 1812, the free states were Pennsylvania, New Jersey, Connecticut, Massachusetts, New Hampshire, New York, Rhode Island, Vermont, and Ohio. Newly admitted to the Union as free states were Indiana, Illinois, Maine, Ohio, Michigan, Iowa, and Wisconsin. The economy of the southern states was based on the plantation system worked by enslaved people. Throughout the first half of the nineteenth century, Congress preserved the Union by ensuring that the balance between free and slave states was maintained, an effort that produced the Missouri Compromise of 1820. As the nation continued to expand westward and new territories, and then new states, were created, the issue of slavery, which had long simmered, was reaching a boiling point.

Several matters were up for discussion in 1850, the year of the publication of the cartoon. First, the United States had acquired a vast amount of territory through the Mexican Cession, referring to the territory in the American Southwest that Mexico ceded in the treaty that concluded the U.S. War with Mexico. The issue was whether the territory and any states formed from it should allow slavery—or whether the settlers should be given the option of deciding the question for themselves. The so-called Wilmot Proviso (which Taylor is holding in the cartoon), proposed by Pennsylvania congressman David Wilmot in 1846, was an unsuccessful effort to ban slavery in any territory acquired as a result of the war, for its passage would have effectively negated the Missouri Compromise of 1820. On three occasions the proposal passed in the House of Representatives, but each time southern senators blocked its passage in the Senate. The Wilmot Proviso stated: "Provided that as an express and fundamental condition to the acquisition of any territory from the Republic of Mexico, by the United States, by virtue of any treaty which may be negotiated between them, and to the use by the Executive of the monies therein appropriated, neither slavery nor involuntary servitude shall ever exist in any part of said territory except for crime whereof the party shall be first duly convicted."

The second issue involved California, which underwent explosive growth because of the gold rush of 1849. California had petitioned Congress for statehood as a free state, but this would upset the balance that had been maintained since the Missouri Compromise of 1820, so it seemed unlikely that the petition would be approved. A third issue involved Texas and its claim of lands extending as far west as Santa Fe, in what is today New Mexico. A final issue involved Washington, D.C., which not only allowed slavery but was the site of North America's largest human trafficking market.

In late January 1850, Senate majority leader Henry Clay of Kentucky, who had brokered the Missouri Compromise of 1820 as a congressman, presented a series of compromise resolutions. He stated that his goal was to "adjust amicably all existing questions of controversy . . . arising out of the institution of slavery." Congress debated his resolutions for months. The key proposal bearing on the slavery issue was the second one: "Resolved, That as slavery does not exist by law, and is not likely to be introduced into any of the territory acquired by the United States from the republic of Mexico, it is inexpedient for Congress to provide by law either for its introduction into, or exclusion from, any part of the said territory; and that appropriate territorial governments ought to be established by Congress in all of the said territory, not assigned as the boundaries of the proposed State of California, without the adoption of any restriction or condition on the subject of slavery."

Taking active parts in the debate were Massachusetts senator Daniel Webster, South Carolina senator John C. Calhoun, and Michigan senator Lewis Cass (Taylor's opponent in the 1848 election and later U.S. secretary of state). Aiding them was Illinois senator Stephen A. Douglas, who helped usher through Congress a series of bills based on Clay's resolutions that collectively constituted the Compromise of 1850. A key bill that passed was the one that organized the territories of New Mexico, Nevada, Arizona, and Utah without mentioning slavery, leaving the decision up to the settlers when they petitioned for statehood. Another key bill that was passed abolished the slave trade in Washington, D.C., although it allowed slavery to continue to exist. The third key bill that passed was the one that admitted California as a free state. However, to appease the members of Congress from slave states, a strict Fugitive Slave Act was also passed, one that required citizens, as well as state and local governments, to aid in the recovery of fugitive slaves and that subjected anyone aiding an escaped slave, in any state, to imprisonment and a fine. Passage of the Fugitive Slave Act enraged abolitionists, increased activity in the Underground Railroad, and turned many formerly ambivalent Americans against the institution of slavery.

Throughout the debate, President Taylor adopted a number of antislavery positions. He particularly opposed the spread of slavery to new U.S. territories, yet at the same time he wavered over the Wilmot Proviso. At one point he came close to forcing armed confrontation between the North and South over efforts to compel New Mexico to become a slave state. In February 1850 he responded angrily at a meeting with southern leaders who threatened to secede from the Union, saying that he would personally lead the army if necessary to enforce the law and that prisoners "taken in rebellion against the Union, he would hang . . . with less reluctance than he had hanged deserters and spies in Mexico."

Explanation and Analysis of the Document

This Currier & Ives print, published in 1850 prior to the death of President Zachary Taylor, depicts the president standing astride a pair of scales. He has a weight in each hand. The weight on the left says "Wilmot Proviso." That on the right says "Southern Rights." The bubble above the president says "Who said I would not make a 'NO PARTY' President? I defy you to show any party action here," suggesting that he tried to put preservation of the Union above the interests of political parties. Indeed, during the 1848 campaign for the presidency, he stated: "If honored by election to the Presidency I will strive to execute with fidelity the trust reposed in me, uncommitted to the principles of either party." The implication is that the president is trying to balance the rights of the slaveholding states with northern interests.

The two scales are evenly balanced. In the tray on the left is an image of Henry Clay and other members of Congress. One of the legislators on the left is singing "How much do you weigh? Eight dollars a day. Whack fol de rol!" "Eight Dollars a Day" was the name of a song at the time but was also the amount of a U.S. senator's salary in 1850. "Fol de rol" was a common refrain in ballads. Another legislator on the left is saying "My patience is as inexhaustible as the public treasury." On the right, one congressman is saying, "We can wait as long as they can." The implication of these statements is that each side in the debate is prepared to wait the other side out. At the bottom of the cartoon, a rotund John Bull (a personification of England, analogous to Uncle Sam in the United States) is saying, "That's like what we calls in old Hingland, a glass of 'alf and 'alf." "Hingland" is a dialect pronunciation of "England," and "alf and 'alf," or "half and half," can refer to any concoction made of a mixture of two ingredients, usually alcohol, implying that Taylor, rather than taking a stand, is trying to have the issue both ways by appeasing both sides in the slavery debate.

—Michael J. O'Neal

Questions for Further Study

1. What is the fundamental message of the cartoon "Congressional Scales"?

2. Would the cartoon likely have influenced a citizen's position on the issue of slavery?

3. How effectively does the cartoon convey the cartoonist's views of Taylor and his handling of the slavery issue?

Further Reading

Books

Birkner, Michael J. "Zachary Taylor in Office: Clay, the Whig Party, and the Sectional Crisis." In *A Companion to the Antebellum Presidents 1837–1861*, edited by Joel H. Silbey, 291–308. Malden, MA: Wiley Blackwell, 2014.

Bordewich, Fergus M. *America's Great Debate: Henry Clay, Stephen A. Douglas, and the Compromise That Preserved the Union*. New York: Simon & Schuster, 2012.

Hamilton, Holman. *Prologue to Conflict: The Crisis and Compromise of 1850*. New York: Norton, 1966.

Maizlish, Stephen E. *A Strife of Tongues: The Compromise of 1850 and the Ideological Foundations of the American Civil War*. Charlottesville: University of Virginia Press, 2018.

Waugh, John C. *On the Brink of Civil War: The Compromise of 1850 and How It Changed the Course of American History*. Lanham, MD: Rowman & Littlefield, 2003.

Websites

"Compromise of 1850." National Archives. https://www.archives.gov/milestone-documents/compromise-of-1850.

"Compromise of 1850." Ohio History Central. https://ohiohistorycentral.org/w/Compromise_of_1850.

"Compromise of 1850: Primary Documents in American History." Library of Congress. https://guides.loc.gov/compromise-1850#:~:text=Senator%20Henry%20Clay%20introduced%20a,Washington%2C%20D.C.%2C%20was%20abolished.

Fling, Sarah. "The Enslaved Households of President Zachary Taylor." White House Historical Association, December 9, 2019. https://www.whitehousehistory.org/the-enslaved-households-of-president-zachary-taylor#:~:text=A%20slave%20owner%20himself%2C%20President,following%20the%20Mexican%2DAmerican%20War.

Documentaries

Henry Clay and the Struggle for the Union: The Compromise of 1850 to the Civil War. Douglas High, director. Witnessing History, 2012.

McCormick's Patent Virginia Reaper Flyer

Author/Creator Cyrus H. McCormick and Co. Date 1850 Image Type Flyers	Significance Illustrates the Virginia Reaper, advertised as a new, efficient way of cradling wheat, demonstrating the importance of agriculture and its advancement with new technology

Overview

This flyer illustrated the Virginia Reaper, a revolutionary new technology for wheat harvesting. The flyer is a broadside, which is a form of an advertisement that is usually printed on one side of a sheet of paper. Often the images used were not as detailed as this one, particularly if due the broadside needed to be reproduced quickly. The intended audience would have been the general population, and everyone was welcome to take one; in fact, this would have been encouraged. It would not have been uncommon for broadsides to be distributed anywhere there was a large gathering of people, including taverns, churches, and town squares. They were a way of communicating something relevant quickly to the public and could convey information related to serious issues, such as government decisions or an upcoming public meeting, promote more lighthearted events, such as a musical concert or other form of entertainment, or advertise a new product.

Advertisements such as this not only would have been helpful to consumers in their day, but they also help historians and scholars understand the social, political, and economic atmosphere of the time. In essence, they act as a sort of snapshot into the past and a physical example of both the substance and methods of communication and advertising.

About the Artist

Cyrus Hall McCormick was an American inventor and businessman who was born February 15, 1809, in Raphine, Virginia, and died on May 13, 1884, in Chicago, Illinois. His father, Robert, a farmer, was highly skilled in using both wood and iron and was constantly looking for ways to improve his existing tools. Thus, it is no surprise that Cyrus McCormick gravitated toward the mechanization of farming and developed the first successful machine for reaping grain when he was only twenty-two years old. McCormick witnessed a slow start in selling his new invention; in 1940, for example, he sold only two machines. By 1845, however, he had expanded beyond Virginia and was selling his reaper in Michigan, New York, Ohio, Illinois, and Iowa.

After his business began to flourish, McCormick decided to move to Chicago. By the time of his death in 1884, the number of reapers sold was a staggering

Document Image

McCormick's patent Virginia Reaper flyer
(Wisconsin Historical Society)

number: more than half a million. McCormick's invention helped farmers keep up with the growing demand for food as the population in America increased. Along with other inventions, the reaper helped the Midwest and Great Plains region in the United States become what was known as the breadbasket of the world—at least until weather, over-farming, and other factors resulted in the drought of the 1930s known as the Dust Bowl. In addition to his invention, McCormick also contributed to society as a local philanthropist who dedicated large sums of money to his church.

Context

In 1848, the Free Soil Party was established after the United States acquired a large area of land, which included present-day California, Nevada, Utah, Colorado, and large portions of New Mexico and Arizona, after defeating Mexico in the U.S. War with Mexico (1846–48). The party's slogan was "Free Soil, Free Speech, Free Labor, Free Men," and it opposed allowing slavery in the newly acquired territory. The party favored settlement by individual farmers, but farming this way was not an easy task. The hours were long, and the work was excruciating. To attract potential settlers, it would help to promote an easier way to clear, plant, and harvest the land. Cyrus McCormick's reaper, which he had developed in the 1830s, could do that.

Over the years, McCormick continued to modify his original invention, but he did not seem concerned about mass producing the reaper. He did not advertise it, and the invention was primarily used to farm his father's land until the latter 1840s. After his father passed away in 1846, McCormick moved to Chicago, a much more urban setting than his family farm in Virginia. It was here that he opened a factory and continued to make improvements to his reaper. Becoming a businessman would prove to be beneficial not only for his individual success as a farmer and inventor but also for the American people. He was able to employ workers, which allowed him to devote even more time to modifying his invention. By 1850, the simple invention McCormick had created in Virginia to help ease the workload on his father's farm, Walnut Grove, was surpassing his initial expectations. The flat plains of the Midwest region proved to be the ideal location for McCormick to sell his reaper because not many workers were available there, and the reaper required only one or two workers to operate it.

Although farmers were used to long hours and hard work, McCormick's invention helped alleviate some of this and ultimately made farming more productive. It was now possible to work more acres of land and produce more staple crops, such as wheat and corn. The increased food supply helped ensure that Americans did not go hungry and helped the Midwest region earn its title as "America's breadbasket," since wheat was used to make bread.

Explanation and Analysis of the Document

Cyrus McCormick began developing his idea in 1831 but did not obtain a patent for his invention, the Virginia Reaper, until 1834. By this time, he had a few rivals, the main one being Obed Hussey; however, McCormick's background proved to give him the edge. His father, Robert McCormick, was a farmer, blacksmith, and inventor, and he was highly skilled at working with lumber and iron, a skill he passed down to his son. Cyrus was twenty-two when he successfully constructed a reaper that was functional; his previous attempts had failed. It had two wheels, a blade that vibrated while cutting, a reel that helped bring the grain within reach of the operator, and a platform that acted as a catchall for the grain. The reaper required only one or two men and just as many horses to function, which drastically reduced the necessary manpower and horsepower compared to earlier tools. For example, in the 1830s approximately 250 to 300 hours were required to farm five acres of land. As the population in the United States continued to grow and as technological advances made both communication and transportation easier, the need to farm more land and do so more efficiently followed. Cyrus McCormick recognized this and decided to move from his family farm in Virginia to Chicago, Illinois, and open a factory to produce his reaper. He made several improvements to the machine, and agricultural productivity drastically increased. By 1850 the amount of labor required to farm five acres had been reduced to 150 hours.

The advertisement for McCormick's Virginia Reaper addresses the improvements made in agricultural production. In 1850, McCormick would have perfected his invention to the point that he felt comfortable with mass producing it in his Chicago factory. The advertisement, known as a broadside, relied heavily on an image, which is why it is centered. Automatically, the viewer's eyes are drawn to the two men and the horses.

Rather than elaborate on a verbal explanation as to what the reaper is capable of doing, instead the viewer can see first-hand. Although the drawing is rather crudely done and lacks detail, the overall message is there: this invention is something that every farmer needs to remain relevant in a country where technological advances had managed to keep up with societal needs and demands. The broadside did not rely solely on the powerful image though.

The brief write-up about the reaper in this broadsheet describes just how this new invention will benefit farmers. The terms "valuable" and "labor-saving" get right to the point. Farming was hard work on many levels, including the financial burden and the back-breaking manual labor. These two adjectives appeal to both of these factors and promise to make a farmer's life easier. In addition, further assistance is guaranteed to every farmer who purchases the reaper. D. W. Brown is listed as the agent and contact person for Ashland County, which is in Ohio. Brown promises not only to help farmers afford the reaper but also to answer any questions they have. This is a useful advertising technique because it provides a potential buyer with a tangible contact, someone to answer initial questions and act as a troubleshooter for potential issues that may arise. The broadside also addresses the issue of affordability, which is something that would have been a worry for most framers, promising to "furnish them with the above reapers on very liberal terms." The broadside would have been an effective advertising technique, appealing to farmers through the use of text and a central image.

—Belinda Vavlas

Questions for Further Study

1. How would Cyrus McCormick's upbringing and his relationship with his father have contributed to the development of his Virginia Reaper?

2. What is the historical significance of Cyrus McCormick's reaper? What was happening in America during McCormick's lifetime that made inventions such as this relevant and necessary?

3. How were advertisements such as this broadside distributed to their audience? Compare this to how advertisements are presented today.

Further Reading

Books

Aldrich, Lisa J. *Cyrus McCormick and His Mechanical Reaper*. Greensboro, NC: Morgan Reynolds, 2002.

Casson, Herbert N. *Cyrus Hall McCormick: His Life and Work*. Chicago: A. C. McClurg, 1909, reprinted, New York: Cosimo Classics, 2005.

Holland, Rupert Sargent. *Cyrus H. McCormick and the Reaper*. [Chicago], 1914, reprinted, Prabhat Prakashan, 2018.

Websites

"Cyrus McCormick." *Ohio History Central*. https://ohiohistorycentral.org/w/Cyrus_McCormick.

"Cyrus McCormick." *Who Made America? They Made America*, PBS. https://www.pbs.org/wgbh/theymadeamerica/whomade/mccormick_hi.html.

"Cyrus McCormick: Mechanical Reaper." National Inventors Hall of Fame. https://www.invent.org/inductees/cyrus-mccormick.

Documentaries

"MBA Cases: Cyrus McCormick: The Business of Agriculture and Reaper Invention." iBiz, February 20, 2017. Available on YouTube. https://www.youtube.com/watch?v=HHIlFuj1yZI.

"Emerson School For Girls" Photograph

Author/Creator Southworth and Hawes	**Image Type** Photographs
Date c. 1850	**Significance** Depicts the state of women's education in the United States through the lens of one of the most advanced schools for girls of the period

Overview

"Classroom in the Emerson School for Girls" is an image produced by the Boston photography firm of Albert Sands Southworth and Josiah Johnson Hawes. It shows a classroom of young women studying under the watch of an instructor. The image is notable in the history of photography because it is one of the earliest pictures taken on location rather than in a studio. It is also notable because it records one of the earliest schools in the United States dedicated exclusively to the education of young women.

The picture was produced as a daguerreotype, a type of chemical image reproduction invented by the Frenchman Louis Daguerre (1787–1851) in 1839. The daguerreotype proved very popular, and for at least the next twenty-one years, it remained the primary form of image-capture technology in use throughout the Western world, from Europe to the Americas.

Daguerreotypes required extensive preparation and chemical expertise. The images were produced on copper sheets treated with silver and polished to a shine, soaked in chemicals to make their surfaces sensitive to light, and then exposed to light in a *camera obscura*. The timing of the exposure depended on the amount of light available on the scene. If the scene was brilliantly lit by sunlight, exposure could be as short as a few seconds. If the scene was in a dimly lit interior, exposure could take much longer—in one famous early image, up to five minutes.

The daguerreotypes were extremely sensitive. The chemicals that made the surface light-sensitive could be washed off easily, taking the image with them. Even accidental scuffing could destroy daguerreotype images. To prevent damage, daguerreotypes were commonly protected by sheets of glass and sealed in wooden containers with a lid that could be lifted to view the image.

About the Artist

Albert Sands Southworth (1811–1894) and Josiah Johnson Hawes (1808–1901) were the founders of one of the first great photographic portrait studios in the United States. The firm operated in Boston for twenty years, from 1843 to 1863. It earned the two photographers a reputation for the highest-quality daguerreotypes produced in the country. The subjects they photographed during their years in business in-

Document Image

"Classroom in the Emerson School for Girls"
(Metropolitan Museum of Art)

cluded such New England luminaries as the minister Lyman Beecher and his daughter, the novelist Harriet Beecher Stowe; Stowe's fellow novelist Louisa May Alcott; the politicians Richard Henry Dana Jr., Edward Everett, and Cassius Marcellus Clay; the philosopher and essayist Ralph Waldo Emerson; and the poets Henry Wadsworth Longfellow and John Greenleaf Whittier.

Southworth and Hawes spent their career working primarily in daguerreotype, ignoring other photographic technologies that used paper or glass in favor of the metal sheet-based format. Daguerreotypes gave the two some advantages. Despite their expense and the careful handling the images required, daguerreotypes provided fine detail and created images that contemporaries ranked alongside fine art. Perhaps the expense associated with daguerreotypes led Southworth and Hawes to concentrate almost exclusively on Boston society and famous contemporaries.

Nonetheless, the photographers were not opposed to registering moments of historical significance. In 1846, physicians at Massachusetts General Hospital asked the pair to record a successful surgery performed under anesthesia to remove a tumor from a patient's neck. The operation was the first public demonstration of using nitrous oxide as an anesthetic. Although the photographers could not record the actual procedure, they did photograph a reenactment of the operation. Southworth and Hawes were asked to photograph an operation in progress the following year.

The photograph taken at the Emerson School for Girls was unusual in part because it was taken on location rather than in a studio. However, it does bear a resemblance in theme to other pictures made by the company. In particular, it concentrates on an elite class of society: in this case, young women who received a liberal arts education. They were likely the children of the upper reaches of Boston society. Despite this, none of the young women, nor their teacher, have been identified.

Context

To understand the role that education plays in U.S. history, especially women's education, we need to look at how American culture has shaped schooling for girls. Education in the West, including America, has always been shaped by the Christian Church, whether Catholic or Protestant. The first school for girls in what would become the United States was founded in the colonial period by the Order of Saint Ursula—the Ursuline Academy in New Orleans. The Academy opened its doors in 1727 and remains open today. It is the oldest continuously operated school for girls in the country. For Protestants, the first all-girls school was opened in Bethlehem, Pennsylvania, by the Moravians—a Protestant sect that arose in Germany—in 1742. Thirty years later, Moravians also opened the Salem Academy and College, another single-sex institution, in Salem, North Carolina.

Much of the study of women's learning institutions has concentrated on New England. In part, this was because the Puritans who settled New England strongly emphasized the ability to read—especially the ability to read the Bible. As a result, founding schools that taught reading and writing was a priority in these colonies. Harvard College was founded in 1636 in Cambridge, Massachusetts, to provide an education for aspiring ministers. By the middle of the next century, statistics indicated that almost 90 percent of colonists in New England, men and women alike, could read and write.

This did not mean that women had the same access to education as men did. Girls were generally taught to read at home or at independently operated schools that taught skills like sewing, weaving, and household management. It was not until 1767 that individual towns in Massachusetts voted to support public schools for girls. The first public high schools for girls in the region did not open for another fifty years.

That school, the Emerson School for Girls, was opened in Boston in 1823. Its founder, George Barrell Emerson (1797–1881), a cousin of the philosopher and author Ralph Waldo Emerson, began his career running an academy for boys in Lancaster, Massachusetts. He also served on the Harvard faculty before becoming head of the English High School for Boys in Boston in 1821. Two years later, he opened the Emerson School for Girls and ran it until he left teaching in 1855. Although Emerson was trained in mathematics, he was also intensely interested in zoology and botany and was a founder and president of the Boston Society of Natural History.

George Emerson was not the only member of his family to support a liberal education for young women. His cousin Ralph Waldo Emerson (1803–1882), while a student at Harvard in the 1820s, taught at a school for girls run by his brother William.

Although some girls managed to receive an elementary education, opportunities for higher education for women was minimal. In 1833, the Oberlin Collegiate Institute opened in Ohio and offered coeducational programs for men and women, both white and Black. Other institutions operated on a seminary or academy model based on the perceived need for moral, literary, and domestic education for young women. After the Civil War, single-sex institutions of higher learning for women multiplied, sparked by a need for the instruction of female teachers. That led to the founding of women's single-gender colleges, such as Smith, Wellesley, Barnard, Vassar, and Bryn Mawr. It was not until a few decades ago, however, that equal access to education for women was established in American law.

Explanation and Analysis of the Document

"Classroom in the Emerson School for Girls" shows at least nineteen young women seated at desks in a large open room. At the right, a man in a high-collared shirt, coat, and tie sits in a chair, balancing a book on his crossed legs. To his right is a desk, covered in books, papers, and a bell. Beyond that is another desk, covered with what appear to be other teaching aids, including an inkwell and an ink blotter. Behind him, the sun shines through a large window, illuminating the first row of students.

At the back of the room, in the middle of the photo, is a long clock sitting in an alcove between two large windows. Screens block off the lower half of the windows, possibly to control the breeze or to help keep insects or birds out of the classroom. Below the clock appears a vase of flowers. Although the picture only shows nineteen young women, it carries an impression that others are just outside the photo along the left-hand margin. The girls pictured seem to be studying intently, primarily reading. Their instructor appears to be speaking to them, perhaps lecturing on a subject from the book he holds.

Although the daguerreotype appears to show a class in session, it is most likely that this picture was staged. Daguerreotypes, as a rule, required lengthy exposures, and the fact that the images of some of the girls are blurred suggests that they could not hold still for the entire exposure. In a nineteenth-century schoolroom, if a teacher were lecturing, students would have been taking notes. If students were reading, then most likely, the teacher would have been calling on one of them to recite, perhaps a translation from Latin or another classical language. Since none of those activities seem to be happening, the picture is more useful as a historical source in what it says about the static parts of the room rather than the educational process of the time.

Without more information about the daguerreotype and why it was taken, especially by such a prestigious photographic firm, it is difficult to determine the picture's intent. Was it taken as a piece of memorabilia, like a modern classroom photo? We know another photograph from Southworth and Hawes shows a class from the Emerson School for Girls. But that photograph is more like a classic class photo, with all the students in rows, facing the camera, and their faces clearly visible. This photo appears closer to modern pictures that serve as school advertisements, demonstrating a school's teaching methods and concern for students. Without more information, such as a way to connect the daguerreotype to an advertisement for the Emerson School, we cannot say for sure.

In fact, what seems to be most interesting about this picture is how little classrooms have changed since the mid-nineteenth century. The essential learning tools are still the same: individual desks, books, and lectures are still the mainstays of American pedagogy. The clock on the wall presages the classic schoolroom clock that still adorns classroom walls today. The young women's dresses are not identical; although their hairstyles are similar, their clothing is not. The school does not appear to require uniforms. In addition, while most girls appear absorbed in their reading, one lone figure is distracted. At the very center of the photo, a young lady stares directly at the camera—the only figure to do so. Even in the 1850s, the allure of learning does not attract every student.

—Kenneth R. Shepherd

Questions for Further Study

1. Look carefully at the students and how they concentrate on their reading. Southworth and Hawes were well known for the ability of their daguerreotypes to capture a subject's character. Do the girls in the photo seem like stereotypes of students, or do you get a sense of their personalities? Please explain.

2. Southworth and Hawes would have scheduled the photo session in advance, and the school would have expected all the girls and their teacher to wear their best clothes. How can you tell, from what the teacher and the girls wear, how much money their families have?

3. Even if the school did not require students to wear uniforms, they would have expected all students to dress modestly, without jewelry. One of the few acceptable ways for the girls to assert themselves would have been through their hairstyles and the ribbons they wore in their hair. What do these say about their individuality?

Further Reading

Books

Howe, Daniel Walker. *What Hath God Wrought: The Transformation of America, 1815–1848*. New York: Oxford University Press, 2009.

Nash, Margaret A. *Women's Education in the United States, 1780–1840*. New York: Palgrave Macmillan, 2005.

Romer, Grant B., and Brian Wallis, eds. *Young America: The Daguerreotypes of Southworth & Hawes*. Rochester, NY: Steidl/George Eastman House/International Center of Photography, 2005.

Rudolph, Frederick. *The American College & University: A History*. Athens: University of Georgia Press, 1990.

Taylor, Alan. *American Republics: A Continental History of the United States, 1783–1850*. New York: W. W. Norton, 2022.

John H. Goater: "Irish Whiskey and Lager Bier" Cartoon

Author/Creator John H. Goater **Date** 1850s **Image Type** Cartoons	**Significance** Shows the racism and anti-immigrant sentiment that became part of the political landscape in the United States during the 1850s and led to the founding of the nativist Know-Nothing Party

Overview

The political cartoon "Irish Whiskey and Lager Bier" dates to the early 1850s. It is an early representation of the anti-immigrant sentiment associated with the Know-Nothing Party. Its featured characters are caricatures of two of the largest ethnic groups in the United States: the Irish and the Germans. Because the two main characters are running off with a ballot box, the cartoon is a commentary on the perceived state of politics in 1850s America.

Political cartoons have a long history in the United States, going back to Benjamin Franklin's 1754 illustration "Join or Die," showing the American colonies as a serpent cut into pieces. Cartooning continued to be an essential part of political commentary in the United States throughout the subsequent centuries. In the early nineteenth century, Andrew Jackson's new Democratic Party was a favorite target of caricaturists. In the 1850s, publishers used politically oriented cartoons to comment on the day's issues.

Part of the reason cartooning became so popular in the early nineteenth century was the advent of lithography. Lithographs, created by drawing with grease or soap on a smooth stone and then coating the stone with ink, made pictures much more complex and elaborate than simple woodcuts, and they were cheap and easy to reproduce. The process also allowed for the production of colored prints for a wide audience.

About the Artist

"Irish Whiskey and Lager Bier" has been attributed to the political cartoonist John H. Goater. Goater was active in and around New York and Brooklyn in the 1850s and 1860s. His initials, JHG, appear in the cartoon immediately behind the right foot of the "Irish Whiskey" figure. Goater worked for several publishers and lithographers in New York, including Thomas W. Strong, publisher of a comics journal called *Yankee Notions*, books for children, and other collections of pictures. Strong also produced a series of publications called *Strong's Dime Caricatures*, collections of what would now be called political cartoons. Goater drew several of these, and they expressed support for the Republican administration of Abraham Lincoln. Little else is known about the artist.

Document Image

The "Irish Whiskey and Lager Bier" cartoon
(Everett Collection Historical / Alamy)

Context

The cartoon "Irish Whiskey and Lager Bier" appeared at a time in American history when the country was undergoing great political change. In particular, waves of immigration from Ireland and central Europe were changing the makeup of the country's population. Beginning in the 1830s in the United States, anti-Catholic feeling grew alongside increased Catholic immigration. In 1830, a northern newspaper asserted that the Catholic Church was secretly plotting to overthrow American democracy. In 1835 Lyman Beecher, the father of novelist Harriet Beecher Stowe and an influential Protestant minister, issued a tract calling for Protestants to send missionaries to the American West to "save" the country for Protestantism. By the mid-1830s, anti-Catholic organizers formed societies explicitly designed to oppose Catholicism in the United States.

The conflict between Catholic immigrants and anti-Catholic societies was no more visible than in New York. By the 1840s, the city had attracted vast numbers of immigrants. The political power of those immigrants, who usually voted with Jacksonian Democrats, sparked the founding of organizations to oppose them. In the early years of the decade, the struggle was rooted in questions about education, especially whether Catholic children could be excused from religious education in Protestant-run schools. By 1844, the anti-Catholic feeling had become so strong that militant Protestants organized a nativist party, called the American Republican Party, to oppose immigrant votes. In May of that year, news of anti-Catholic riots in Philadelphia sparked a similar riot in New York City. It was stopped when the city's Catholic bishop asked the city's leaders who would be held liable for any damages to church property.

The situation got worse as immigration from Germany and then Ireland expanded in the middle of the nineteenth century. German immigration was spurred by political and social unrest in the region following the Napoleonic wars. The Revolution of 1848, which threatened to unseat conservatives in power since Napoleon's defeat in 1815, forced large numbers of Germans to flee their home countries. In Ireland, on the other hand, people were driven out by famine when the potato crops they relied on failed in the mid-1840s. British landowners, who had forced Irish tenants onto marginal land, did nothing to relieve their poverty.

By 1850, nativists in New York felt pressed by the political power of Irish and German immigrants. German Americans used their new political power to call for reforms that had been denied them by the Revolution of 1848. They petitioned for universal manhood suffrage, complete religious freedom, a faster track to citizenship, popular election of all officials, and several other proposals considered radical for the time. Some even went so far as to condemn the country's fugitive slave law and to call for women to receive the right to vote.

The nativist response to these suggestions came in the formation of secret societies. They had elaborate names, such as the Native Sons of America, the Order of United Americans, the American Brotherhood, the Order of the Star-Spangled Banner, and even the Order of the Sons of the Sires of '76. By 1852, nativists had organized sixty different societies in New York, with the aim of electing only "true Americans" to office. They also did not hesitate to turn to violence. By the time elections were held in 1853, the political power of these nativist societies had spanned the nation. Since the societies were secret, members who were questioned about their activities simply responded, "I know nothing." As a result, they became known as the Know-Nothings, and their political party—at first known as the Native American Party—fielded candidates in national elections for the rest of the decade.

The Know-Nothings arose at a time when the previous two-party political system in the United States was falling apart. The conflict over slavery, including whether it should be expanded into U.S. territories, had virtually destroyed that system. Nativists across the United States saw political opportunities in the void created by the degradation of the Whig Party. In the end, however, they proved no more able than the Whigs to bridge the sectional gaps that increasingly divided Americans. While Nativism in the North and East was synonymous with anti-Catholicism, it was almost the opposite in places like Louisiana. In New Orleans, the nativist Native American Party openly admitted French Catholics. In Maryland, pro-union voters quashed anti-Catholic policies in order to attract the Catholic vote. By the end of the decade, it was plain that Nativism was too divisive to form the basis of a national party. The goals of the Know-Nothings were instead wrapped into the new Republican Party platform.

Explanation and Analysis of the Document

The cartoon "Irish Whiskey and Lager Bier" shows an urban street with two prominent figures in the foreground. One is encased in a barrel labeled "Irish whiskey" and waving a club (a shillelagh), and the other is wearing a barrel marked "Lager Bier" and carrying a long-stemmed pipe. The two carry a ballot box, presumably stolen from the public square behind them. At the same time, other figures behind them are engaged in a brawl. The implication is that the Irish and German immigrants are stealing the votes of native-born Americans while those Americans fight among themselves.

The Irish and German figures are caricatures, drawings that greatly exaggerate characteristics associated with the two ethnic groups. The Irish figure, for instance, is shown with tousled hair and a wild-eyed expression; he may be drunk. His working-class boots show hobnails driven into the soles. The German carries a long-stemmed meerschaum pipe, showing that he is addicted to tobacco in addition to his drinking. The signage behind him advertises cigars as well as other forms of tobacco.

The primary characteristic associated with the two figures, however, are the barrels of alcohol they wear. The barrels imply that the key element of both the German and the Irishman is their love of drink. The implication that immigrants abuse alcohol is another form of commentary that would have spoken to the nativists to whom the cartoon was directed. The image says the immigrants are not only stealing the votes of "true Americans," but their love of alcohol makes them unfit even for self-government. Therefore, they ought to have no right to vote.

"Irish Whiskey and Lager Bier" appears, at first glance, to be a commentary about drinking. However, it is better understood as a statement about immigration and the fear of immigrants. By the middle of the nineteenth century, parts of the U.S. electorate had come to fear the rising population of immigrants arriving in the country. Many of these immigrants were from places like southern Germany and Ireland. They were poor, predominantly Catholic, and spoke English with strong accents or did not speak it at all. For many American workers in the midst of an economic upheaval (the rise of capitalistic industry), the immigrants represented an easily identifiable and easily caricatured threat.

The cartoon is designed to speak to the fears that some immigrants—different in language, habits, and religion—sparked in native-born Americans. It works on several different levels. At its most basic, the cartoon suggests that immigrants steal votes from ordinary citizens. It also suggests that these immigrants are not only strange but immoral. They drink too much, and they drink strange drinks like "Wein" in addition to "Lager Bier" (as the German-language sign behind the "Lager Bier" figure suggests). Neither of those was the tipple of choice of ordinary American citizens. In addition, the two appear to be getting away with a ballot box while ordinary citizens are fighting in the background. That suggests that native-born Americans need to unite to preserve their rights from the threat of immigrants.

Although the cartoon does not emphasize it, there is a subtext that shows that "Irish Whiskey and Lager Bier" is on some level a plea for political action. The first sign is, of course, the ballot box itself. But, in the background behind the fighting figures, a polling station advertising an election also appears. These political elements show that "Irish Whiskey and Lager Bier" calls for national unity in the face of the perceived threat of immigrant political power.

—Kenneth R. Shepherd

Questions for Further Study

1. What do you think is the significance of the American flag flying in the background of this cartoon?

2. A caricature is a cartoon that emphasizes certain elements of a character, primarily for comedic or political purposes. What elements of the German and Irish characters are emphasized? Are they so stereotyped that they should be considered offensive?

3. How effective is the cartoon at communicating its message?

Further Reading

Books

Billington, Ray Allen. *The Protestant Crusade, 1800–1860: A Study of the Origins of American Nativism*. Gloucester, MA: Peter Smith, 1952.

Howe, Daniel Walker. *What Hath God Wrought: The Transformation of America, 1815–1848*. New York: Oxford University Press, 2009.

McPherson, James A. *Battle Cry of Freedom: The Civil War Era*. New York: Oxford University Press, 1989.

Rorabaugh, W. J. *The Alcoholic Republic: An American Tradition*. New York: Oxford University Press, 1995.

Tyler, Alice Felt. *Freedom's Ferment: Phases of American Social History from the Colonial Period to the Outbreak of the Civil War*. New York: Harper & Row, 1980.

Websites

"Nativist Political Parties and Organizations." Young American Republic, http://projects.leadr.msu.edu/.

George Caleb Bingham: *The County Election* Painting

AUTHOR/CREATOR George Caleb Bingham	IMAGE TYPE PAINTINGS
DATE 1852	SIGNIFICANCE Presents a romanticized view of the way frontier democracy worked in the mid-nineteenth century Midwest

Overview

George Caleb Bingham's *The County Election* dates from the year 1852 and shows an idealized portrait of the democratic process in the United States at the century's midpoint. The canvas shows not only the ways democracy works but also the ways it fails. The large oil painting, which measures 38 inches tall by 52 inches long, is the first in a series of three paintings that Bingham completed in the 1850s that depict U.S. democracy in action. The other canvases are titled *Stump Speaking* (1853–54) and *The Verdict of the People* (1854–55). Bingham's "Election" series of paintings demonstrate the vitality—and the rampant corruption—of nineteenth-century American democracy.

Although *The County Election* is usually considered a composite image that draws on archetypes of the American West, it also serves as a record of a historical event. Bingham had been elected to the Missouri state legislature for Saline County in 1848, after having tried for a seat in 1846 and lost. In the election of 1850, the artist and politician ran to defend his office but lost his reelection bid to E. D. Sappington. Sappington, it turned out, was a relative of the judge and a county clerk, who together shared responsibility for conducting the election. Although Bingham's contemporaries recognized the irregularities that accompanied Sappington's election, the artist chose not to contest the results.

Although Bingham's reputation as an artist declined after his death, his work underwent a revival starting in 1933 when the New York Metropolitan Museum of Art acquired one of his best-known early works. In the early twenty-first century, Bingham had taken his place as one of the foremost American artists of the mid-nineteenth century.

About the Artist

George Caleb Bingham (1811–1879) had a dual career as an artist and a politician in Missouri for years in the middle of the nineteenth century. He was born in Virginia, the son of a couple who owned extensive land and enslaved people in Augusta County, located in the Shenandoah Valley. The family lost the lands after they were pledged to repay a debt in 1818. The following year, the entire family relocated to Franklin, in Missouri territory. By 1823, Bingham's father had become a tavern owner and a judge in the new state. When he died suddenly, however, he left his family deeply in

Document Image

George Caleb Bingham's The County Election
(George Caleb Bingham)

debt. As a result, George and his siblings had to sell the family lands in and around Franklin.

By this time, Bingham had already demonstrated some artistic talent. When he was sixteen, however, he had to start work as a cabinetmaker's apprentice, serving first Jesse Green in Boonville and then Justinian Williams. During this time, Bingham kept up his artistic training. By 1830 he was painting portraits so rapidly that he completed some of them within a single day, and by 1833 he supported himself solely through his painting. Sometime before 1838, he set up shop in St. Louis, where he worked for some years. In the early 1840s he traveled to Philadelphia, Pennsylvania, to seek formal training. He then relocated to Washington, D.C., where he painted portraits of famous politicians.

Bingham returned with his family to Missouri in 1845, having established a reputation as a delineator of the American West. The prints of *The Jolly Flatboatmen*, distributed by the American Art Union in New York, had reached 10,000 customers. He then turned his attention to politics. He stood as a Whig for the Missouri House of Representatives in 1846, 1848, and 1850. He won his seat in 1848 but was defeated in 1850. In the later 1850s he toured Europe, visiting Paris, France, and Dusseldorf, Germany.

When Bingham returned to Missouri in 1959, he re-involved himself in state politics. In 1861, following the inauguration of pro-Confederate Governor Claiborne Fox Jackson, Bingham helped raise troops for the Union army. In 1861 Jackson's replacement, Hamilton Gamble, named Bingham the state treasurer, an office he held for the remainder of the war.

Throughout the Civil War and into the postwar period, Bingham maintained his artistic work and continued to serve in political offices. In 1874 he was named president of the Kansas City Board of Police Commissioners. The following year, he was appointed adjutant general of Missouri. A few years before his death, Bingham accepted the position of professor of art at the University of Missouri–Columbia. He held that post until he died on July 7, 1879.

Context

Bingham painted *The County Election* during a particularly tense era in American political history. At the time, Americans were divided perhaps more deeply than they ever had been before. Bingham understood this; he began his political career as a Whig, one of the precursors to the Republican Party in American politics, and then re-aligned with the Democratic Party following the Civil War. His canvasses show the chaotic ways in which ordinary Americans expressed their political will through the ballot.

The artist worked at a time when party politics was growing in popularity. The party-based political system that had developed during the two terms of Andrew Jackson from 1829–1837, and solidified under Martin Van Buren, was fracturing under the stresses of the institution of slavery. Professional politicians regarded parties as a necessary evil. They had been condemned in the republic's early years by no less than George Washington. Still, in the decades since Washington's terms in office ended, parties had become a staple of American politics. As the young republic developed its democratic institutions, parties provided an outlet for people to disagree with officeholders while remaining faithful citizens.

The destruction of the party system that Bingham witnessed in the 1850s was rooted in the institution of slavery. Slavery had been accepted by many of the founding fathers, many of whom were slaveholders themselves, as at best a necessary evil. The colonial economy, based on exporting crops and raw materials to Europe, was made possible through the labor of enslaved Black laborers. The founding fathers hoped that slavery, which they recognized as antithetical to their principles, would become extinct within a few generations. But, with a few exceptions, they did not see a way in which they could free all enslaved people within their own lifetimes.

Contributing to the reliance on slavery was the invention of a Connecticut experimenter named Eli Whitney: the cotton engine, or cotton gin, patented in 1794. This simple hand-cranked combing device sped up the process of separating cotton fibers from the seed, but in doing so it created even more demand for the cotton itself. The result was an even greater demand for enslaved labor and for southern land—much of which was still in the hands of the Native Americans who had lived on it from time immemorial. By the end of the War of 1812, millions of acres of Native American territory had fallen into U.S. hands, and most of it was prime cotton-growing soil.

Early in this process, many American politicians believed that slavery was doomed to extinction. But the expansion of cotton farming meant that not only would slavery not go extinct, but many people began arguing for its extension. The creation of the cotton gin and the hunger for raw cotton in newly industrializing Europe and New England gave slavery new vitality.

By the 1830s, new states were being admitted to the Union. Many offered settlers the possibility of extending cotton production into new regions. Missouri, Bingham's home state, sat squarely on the border between the cotton lands of the South and the agricultural-industrial lands of the north. In 1820, when Missouri became a state, Congress negotiated a compromise line—the Missouri Compromise—through Louisiana Territory to stop slavery at Missouri's southern border. That was the theory; in practice, Missouri became a slave state.

Missouri served as an epicenter for questions involving slavery. In 1846, an enslaved person in Missouri known as Dred Scott sued for his freedom from his owner, a United States Army surgeon. Dr. John Emerson had lived with Scott in territories and in states where slavery was outlawed. Under Missouri law, slaves could sue for their freedom if they were held illegally in bondage. The case dragged on till 1857, when the Supreme Court decided that not only was Scott legally a slave, but that Black Americans could not sue in court because they were not considered citizens.

The stresses over slavery fractured both Andrew Jackson's Democratic Party and the Whig Party that had opposed it for decades. In 1860, Republican Abraham Lincoln was elected president—the first party member to achieve office. During the Civil War, parties fractured along sectional lines. At the end of the war, a new two-party system of Republicans and Democrats, the same two-party system that exists today, emerged.

Explanation and Analysis of the Document

Bingham's *The County Election* shows a multifaceted scene depicting Election Day in a small, mid-nineteenth century American town. His canvas shows the many ways in which rural Americans in the nineteenth century expressed their political will. The picture includes individuals from all walks of life, from local officials and landowners to ordinary farmers. It suggests that participatory democracy, and the equality it requires, is at the root of American society.

Although Bingham's painting can be understood as celebration of the democratic spirit, in fact the details suggest the irregularities that plagued voters at the time. At the center of the scene is the entrance to the county courthouse, where votes are cast. A voter is being sworn in by a judge, his hand resting on a Bible. There is no secret ballot; the voter casts his vote orally, and everyone within earshot knows who he votes for. The vote is recorded by the clerks behind the judge at the courthouse entrance.

To the left of the voting scene is a variety of characters engaged in activities related to the election, either directly or indirectly. An old man, possibly a veteran, descends the steps of the courthouse, having just voted. In front of him on the courthouse steps is a man, possibly a candidate, handing out cards and soliciting votes. Further to the left, we see a drunken man supported by two comrades who are bringing him to cast his vote, despite his condition. At the left-hand margin of the painting, we see a man being served a glass of cider. Such drink, along with the barrel and the basket next to the table, was common at voting parties. It was not unusual for candidates to solicit votes by offering free drinks and free food. At the right-hand margin of the painting, a man sits with his head bowed and a bandage around his brow. He may have been in a fight; violence was also not uncommon at the polls on voting day. In the very center of the painting, wearing fawn-colored pants, a white jacket, and a gold hat and vest, sits a figure who appears to be writing or drawing. That may be Bingham, the artist himself, who was a candidate in the county elections of 1850.

Many of the practices depicted by Bingham would not be tolerated in modern elections. Some of them were frowned on even during the artist's time. Bingham's point seems to be not that American elections are the epitome of fairness but that, despite the chaos and the cheating, the electoral process works. American democracy is neither clean nor nice, Bingham seems to be saying, but it is uniquely American.

So what is it, exactly, that *The County Election* represents? Is it a satire of the idea of a democracy in which citizens do not care enough to take their own vote seriously and instead auction it off to the highest bidder? Or is it a celebration of the chaotic but class-spanning process of voting in the United States? Art critics and historians have differed in their interpretation of the picture, and interpretations are rooted in their understanding of Bingham's own political identity.

At the beginning of his political career, Bingham was a Whig, a member of a party that defined itself partly through its fiscal ideas and its commitment to infrastructure, but mostly through its opposition to the Democratic Party. Bingham may be expressing his Whig ideals through his satiric critique of democracy as practiced by the Democrats. On the other hand, the painting also demonstrates a unity of purpose, with all sections in society coming together to vote for the common good. That too was a Whig principle. Bingham both celebrates the democratic principle of American society and at the same time displays its shortcomings

—Kenneth R. Shepherd

Questions for Further Study

1. Describe the mood of Bingham's painting. What do you think he was suggesting about the atmosphere and environment of a historical American election? In your response, cite visual elements that support your interpretation.

2. Analyze the visual elements of this painting. Then, when you have completed your analysis, compare and contrast the voting scene Bingham presents with a contemporary American election. Note both similarities and differences in your response.

3. There are a variety of clues in Bingham's painting that suggest class differences between the figures presented. Hats, clothes, and decorative items all communicate the status and station of their owners. What messages do you think Bingham was trying to express about political participation, civic responsibility, and American democracy through his painting?

Further Reading

Books

Baker, Jean H. *Affairs of Party: The Political Culture of Northern Democrats in the Mid-Nineteenth Century.* New York: Fordham University Press, 1998.

Howe, Daniel Walker. *What Hath God Wrought: The Transformation of America, 1815–1848.* New York: Oxford University Press, 2009.

McPherson, James. *Battle Cry of Freedom: The Civil War Era.* New York: Oxford University Press, 1989.

Nagel, Paul C. *George Caleb Bingham: Missouri's Famed Painter and Forgotten Politician.* Columbia: University of Missouri Press, 2005.

Taylor, Alan. *American Republics: A Continental History of the United States, 1783–1850.* New York: Norton, 2022.

Articles

Husch, Gail E. "George Caleb Bingham's 'The County Election': Whig Tribute to the Will of the People." *American Art Journal* 19, no. 4 (Autumn 1987): 4–22.

Documentaries

The American Artist: The Life & Times of George Caleb Bingham. Wide Awake Films, 2016.

John L. Magee: "Forcing Slavery Down The Throat Of A Freesoiler" Cartoon

Author/Creator John L. Magee	**Image Type** Cartoons
Date 1856	**Significance** Illustrates the violence between antislavery supporters and those who favored extending slavery after the passing of the Kansas-Nebraska Act

Overview

This political cartoon from 1856 depicts the violence at the heart of the battle between slavery opponents. The significance of political cartoons can be traced back to Ancient Greece, where the use of satire was used in tragedies and comedies. Satire was a lighthearted way of making the people aware of what was happening in society on the political, economic, cultural, and eventually global spectrum. Political cartoons combine satire with caricature in a reference to a timely and often controversial event. In other words, the cartoon is meant to enlighten the public in a (usually) whimsical manner.

Caricatures are meant to be a little over the top and rather exaggerated, but caricature is only one of the two main elements associated with a political cartoon. The other is relevance to a current event that will be familiar to the audience. At first glance, a political cartoon may appear to be humorous, but it is important to analyze the details of the image for clues about the societal atmosphere of the time. Politics can highly nuanced, to the point that many people find it difficult to understand the major issues or the political jargon that often accompanies a written explanation. Political cartoons provide an alternative way to present and explain such issues; they illustrate topics that are often controversial in a way that simplifies or humanizes them and makes them relatable.

About the Artist

This political cartoon was created by John L. Magee, an artist who was born in New York. The year of his birth is rather a mystery, with some sources citing 1804 and others citing sometime in the 1820s. Early in his career he created various lithographs and engravings for publishing companies in New York, including the firm of James Baillie and Nathaniel Currier. During the 1840s through the 1850s, Magee produced illustrations for various children's books. Three of his works, including perhaps his most famous painting, *The Mischievous Boy*, were on exhibit at the National Academy of Design, and he also exhibited at the American Art Union. For at least two years, from 1850 to 1852, he is credited as having his own business in New York at 34 Mott Street. Around 1852, Magee decided to move to Philadelphia, Pennsylvania, where he also established his own firm and continued to work as a lithographer and political cartoonist. His work became more politically focused in his later years, reflecting the volatile

Document Image

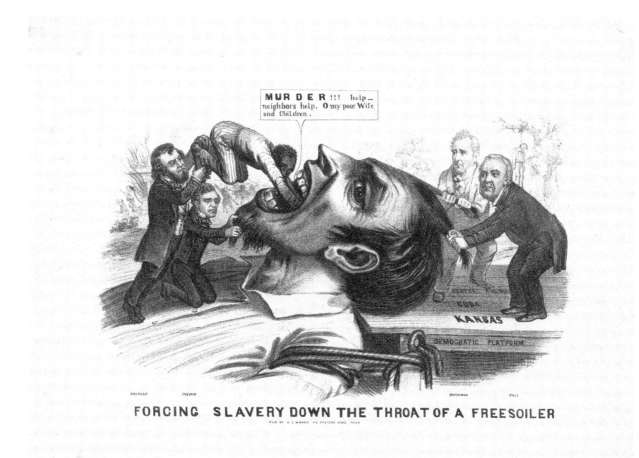

"Forcing Slavery Down the Throat of a Freesoiler"
(Library of Congress)

time in the United States. In addition to "Forcing Slavery Down the Throat of a Freesoiler," Magee also created "Satan Tempting Booth to the Murder of the President" and "Death Bed of Abraham Lincoln." He was listed as a genre lithographer as late as 1870 in the Philadelphia census report; however, after the 1860s there is no record of new material from Magee.

Context

"Forcing Slavery Down the Throat of a Freesoiler" was created to reflect a turbulent time in United States history. By 1856, when John Magee produced this political cartoon, the American political system was deeply divided on the issue of slavery. In fact, up until Congress passed the Missouri Compromise of 1820, slavery had been dealt with in a precarious manner, if at all. The Missouri Compromise was the first legislation that attempted to face the slavery issue head on, and its very attempt to do so illustrated the deep divide within the country. The divide extended to government itself, as could be seen in the political platforms of the two major parties at the time, the Whigs and the Democrats. The Whigs were not necessarily the party of abolitionists, but they did believe that the federal government should retain more control over the nation's affairs. The Democrats, on the other hand, felt that the power of the federal government should be limited and that individual states should have more power. This was a time of clear-cut division within America: federal government versus state governments, antislavery versus slavery, and Whigs versus Democrats. The Missouri Compromise merely quieted the storm temporarily.

After the U.S. War with Mexico ended in 1848 with the signing of the Treaty of Guadalupe Hidalgo, the shortcomings of the Missouri Compromise became apparent. The United States acquired over a half million square acres of land, including present-day California, Utah, Nevada, and parts of Colorado, Wyoming, New Mexico, and Arizona. The question arose as to whether these new territories should be admitted as states that allowed or disallowed slavery after criteria for statehood was achieved. The Compromise of 1850 temporarily settled the turmoil but ultimately caused more issues than it solved, particularly in the Kansas and Nebraska territories.

As more settlers migrated into the Kansas and Nebraska territories, the question of slavery was once again a main issue. A proposal from Senator Stephen Douglas of Illinois was to allow settlers, primarily white males, the power to determine whether the territories should be admitted as free states or as slave states. This was known as popular sovereignty and essentially removed the decision over slavery from the government and placed it directly with the settlers. The Kansas-Nebraska Act was passed in 1854 and emphasized the idea of popular sovereignty within each of the respective territories. Violence erupted as settlers representing both sides infiltrated Kansas and Nebraska, each feeling justified to have the ultimate decision in response to the slavery question. Kansas was nicknamed "Bleeding Kansas" as the violence escalated and the already existing divisions became even deeper.

Explanation and Analysis of the Document

After the Kansas-Nebraska Act was passed in 1854, violence erupted in the United States, and the primary targets were antislavery settlers, known as freesoilers, in Kansas. The violence stemmed from the policy of popular sovereignty, proposed by Senator Stephen Douglas in the Compromise of 1850, which directly placed the slavery decision in the hands of the white settlers in Kansas and Nebraska. As the population within each of the territories grew, the violence against the freesoilers escalated, earning Kansas the nickname "Bleeding Kansas." This was a popular topic among artists such as John Magee, and several political cartoons were created to explain and make sense of the bloodshed that occurred between those who favored and those who opposed the extension of slavery.

The Free Soil Party was rather short-lived, lasting only from 1848 to 1854, but it had an enormous impact in the years leading up to the Civil War. The party was created after the Treaty of Guadalupe Hidalgo was signed, which ended the U.S. War with Mexico. Although the treaty may have silenced any disputes with Mexico, the slavery question about the newly acquired territory was not settled. Those who supported the Free Soil Party opposed the extension of slavery, reasoning that even though the federal government could not end slavery in states where it existed already, it should take an active stance in disallowing slavery in new territories. This was reflected in the party's slogan "Free soil, free speech, free labor, and free men." The Free Soil Party felt that the federal government should exercise more control and have more of a voice on the matter the individual states. This voice deepened the divide between the main two political parties at the time, the Whigs in the North and the Democrats in the South.

This political cartoon showcases a freesoiler bound to a platform labeled "Democratic Platform" and featuring Kansas and other place names, representing the Democratic platform that supported the movement of slavery into western territories. The freesoiler is being restrained by two recognizable men from the Democratic Party: presidential nominee James Buchanan and Senator Lewis Cass. The two men who are shoving a Black man into the gaping mouth of the freesoiler are Senator Stephen Douglas and President Franklin Pierce, also prominent members of the Democratic Party. This demonstrates the clear division between the two political parties, the division between the federal government and the state governments, and the power difference between the Democrats and the bound and helpless freesoiler. While this scene is the most noticeable at first glance, there are several other details worth mentioning.

Although the platform clearly spells out "Kansas," the words "Cuba" and "Central America" can also be seen upon closer examination. This is in reference to the Democratic Party's future ambitions to extend slavery not only into western territories within the United States but also into areas outside the United States. This also suggested the desire to acquire more territory, thus growing America's status in global markets.

Two other mini scenes are illustrated in the background: to the left is an image representing the burning and destruction of land, and to the right a dead man is portrayed hanging from a tree. The former refers to the literal destruction of land owned by freesoilers and the violence that resulted from the Kansas-Nebraska Act. The latter refers to lynching, which was used as a terrorist tactic by white supremacists. Lynching was especially prevalent in the South from the 1830s through 1960s. The Kansas-Nebraska Act escalated such behavior, but more people were made aware of these atrocities thanks to the efforts of investigative journalist Ida B. Wells (1862–1931), who documented and published widely about the prevalence of lynching as part of her anti-lynching campaign. This awareness also made it possible for artists such as Magee to incorporate such themes into their work.

—Belinda Vavlas

Questions for Further Study

1. Why do you think John Magee drew the freesoiler larger in comparison to the men who represented the Democratic Party? What does this suggest about Magee's viewpoint on the subject?

2. Why would Magee have included Cuba and Central America on the platform along with Kansas? What does this imply about imperialism in general and the United States' role in it?

3. After examining the expressions on each of the men, relate them to the turbulent time in 1856 following the Kansas-Nebraska Act. How would you describe each of their expressions, including that of the freesoiler? Now examine the size of the slave compared to the size of the freesoiler's mouth. What is Magee trying to convey to his viewers?

Further Reading

Books

Etcheson, Nicole. *Bleeding Kansas: Contested Liberty in the Civil War Era*. Lawrence: University Press of Kansas, 2004.

Foner, Eric. *Free Soil, Free Labor, Free Men: The Ideology of the Republican Party before the Civil War*. New York: Oxford University Press, 1970.

McArthur, Debra. *The Kansas-Nebraska Act and "Bleeding Kansas" in American History*. Berkeley Heights, NJ: Enslow, 2003.

Websites

Garrison, Zach. "Kansas-Nebraska Act." *Civil War on the Western Border: The Missouri-Kansas Conflict, 1854–1865*. The Kansas City Public Library. https://civilwaronthewesternborder.org/encyclopedia/kansas-nebraska-act.

"Kansas-Nebraska Act." History, June 14, 2021. https://www.history.com/topics/19th-century/kansas-nebraska-act.

"Kansas-Nebraska Act (1854)." National Archives. https://www.archives.gov/milestone-documents/kansas-nebraska-act#:~:text=In%20January%201854%2C%20Senator%20Stephen,slavery%20would%20be%20legal%20there.

Documentaries

The Kansas-Nebraska Act. "Legacies of the Civil War" series, Johnson County Library. https://www.youtube.com/watch?v=8S4GAjWkWwo.

"Picking Cotton, Georgia, 1858" Illustration

Author/Creator
Unknown

Date
1858

Image Type
Illustrations

Significance
Image produced for a northern magazine in the late 1850s showing enslaved men, women, and children working on a cotton plantation, indicating the general awareness of slavery but not its many brutalities

Overview

This image offers an idealized version of the life of enslaved people living on a Georgia cotton plantation. It appeared in a widely circulated magazine published in Boston in the first half of the 1800s, a time when increasing literacy encouraged the production of more books, newspapers, and other print material. Such illustrations were common until photography, still in its infancy, became more commonplace and photographic equipment more reliable and portable. By 1858, the year this image appeared, the American South was in many respects isolated from the rest of the nation, with a distinctly different economy and culture defined by the area's use of enslaved labor.

The twin forces of industrialization and urbanization brought about significant changes to the northern United States during the first half of the nineteenth century that impacted its economic, political, and cultural institutions for generations to come. While southern states did not experience the building of factories and expansion of cities on the same scale as those to the north, it was not exempt from transformative events and processes that greatly increased the wealth and political power of the region's most powerful families. But the American South continued to cling tenaciously to the very things that had first brought prosperity to its earliest European inhabitants: the vast production of cash crops such as cotton, sugar, and tobacco, and the use of a large, enslaved workforce to plant, tend, and harvest those crops.

Tobacco, first grown at Jamestown in the 1600s, was the South's most lucrative crop until the late 1700s, when the production of cotton, beginning in deep southern states like Georgia, exploded with the invention of the cotton gin, a device that deseeds cotton. These developments, combined with the forced removal of Indigenous people in the South to reservations to the west in the 1820s and 1830s, encouraged thousands of ambitious, would-be cotton tycoons to purchase land for relatively low cost in Alabama, Mississippi, Louisiana, and other southern states. With the demand for cotton growing in concert with the rise in textile production in New England and Great Britain, the only missing element was enslaved workers to perform the backbreaking labor needed to produce the cotton. By 1835, cotton held the distinction of being the United States' most important export, a position it retained until the start of the Civil War.

Document Image

"Picking Cotton on a Georgia Plantation"
(Ballou's Pictorial)

About the Artist

This image appeared in an 1858 issue of *Ballou's Pictorial Drawing-Room Companion*, a popular illustrated periodical based in Boston. The artist is unknown.

Context

Slavery was not new to the South when cotton so thoroughly transformed it after 1800; the first ship carrying enslaved Africans arrived in Jamestown in 1619. But cotton production both increased the use of enslaved people and altered how slavery came to be viewed by both southerners and northerners. In 1790, more than 650,000 enslaved individuals were held captive in the South. That number nearly doubled by 1810, and despite the federal ban on the importation of enslaved people in 1808, it stood at roughly four million at the outbreak of the Civil War in 1865. This rapid increase in practice of slavery was correlated directly to the growing production of cotton. And as the price of previously inexpensive farmland rose, so did the price of purchasing enslaved workers, doubling between the 1820s and the 1850s, with robust young males tending to cost the most.

When Senator James Henry Hammond, a prosperous owner of multiple plantations and hundreds of enslaved people, famously declared in 1858 that "Cotton is king," it was at a time when the South's economic fortunes were utterly dependent upon the continued production of the crop, which necessitated the continuance of slavery, as there were not enough free laborers able or willing to toil in the fields should the federal government abolish slavery. Profits from cotton consolidated the political and social dominance of the "planter class," the largest landowners, whose members filled positions in state governments and populated much of Congress.

The rapid increase in the use of enslaved labor in the early decades of the 1800s led to it becoming more deeply ingrained in southern society, to the point where it came to be seen as a practice worth defending with force if necessary. White southerners, even those who were not slaveowners, grew increasingly sensitive to any criticism made against slavery and militant in their commitment to ensuring its continuance. Their anger mounted as abolitionist groups emerged in the 1830s and 1840s, hosting lectures by those who had escaped from captivity and circulating pamphlets and newsletters that included accounts of cruelties committed against enslaved people, including vicious beatings and the separation of children from their parents. Northern awareness of slavery's many evils grew, as did opposition to its continued expansion to western states and territories.

Slavery's defenders sought to fend off the northern abolitionists' criticism by contending that the dehumanizing practice actually offered benefits to its victims. Apologists claimed that a life of enslavement enabled supposedly inferior people of African descent to lift themselves up by living near whites and following their example, that it offered exposure to Christianity and a chance for eternal salvation, and that it provided the enslaved with all the essentials necessary for a fulfilling life: food, shelter, and a sense of purpose. Some white southerners went so far as to argue that the life of an enslaved person was far superior to that of a northern industrial worker, who performed mind-numbing tasks in a stifling factory for such low pay that their basic needs might not be met.

For enslaved people themselves, such justifications were absurd. Nearly all African Americans were Christian by the early nineteenth century, some by choice and others under force from their owners, usually as members of Baptist or Methodist churches typically led by white ministers. But African Americans developed new forms of Christian worship that often drew upon African religious traditions and organized their own worship services that offered hope in times of crushing despair. The inner lives of enslaved people were far more complicated than their captors and most white southerners ever bothered to realize.

Explanation and Analysis of the Document

A sanitized depiction of a dehumanizing practice, this image, captioned "Picking Cotton on a Georgia Plantation," seemingly reveals relatively little about the practice of slavery as it existed in the mid-nineteenth century beyond the sort of labor performed by a great many enslaved persons on plantations across the South. Despite the strong association between slave labor and the production of cotton that persists in popular culture, enslaved people living in the "Old South," particularly on larger plantations, worked in a variety of settings well beyond the cotton fields, including mines, factories, and inside the homes of their owners. But the vast majority of those who toiled as enslaved workers did so outdoors, preforming agricultural labor, and most did not live on large plantations like those that tended to be represented in illustrations like this one, reinforcing an overly romantic notion of the South in the minds of northerners who never traveled to the region. In 1860, only one-fourth of enslaved people lived on plantations with fifty of more people held in bondage; half of enslaved people lived on smaller farms where twenty or fewer lived in servitude, typically five or less.

In terms of what the engraving gets right about slavery, it shows men, women, and children on a Georgia plantation sharing in an assigned task, which was common for enslaved people assigned to work in the fields. Tending such crops as rice was generally carried out according to the principles of the "task system," which involved designating an undertaking, perhaps a set poundage of cotton to be picked, to be completed by each enslaved person, who was then allowed to enjoy any free time left in the day once the chore had been completed. When working under the task system, enslaved people generally enjoyed less supervision and could generally set their own work tempo. This was not the case when they worked under the "gang system," which was far harsher than the task system. It divided enslaved laborers into three groups: the most efficient, the least efficient, and children, assigned a task of specific difficulty based on which group was to complete it. Each group was expected to work through the entire workday under much closer supervision than under the task system. Plantations growing high-maintenance crops such as sugar, tobacco, and cotton tended to rely upon the gang system. In the case of cotton, a speedy harvest was of paramount importance; the plantation owner who succeeded in getting his cotton bales to market first usually could usually command a higher price than those who delivered their crop later. Denied any sort of formal education, enslaved children were expected to perform less-demanding chores compared to their adult counterparts. The girl shown at the left of the image is picking cotton while the girl on the right sits contentedly under a tree. Quarters for the enslaved people can be glimpsed in the background on the right.

The image is misleading in terms of what it depicts and the absence of larger context. All the enslaved people appear healthy, well-fed, and provided with adequate clothing, none of which were legally guaranteed by the slaveowner. An average workday for a field hand on a cotton planation began at sunrise and concluded at sunset, which meant increasingly longer and more arduous days of toil during the spring and summer months, picking hundreds of pounds of cotton each day. When it was time to harvest the cotton crop, usually in August or September, an owner would often send his "house slaves" to assist the "field slaves" in completing their work. Once the harvest was completed, enslaved people were expected to immediately pack the cotton into bales and begin preparations for next year's crop. The engraving fails to include an overseer armed with a whip, pistol, or shotgun, monitoring the pace of the enslaved workers and ensuring that they don't shirk their duties. There is nothing to suggest that those depicted are experiencing distress or misery, which is precisely the sort of image slaveowners of the late 1850s would want to foster as the nation grew increasingly divided over the issue of slavery based on economic, political, and moral considerations.

This image appeared in an 1858 issue of a popular illustrated periodical based in Boston, *Ballou's Pictorial Drawing-Room Companion*. Each copy of the magazine contained attractive engravings and stories from around the United States and the larger world. It was hardly the sort of publication to provide anything other than a superficial survey of slavery, which was largely an abstract practice for most northerners. While the growing abolitionist movement and fugitives along the Underground Railroad, such as famed orator Frederick Douglass, increased northerners' knowledge of slavery, the vast extent of slavery's true horror would not become clear until the Civil War when Union troops came into regular contact with those who suffered under it.

—Michael Carver

Questions for Further Study

1. How might a photograph of enslaved persons picking cotton have elicited a different response from a viewer compared to this image? Why?

2. What might have been the dangers of depicting slavery without any attempt to address its many abuses to the readership of the magazine?

3. By the end of the 1850s, white southerners increasingly argued that the enslavement of African Americans was to their benefit. Are there any aspects of the image that seem to reflect this attitude?

Further Reading

Books

Faust, Drew Gilpin. *The Ideology of Slavery: Proslavery Thought in the Antebellum South, 1830–1860*. Baton Rouge: Louisiana State University Press, 1981.

Jennison, Watson W. *Cultivating Race: The Expansion of Slavery in Georgia, 1750–1860*. Lexington: University Press of Kentucky, 2012.

Morrison, Fred W. *From Slavery to Agrarian Capitalism in the Cotton Plantation South: Central Georgia, 1800–1880*. Chapel Hill: University of North Carolina Press, 2000.

Websites

"The Spread of Cotton and of Slavery 1790–1860." Mapping History, University of Oregon. Accessed August 12, 2022. https://mappinghistory.uoregon.edu/english/US/US18-00.html.

Documentaries

"Seeds of Destruction." Episode 3 of *Slavery and the Making of America*. Chana Gazit, director. PBS, 2004.